The Continuing Conversion
of the Church

DARRELL L. GUDER

William B. Eerdmans Publishing Company

Grand Rapids, Michigan / Cambridge, U.K.

© 2000 Wm. B. Eerdmans Publishing Co.
255 Jefferson Ave. S.E., Grand Rapids, Michigan 49503 /
P.O. Box 163, Cambridge CB3 9PU U.K.

Printed in the United States of America

05 04 03 02 01 00   7 6 5 4 3 2 1

Library of Congress Cataloging-in-Publication Data

Guder, Darrell L., 1939-
    The continuing conversion of the church / Darrell L. Guder.
        p. cm. — (The gospel and our culture series)
    Rev. ed. of: Be my witnesses. c1985.
    Includes bibliographical references and indexes.
    ISBN 0-8028-4703-X (pbk. : alk. paper)
    1. Church. 2. Mission of the church. 3. Evangelistic work.
    I. Guder, Darrell L., 1939-   Be my witnesses. II. Title. III. Series.

BV600.2 .G83 2000
262'.001'7 — dc21
                                        99-462213

THE CONTINUING CONVERSION
OF THE CHURCH

THE GOSPEL AND OUR CULTURE SERIES

A series to foster the missional encounter of the gospel
with North American culture

Craig Van Gelder

General Editor

•   •

Volumes now available

Darrell L. Guder, *The Continuing Conversion of the Church*

Darrell L. Guder et al., *Missional Church: A Vision for the
Sending of the Church in North America*

George R. Hunsberger and Craig Van Gelder, editors, *The Church between
Gospel and Culture: The Emerging Mission in North America*

George R. Hunsberger, *Bearing the Witness of the Spirit: Lesslie Newbigin's
Theology of Cultural Plurality*

Craig Van Gelder, editor, *Confident Witness — Changing World*

Forthcoming

Alan Roxburgh and Mike Regele, *Proper Obsession:
Refounding the Church for a Postmodern World*

Contents

Preface

"This is a book about the mission of the church." With that sentence I began my first book on the theology of evangelistic ministry, *Be My Witnesses*.[1] It is the most appropriate way to introduce this book as well. When I began work on this manuscript in 1995, my intention was to rewrite *Be My Witnesses*. Mr. Eerdmans had called me in 1994 to ask if I might be interested in doing a revised version of that volume. With a sabbatic semester coming up the next year, I gratefully agreed to make the revision my project.

In February 1995 I began the reading and research necessary for the envisioned revision. We were located at the University of Tübingen, Germany, with excellent research resources and a very supportive working situation at the Theologicum made possible by the then Dean of the Protestant Theological Faculty, Prof. Dr. Peter Stuhlmacher. Within a few weeks, it became very clear to me that it was not going to be possible to revise my first book, at least not at that point. Rather, I needed to write a sequel, a continuation of the basic exposition of the church's evangelistic mission as "incarnational ministry." I would not have to change substantially the basic ideas and argument of that book. On the contrary, it was clearer to me than ever that I needed to presuppose the understanding of evangelistic ministry as "being, doing, and saying the witness to the gospel," which was my basic theme.

1. Darrell L. Guder, *Be My Witnesses: The Church's Mission, Messenger, and Messengers* (Grand Rapids: Eerdmans, 1985).

Yet, since 1983 when I wrote that book, several things had happened which called for a sequel rather than a revision.

In the preface to *Be My Witnesses,* I provided my readers a survey of the theological and ecclesial experiences that shaped my understanding of the church's mission. It was my conviction then, as it is now, that one should always let one's students or readers know the assumptions and presuppositions which are shaping one's ideas. The responses to that preface over the years encourage me to continue the exercise. I can recognize three major areas of experience and exploration that have helped me to develop further my own understandings of evangelization, building upon *Be My Witnesses.*

There has been, first of all, the continuing discussion with those who read and reacted to *Be My Witnesses.* I have been particularly helped and challenged by the questions raised by colleagues in seminary classes, both faculty and students. For many years, the book was used in one of the basic courses of the Institute of Youth Ministries of Fuller Theological Seminary and Young Life. Mr. Lester Comee, one of the ablest teachers and interpreters of incarnational youth ministry I know, taught that course. His reflections on his students' work with incarnational understandings of evangelization confirmed that the direction was right. It was encouraging to see that the men and women doing youth outreach in Young Life were helped to put biblical and theological foundations under their practice of ministry. At the same time, the experience with an evangelistic parachurch organization began to raise questions about the separation of evangelization from the basic mission community, the local congregation. These questions became more compelling as every year I taught the course on ecclesiology in the Institute.

An organization like Young Life quite rightly emphasizes that it is not a church, but a ministry in partnership with the churches. Much of my work with that organization involved the implications and challenges of that partnership. The very concept of a "parachurch" raises important issues for the theology of the church, issues to which classical systematic theologies, traditional denominational structures, and most parachurch organizations rarely give any attention. Certainly the men and women doing Young Life's evangelistic youth ministry were struggling honestly with the biblical and theological dimensions of communicating the gospel to North American teenagers. In fact, a considerable number of the leaders and colleagues in Young Life in those years (1975-1985) were exploring the whole theme of "mission community," looking at the integral relationship between the community of faith which evangelizes and the evangelistic outreach which such a community does. These important issues strongly influenced what we were doing in the Institute of Youth Ministries at that time. However, it became clear to me (and many others) that any evangelistic parachurch movement which specializes in a particular constituency or approach to evangelistic ministry must shape what it does as a program, rather than as the expression of the very life and calling of a mission community.

When this happens, evangelization tends to be understood in terms of methods, effectiveness, and measurable results, and the gospel itself becomes a manageable "product." I began to see this separation between evangelization and community as a problem of "reductionism," with questionable consequences for all concerned. The church, which is intended to be the evangelizing community, tends to reduce or neglect its essential missionary character. The evangelistic organization, with no negative intention, tends to proclaim something less than the full gospel. Such reductionisms stand in obvious tension with an incarnational approach to mission, which is committed to biblical integrity and faithfulness.

Dr. George Hunsberger, professor of missiology at Western Theological Seminary in Holland, Michigan, has used the book in an introductory course on the mission of the church at his seminary. His students have compared the approach in *Be My Witnesses* with Hans Küng's theology of the church's mission (the idea of such a comparison continues to intimidate me!). The students' findings, as reported to me by their professor and my good friend, interacted with the questions that were crystallizing for me in my work with an evangelistic para-church. They sharpened and focused my thinking about the theology of evangelization by helping me to see it within the larger theological context of the mission of God *(missio Dei)* as it defines the missionary nature of the church. The students' work, in particular, revealed the inadequate exposition of the kingdom of God in my approach, especially in view of the way that theme dominates Jesus' own proclamation of the gospel. That has led me to explore the curious separation of salvation from the kingdom of God in the church's evangelistic proclamation, going back a long time. This major theme is more than enough reason to move from a revision to a sequel.

The second area of experience that has shaped my thinking since *Be My Witnesses* appeared was the surprising opportunity to become a seminary professor of evangelism and mission. In 1991, I accepted the call to become the Benfield Professor of Evangelism and Mission at Louisville Presbyterian Theological Seminary. President John M. Mulder had concluded, after reading *Be My Witnesses,* that what I was trying to do in that book should be explored further in the context of a seminary curriculum. With that gracious and humbling invitation, he and his seminary helped me to discover that I had been, in fact, becoming a missiologist all along. The contemporary global exploration of the mission of the church, for which David Bosch's magisterial *Transforming Mission: Paradigm Shifts in Mission Theology*[2] is the most helpful overview, has proven to be a rich exploration as well as a theological homecoming. I have come to realize that one cannot address evangelization with theological integrity unless one approaches the subject missiologically, that is, within the context of the mission of the church as God's sent people. In a sense, it is like starting one's theological formation all over again, when one begins to work from the basic assumptions of the *missio Dei.* Part of the excitement of this pilgrimage is the ongoing discovery that Scripture is appropriately read and interpreted as the Spirit-empowered testimony that equips God's people for their mission, that is, for their incarnational witness. I found, as I was doing my research in Tübingen, that there were many voices in the theological discussion who, while they might not use words like "missiological" or "missional," were in fact involved in a fundamental reshaping of both biblical studies and our theological understanding of the church (ecclesiology). What I sensed was a convergence of insights: the growing consensus about the centrality of the reign of God in the biblical witness to the gospel, interacting with the radical change in our North Atlantic context as we clearly were moving out of (or being ejected from) Christendom. For someone who focused on evangelization as a theological theme, this convergence raised all kinds of questions about the individualism of most evangelistic work in the West. This was already a

2. David Bosch, *Transforming Mission: Paradigm Shifts in Theology of Mission* (Maryknoll, NY: Orbis Books, 1991).

major concern in *Be My Witnesses,* where I explored this problem under the rubric of "the false dichotomy between mission and the benefits of salvation." All of this was further reason for a sequel rather a revision, as the argument of this book will demonstrate.

The third area was the emerging discussion of gospel and culture. After I arrived at Louisville, John Mulder suggested that I get in touch with George Hunsberger, because he was involved in something called the "Gospel and Our Culture Network," which John thought might be interesting to me. It proved to be not only interesting but crucial. With several other missiologists, George had been engaged since the late 1980s in a continuation of the discussion of gospel and culture initiated in Great Britain in the early 1980s by Bishop Lesslie Newbigin. His work, and especially his missiological analysis of the situation of Western culture, are by now a major and much discussed part of our Western theological scene (see the bibliography at the end of this book). He had been my mentor ever since 1960, when I heard him lecture at the University of Hamburg on the occasion of his receiving an honorary doctorate from my alma mater. Later, when I was teaching ecclesiology to Young Life colleagues in the Institute of Youth Ministries, his *The Open Secret* became a basic textbook, because I had been so profoundly challenged by its missional vision of the church. I felt that it was one of the few theological resources that could speak to the particular task of youth evangelists who want to work with biblical integrity. Newbigin's *The Other Side of 1984: Questions for the Churches* had appeared in 1982 and was stimulating the British discussion which led to the Gospel and Culture movement on both sides of the North Atlantic. I went to Whitworth College as academic dean in 1985, and at my first faculty retreat there, I gave the book to all the professors and asked them to begin a discussion with me of the implications for Western liberal arts education of both the end of Christendom and the emerging critique of the Enlightenment. During the six years of my tenure at Whitworth, that discussion constantly prodded us. My own understanding of the "paradigm shifts" we are undergoing was much deepened by the exchange with scholars from all the major disciplines who were willing to sustain the tension created by asking such sweeping and threatening questions. We were and are like fish who are learning to analyze and criticize the water in which we swim.

Now, in the Gospel and Our Culture Network which has emerged in North America, this theological exploration of the critical and complex interactions between gospel, church, and culture is being pursued in a disciplined way by people from all across the ecclesial and theological spectrum. For several years, this growing circle of people concerned about the missionary faithfulness of the church in North America met, presented papers, and tried to chart the contours of the task which was looming on the horizon. The results of those initial years of discussion are summarized in the first book of essays published by the Gospel and Our Culture Network, in cooperation with the Wm. B. Eerdmans Publishing Company: *The Church Between Gospel and Culture* (1996).[3]

Then the Network, through George Hunsberger's remarkable leadership, received a generous grant from the Pew Charitable Trust to continue and intensify its work. George asked me to work on the research component made possible by this funding. We agreed that the crucial issue was an ecclesiological one. While there was an emerging consensus about the missiological crisis of the church — Christendom was truly over! — the classical theological discipline of ecclesiology was largely unaffected by these changes. We asked ourselves, What would a missiological ecclesiology for the church in North America look like if we were to take the missionary context we are now in seriously? Beginning in 1995 (paralleling my work on this manuscript), a group of six missiologists from diverse traditions began to examine all the questions raised by this basic curiosity about a missiological ecclesiology. We tried to survey the context of North America and the emerging theological struggle with that context, such as it is. The outcome of that work was the publication, in 1998, of *Missional Church: A Vision for the Sending of the Church in North America.*[4] Our hope with that project was that it would be a catalyst for discussion which would go far beyond the limitations which were obviously present in a group of six who represented a sampling of the ecclesial diversity of our society. It appears that our hopes are being affirmed as we now experience a much broader debate that moves from and beyond the platform provided by *Missional Church.*

3. George Hunsberger and Craig Van Gelder, eds., *The Church Between Gospel and Culture: The Emerging Mission in North America* (Grand Rapids: Eerdmans, 1996).

4. Darrell Guder, ed., *Missional Church: A Vision for the Sending of the Church in North America* (Grand Rapids: Eerdmans, 1998).

Obviously that project and my own concerns in this book have been in constant interaction. Our work on the reign of God and the church's calling to be its witness has profoundly shaped my thinking as reflected in the first third of this book. My concern about the reductionism of the gospel was shared by my colleagues in that project and is addressed in a variety of ways as we sorted out basic implications of the missionary vocation of the church. But I have found, as I have re-worked this manuscript after the completion of *Missional Church,* that the biblical and theological concerns that were pushing me toward a se-quel rather than a revision have only been confirmed and deepened by our project. It has been for me a remarkable and exciting convergence of convictions. Further evidence of that growing convergence can be seen in two further books emerging out of the Gospel and Our Culture Network's labors: George Hunsberger's treatment of the essential the-ology of Lesslie Newbigin for our situation, *Bearing the Witness of the Spirit,* and a volume of essays edited by Craig Van Gelder, *Confident Wit-ness — Changing World.*[5] As I have often said, the most stimulating theo-logical conversation I experience today is within the context of the Gos-pel and Our Culture Network. The publications in this series are the tangible evidence of that conversation.

It should be clear now why it was necessary for me to move on to a sequel to *Be My Witnesses,* rather than attempt a revision. Perhaps I am moving gradually into a passage in which such a revision would be good stewardship. At this point, I am primarily concerned that the dis-cussion which has emerged in the last years should continue with the same vitality and more risk-taking if we are to be faithful to our call-ing.[6] I am also very anxious to make it clear that this book has many of the marks of a "joint production." It has been shaped all along by so many people, experiences, and conversations, many of them referred to in the paragraphs above. The discussion is a very dynamic one, and it is difficult to end a manuscript, knowing that virtually everything one is writing about calls for reactions which will lead to further insight and

5. George Hunsberger, *Bearing the Witness of the Spirit: Lesslie Newbigin's Theology of Cultural Plurality* (Grand Rapids: Eerdmans, 1998); Craig Van Gelder, ed., *Confident Wit-ness — Changing World* (Grand Rapids: Eerdmans, 1999).

6. It is reassuring that, as a result of a generous grant from the Lilly Endowment, the Network is able to continue its research in a project entitled "Moving Congregations Toward Mission."

the definite need to revise. My hope is that this book will stimulate and contribute to the discussion already unfolding.

It remains only to thank those who in particular ways have made this book both possible and necessary. Certainly I must acknowledge gratefully the initial suggestion made by Mr. William Eerdmans, and couple that acknowledgement with my profound appreciation for the way he and his colleagues are enriching our theological work with the publication not only of our series but of a wide range of important books. Dr. Peter Stuhlmacher, professor of New Testament at the University of Tübingen, was our host and sponsor for a six-month sabbatical leave in 1995, during which the basic work on this manuscript was completed. As will become clear to the reader, I am indebted to him not only for his hospitality but for the important New Testament work he is doing, which is helping me to understand what a "missional hermeneutic of the Bible" is and how it works.

I wish to thank my colleagues in Young Life for their part in this dialogue, especially Lester Comee, who read this manuscript and provided important criticism. My colleagues at Whitworth College, Louisville Presbyterian Theological Seminary, and now Columbia Theological Seminary have all been an important part of this discussion in a great variety of ways. With them the fascinating process continues of finding a way to do theology missionally, after centuries in which the missional nerves of the Western church have largely atrophied. Among the many who have been important to me in these institutions, I must especially acknowledge John M. Mulder, without whose vision I would never have discovered that I am a missiologist, and my Louisville colleagues Marion Soards and Milton J Coalter. Marty Soards has been a gracious sounding board as I have tried to sort out the biblical foundations of mission and learn to do missional hermeneutics. Joe Coalter read the manuscript with a sharpened editorial pencil and greatly helped me to say what I wanted to say much more clearly — he is truly that rare gift, a genuinely honest critic whose insights instruct, stimulate, and not seldom humble one.

This manuscript has served as a teaching text in several courses since 1996, and the students in those courses have become valued and important critics as I have reworked the content. I wish to thank my students at Louisville Seminary and Columbia Seminary, who worked through the entire manuscript in courses on the theology of evangelistic ministry. I hope that they will recognize their influence on the final draft. One of my students provided important criticisms, especially in the area of New Testament interpretation, after his careful reading of an early draft of the book; I thank Michael Barram for his theological partnership and encouragement.

I was also privileged to teach a course using this text in a summer school of the Churches of Christ Theological College in Mulgrave, Melbourne, Australia. I thank those valiant students for their hard work and thoughtful engagement of my subject matter, and I especially thank the principal of the College, Dr. Greg Elsdon, and the faculty colleagues and their families, especially Graeme and Eileen Chapman. An invitation to teach an intensive course in missional theology at the Coptic Evangelical Seminary in Cairo provided another opportunity to test the basic ideas of this book, in conversation with pastors and students seeking to carry out faithful witness as a small minority in an Islamic culture. I am sure that I learned more than my students during that fascinating and very stimulating encounter. I am indebted to the Rev. Dr. Tharwat Kades, pastor in the Church of Hesse, Germany, who made that visit to his home church possible.

The five colleagues who joined me in the *Missional Church* project became close friends and valued critics. I thank them for the numerous ways they have shaped and corrected my own thinking. They are Lois Barrett, Inagrace Dieterrich, George Hunsberger, Alan Roxborogh, and Craig Van Gelder. Everyone involved in the Gospel and Our Culture Network will join me in acknowledging our dependence upon our gracious and patient administrator, Judy Bos.

My particular thanks go to my wife, Judy; I have no more honest or supportive theological critic than her. Her willingness to share this missiological pilgrimage has made our life far more nomadic than she (or I) ever dreamed it would be. She continues to broaden and deepen my life and thinking as she ensures that my scholarship not take place in isolation; through her encouragement and interests I am constantly drawn out of my rut into a much more wholesome experience of our modern world.

I would like to dedicate this volume to my students at Louisville Seminary between 1991 and 1997, many of whom have continued their journeys in ministry as missiological servants of the church. As representative of many, I name in particular Alan Adams, Michael Barram,

Bruce Brown, Kurt Helmstedt, Michelle Kolhoff James, Ann Mayo, Eunice McGarrahan, John Owen, Jim Porter, and "like one lately born" Clay Stevens.

Holy Week 1999   DARRELL L. GUDER

PART I

Foundations: The Church's Calling to Evangelistic Ministry

For many years, when teaching the Bible I would assert that the New Testament did not contain evangelistic literature. I believed that the New Testament writings were only directed to believing communities. I can no longer make that statement. In fact, I would now say that such an interpretation is based on a much too narrow understanding of evangelization. Now, based on the theology of evangelistic ministry that I will seek to develop in this book, I would say that the New Testament is evangelistic from beginning to end. (The Old Testament can be defined as evangelistic as well, but that will not be the burden of the discussion in this book.) What all this means will depend, of course, upon how evangelistic ministry is defined.

In the first third of this book I will lay the foundations for a theology of evangelistic ministry rooted in Scripture. I will start in chapter 1 by putting the discussion in the context of the twentieth-century debate about the church's mission. This missiological discussion will provide the framework for a definition and interpretation of evangelism as the heart of the church's ministry. But it will also reveal how much work needs to be done if we are to understand evangelism as a serious theological discipline.

The definition of evangelism must start with the "evangel," the good news. In the second chapter, I "begin at the beginning" by drawing together a survey of the biblical proclamation of the gospel. This good news is rooted in God's self-disclosure as loving, saving, reconciling, and redeeming. The incarnation of Jesus is the climax of that self-disclosure. Jesus' message of the kingdom of God, the cross and resurrection, and the basic Christian confession that Jesus is the Savior and the Lord who is bringing in the kingdom all define the evangel. That evangel is the heart of Christian mission.

God's gracious work unfolds in the calling and forming of the church to carry the good news of Jesus Christ as Savior and Lord into all the world. In the third chapter, I will argue that the concept "witness" serves as the overarching definition of the church's calling. This way of understanding Christian identity and vocation brings together the centrality of Christ with the sending out of the church. It is a truly integrative way to think theologically about the church and its ministry. Jesus' definition of the church in Acts 1:8, "You shall be my witnesses," forms the biblical foundation for our understanding of evangelization as the heart of ministry.

Chapter One

Mission and Evangelism: The Emergence of the Theological Challenge

Mission is the mother of theology.

MARTIN KÄHLER

The Optimism of Modernity

The twentieth century began, in the Western world, with a pervasive sense of optimism. Buildings began to soar upward, "scraping the sky." Railroads and steamships, those great accomplishments of nineteenth-century industrial ingenuity, were making the entire world accessible, while the telephone and telegraph were beginning to transform communication. Technology was translating the advances of science into daily life as electricity began to revolutionize housekeeping. Life was enhanced as medical research conquered one threatening disease after another.

Western societies had every reason to assume that they had reached the highest level of social, cultural, technical, and political achievement within human history. This civilization was also spreading throughout the whole world, thanks to the efforts of European and North American colonists and empire builders. These representatives of the West understood themselves as fulfilling their own racial and cultural destiny, which was to "bring the benefits of civilization" to the backward non-Western societies of the world which could now be reached so quickly. There was a great moral energy to their efforts. Not only were they building the wealth of their various Western empires, but they were pulling and pushing the "primitive" cultures of the non-Western world into the undoubted blessings of modernity. It was a vision that mobilized thousands of young men and women to go abroad and evangelize the world. The linkage between their labors and the colonial enterprise was a complex one: sometimes a partnership, sometimes opposed by commercial and military colonial interests, and often in conflict with the cultural imperialism of Western expansionists.

The achievements of Western science and technology, which had been accumulating impressively for two centuries, confirmed this sense of "manifest destiny" as we turned our calendars to 1900. In the eighteenth century, the intellectual development of the West culminated in the Enlightenment, which recognized and implemented the vast resources of human reason. Trusting in the reliability of human reasoning, Western scientists developed the scientific method. As their experiments became more sophisticated and their explorations more daring, they unlocked, one by one, the secrets of nature. They found new and vastly expanded sources of energy. They developed manufacturing techniques of unimagined quantity and speed. By the end of the nineteenth century, they had reduced the meaning of time and distance with the development of the steam engine. The idea of "the global village" began to emerge on the horizon as modern transportation expanded.

Darwin's exciting doctrine of evolution fueled this visionary enthusiasm: it was now clear that the human species (at least, in its "superior" European mutations) had advanced to the point that it could govern its further development to perfection. The outcome was certain to be a modern human society that was truly enlightened, truly civilized, probably democratic, and certainly European or Europeanized. No one could reasonably dispute the claim that this modernity represented the highest and most desirable form of human civilization.

The Christian religion continued to dominate Western culture until early in the twentieth century. This was mostly for institutional reasons. The network of established churches and their various forms of partnership with the states and social orders managed this cultural domination. Most of institutional Christendom adapted itself readily to the assumptions of modern Western thought. It equated Western cultural superiority with the Christian religion. The cultural optimism of the nineteenth-century European scientist, artist, philosopher, and politician combined convincingly with the faith conviction of the Christian theologian, church leader, and missionary. The Western world felt obligated to share its blessings, which included the gospel, with the rest of the world.

Looking backward from the perspective of the year 1900, the churches of the West had good reason to praise God and enter confidently into the new century. They surveyed two centuries of missionary activity that generated the most extraordinary expansion of Christianity in its history. Revival movements during the eighteenth and nineteenth centuries had produced a broad range of societies, organizations, and programs designed to advance the kingdom of God on earth. Thousands of young European, British, and North American men and women spread across the globe to pursue the goal of "the evangelization of the world in this generation."[1]

In North America, the distinctive institution called the denomination expanded and restructured itself after the model of the American corporation, confident that it possessed the know-how to organize the continuing Christianization of American culture.[2] With similar confidence, a major American Christian journal changed its name in 1900 to *The Christian Century*. At the same time, the German kaiser built himself a cathedral alongside his Prussian palace in Berlin. Its interior decoration confidently celebrated an alliance between throne and altar that would guarantee the continuation of "Christian civilization" in what was certain to be a universally Christian century. The emperor, sitting in a loge facing the altar and pulpit, looked up to see statues of the four great Reformers — Zwingli, Luther, Calvin, Melanchthon — and facing them, statues of the worldly lords, his ancestors, who supported the Reformation. Here was the constant reminder that the political leader and his people had a role to play in the life and direction of the

1. John Mott, *The Evangelization of the World in This Generation* (New York: Student Volunteer Movement for Foreign Missions, 1900; reprint, New York: Arno Press, 1972).

2. See Darrell Guder, ed., *Missional Church: A Vision for the Sending of the Church in North America* (Grand Rapids: Eerdmans, 1998), pp. 61-76.

church as its public partners. Just as the mighty cathedral dome dominates the landscape, so this system of partnership would continue to dominate culture.

This same Christian tradition reacted to modernity's emerging social problems by confidently proposing Christian solutions. The abolition of slavery had already been achieved, and the role of Christians was significant in the process. But the unjust underside of modern technological success — deplorable industrial ghettos, the human misery of child labor, disintegrating family structures, and systemic poverty — remained to challenge society. In central Europe, prophetic Christian leaders like Fliedner (1800–1864) and Bodelschwingh (1831–1910) formed diaconic brotherhoods and sisterhoods for impressive institutional ministries committed to gospel service in areas of dire need. Social welfare legislation gradually emerged in most of western Europe, much of it shaped by Protestant understandings of the just Christian society. In North America, the same challenges were countered by a newly formulated "social gospel" together with the optimism that the Christian West would bring about the promised kingdom of God — in fact, it was likely to look like North American democracy, cleansed of its last remaining problems.

Christendom in Question

There were, however, threatening clouds on the horizon. The optimism with which the twentieth century began was threatened by the profound tensions in the relationship between Western Christianity and its European cultural forms. One of the most fundamental of these tensions, from the sixteenth century onward, was the complex relationship between the legacy of Christendom and the progressive secularization of Western societies. This secularizing process was both institutional and intellectual. Its roots lay in the Renaissance, when new concerns about human potential and individual freedom began to emerge. The Reformation joined in the process leading toward modern secularization by questioning the authority and certainty of medieval Christian culture. Since the Reformation, the place and power of the institutional churches within their societies have gradually diminished. The fury and suffering of the religious wars of the sixteenth and seventeenth centuries greatly weakened the hold of the Christian tradition on its host societies. Under the absolute rulers of many emerging central European nation states in the eighteenth and early nineteenth centuries, the church was both protected and managed for political purposes. The long-term effect was to diminish the cultural and political power of the church.

"Disestablishment" is the process by which the organized church loses its special legal privileges within a state and becomes a private association in some sense. This process has been a threat if not a reality for all the churches rooted in the *corpus Christianum* (the structure of Western Christian societies). It has proceeded in different ways, ranging from the radical disestablishment of the Roman Catholic Church in France during the Revolution, to the gradual reduction of churchly power in Britain in the nineteenth century, to the abrupt ending of Russian Orthodox dominance after the Communist Revolution.

In the newly formed United States, disestablishment became the law of the land with the adoption of the American Constitution and its separation of church and state. At the same time, absolute monarchs in central Europe claimed and wielded power over the churches in ways which medieval popes would have condemned. Political thinkers and practitioners began to expound the previously unheard-of idea that the state should be religiously neutral. The papacy receded from its position of temporal power as the Vatican State gradually shrank to the size of a large urban park in Rome. In many countries free churches emerged to compete with the privileged traditional churches. Many forms of ministry arose outside the traditional institutions of the churches, in order to meet emerging modern needs that the established churches would or could not address. Most of the missionary societies were a case in point. The power of the churches to define and control public morality began to recede. Dissent spread, and with the enactment of various forms of legal toleration, it became a protected part of the value system of modern Western culture. Blasphemy ceased to be a crime. Religious heretics would never again be executed by the state at the behest of the Christian church. Education, which had been the privileged obligation of the church for centuries, gradually shifted over to the public sector.

Intellectual secularization was equally complex. The Enlightenment of the seventeenth and eighteenth centuries surfaced doubts about Christian thought and practice that had long been anticipated in the late Middle Ages and Renaissance. It was prefigured by the conflict between emerging modern science and the church's claim to authority in all areas of knowledge; the trial of Galileo is perhaps the best-known example of this tension. The cruelty of the religious wars of the seventeenth century left many thinkers questioning the absolute truth claims of the Christian tradition. Skepticism about the biblical record emerged as the methods of historical and literary criticism, long since applied to the great classic texts of Greece and Rome, were now applied to Scripture. The discovery of the other great world religions generated not only missionary zeal but also the rationalist ideal of a universally true religion which might underlie all religions. Christianity's claim to be uniquely true began to be doubted, or at least qualified. Continental universities continued to teach theology as the queen of the sciences, but philosophy freed itself from the dominion of theology and often became a radical intellectual force, placing in question much that Christianity held dear.

Among the many reactions of Christian defenders were learned attempts to adapt the faith to these new circumstances. That, in turn, produced reactions and tensions within the churches. Descriptive terms such as "liberal," "conservative," "radical," and "moderate" appeared. Religious pluralism emerged, composed of divided strands of Christianity as well as secular ideologies that now competed quite openly with Christianity. Religious toleration, now a political necessity, became also a supreme ethical value of what had once been a monolithically Christian culture.

For many theologians in the nineteenth century, it appeared patently clear that the Christian ethic was the important legacy of the ancient tradition. But it needed to be refined, freed of its mythological trappings, and modernized. Jesus, the great model and teacher, needed to be liberated from the unacceptable context of the cross and revisioned as the mentor of modern humanity on its way to moral perfection. While erudite thinkers on both sides of the North Atlantic revised the creeds to fit such modern expectations, revival preachers called people to the cross and new birth. The tensions of the pluralism of Christendom would inevitably emerge as the polarities of liberal, modern, conservative, and fundamentalist Christianity.

The New Questions of Mission and Evangelism

This rapidly changing context of Western modernity, especially in the nineteenth century, raised questions for Christendom for which its traditional language and thought were inadequate. In particular, the expansion of Western cultural hegemony around the globe and the growing secularization of European culture itself confronted the church with the issue of mission and evangelism. The vocabulary of traditional Christianity now became a problem.

Terms like "mission" and "evangelism" were absent from the language of medieval Christian culture. European theology had not really dealt with the "missionary nature of the church" for over a thousand years. To be sure, the church had always carried on mission, but its missionary strategies changed when Constantine began the process that made Christianity the official religion of Western cultures. From the "Constantinianization" of Christianity in the fourth century onward, Christian mission was the outward expansion of the Christian culture that was the established religious force in Europe. This was mission "by diffusion," as Lamin Sanneh describes it.[3] It is clearly seen in the progressive expansion of Latin Christian culture in the early Middle Ages.

The process was a complex one, but the effect was that the pagan cultures which encountered Latin or Roman Christianity in western and central Europe adopted it, whether they were the military victors (the Franks) or the vanquished (the Saxons). Much of this mission (not all) was carried out by coercion. Charlemagne's (742-814) armies conquered the tribes on the fringes of his expanding empire and baptized them by force. The biblical mandate was "compel them to come in" (Luke 14:23). As they "came in," they became Roman Catholic Christians.

The theology of such diffusionist mission was not really missional; it assumed that the creeds and dogmatic works of the church fathers defined Christianity in a final and valid sense. Further, it assumed that the Christian culture that had been developing since Constantine was God's design for Christian existence. To become

---

3. Lamin Sanneh, *Translating the Message: The Missionary Impact on Culture* (Maryknoll, NY: Orbis Books, 1991), pp. 28ff, 35-36, 54ff.

Christian in the western half of Europe was to become a bearer of Western Christian culture and a citizen of a Western Christian state. There were similar linkages in the development of Eastern Orthodox Christendom, although national cultural identities were a stronger element than in the West. Western Christendom continued (and continues) to make such assumptions about its own grasp of the gospel and its meaning, to see itself as the normative Christian culture.

Modern secularization created profound theological problems for the heirs of Christendom. They struggled with the challenges of modernity, burdened by the assumption that all truly civilized people had been, for centuries, already Christian. In emerging modern Western culture, they encountered Europeans whose faith had lapsed or who even consciously rejected the Christian tradition that had molded Europe. At the same time, the colonial enterprise and its missionary partners discovered vast worlds of non-Christian religions in the non-Western cultures they occupied. These new forms of domestic and foreign paganism were a challenge for traditional Christian thought and language: they required that at least some Christians think and talk about "mission" and "evangelism."

 Those who did begin to talk about mission and evangelism were, for the most part, the Christians who organized, supported, and engaged both in foreign mission and in the gradually emerging varieties of home mission. They were seldom the leaders of the church establishments and almost never a part of the academic and intellectual theological guild. For a very long time, well into the twentieth century, this conversation took place primarily among the practitioners of Christian ministry and mission, many of them outside the established church structures. Very few theologians, in the formal sense, took mission and evangelism seriously. The question of mission is not found in the major confessional documents of Western Christendom before the early twentieth century. But thousands of Christians in Europe and North America were taking mission very seriously. Both internationally and at home, Christians were becoming concerned about soul winning and church planting. Their actions generated theological questions and demonstrated the need for theological vocabulary that largely did not exist.

The term "evangelism" was, therefore, a relatively new word in the Christian vocabulary whose emergence in the nineteenth century is linked with the changing challenge just described. Although the New Testament frequently uses the word "evangelize," Western churches customarily translated it with terms like "preach" and "proclaim."[4] Such language demonstrates one of the basic assumptions of the Western Christian civilization, the *corpus Christianum*, which evolved from Constantine onward: the apostolic commission of the early church had been fulfilled with the Christianization of the West. The church's ongoing task was to proclaim this word within the Christianized world, to expand its boundaries by diffusion, and, very importantly, to ensure that everyone within these boundaries thought and acted in accordance with the church's dogma and strictures. "Evangelizing" thus became the task of those Christians who were assigned responsibility for this activity. It was priests and bishops who "preached" and "proclaimed," not ordinary lay believers. When that preaching and proclaiming took place among nonbelievers, say, on the boundaries of Christian Europe in the Middle Ages, then it was normally done by monks who "civilized" (i.e., made into Constantinian cultural Christians) as they evangelized.[5]

The Reformation of the sixteenth century did not change the situation with regard to the language of evangelism. It was still largely the priests and pastors who preached and proclaimed. The definition of the true church in the Augsburg Confession (1530) emphasized the preaching of the Word and the administration of the sacraments, and thereby underlined the clerical nature of all gospel communication in the Reformation churches.

Only when the missionary movement began in earnest (for Protestants, about two hundred years after the first generation of Reformation) did Christians begin to speak again of evangelizing and evangelism, and then only gradually did this language expand into more or less common usage. Because the gospel, the evangel, was being pro-

---

4. For a detailed study of the terminology of "evangelize" and "evangelization," see David B. Barrett, *Evangelize: A Historical Survey of the Concept* (Birmingham, AL: New Hope, 1987).

5. David Bosch, "The Medieval Roman Catholic Missionary Paradigm," in *Transforming Mission: Paradigm Shifts in Theology of Mission* (Maryknoll, NY: Orbis Books, 1991), pp. 214-38. For a detailed survey of medieval mission, see Kenneth Scott Latourette, *The Thousand Years of Uncertainty,* vol. 2, *A History of the Expansion of Christianity* (Grand Rapids: Zondervan, 1970).

claimed among former believers and nonbelievers, one needed to speak of "evangelism." This new fact confronted the Western churches in two ways: in the expanding missionary endeavors in non-Western cultures, and in the new challenges to established Christianity created by the secularization discussed above.

When missionaries carried the gospel into places where it had never been heard before, it made sense to describe their task as "evangelizing" in the pattern of the New Testament. Many of those "missionaries" were lay people, since the Western missionary movement began and was strongly carried by lay Christian leadership. These Christian missionaries were, once again after many centuries, doing what the original apostolic community had been all about. They were calling people to faith from unfaith. They were not just preaching in the traditional forms of that activity in Western churches. They were communicating the gospel in a great variety of ways. Evangelistic ministry included, for instance, education, medical ministry, and agricultural development. These missionaries were forming Christian communities and founding churches where there was no Christendom tradition. They were saying and doing evangelism.

Similarly, when Christians encountered secularization within their own Western culture, that is, when they met people who no longer were confessing Christians, then some saw the necessity to evangelize. These activities were also often conducted by lay Christians, or by specialized Christian organizations on the margins of the established churches. In some cases, whole new strands of the Christian church, such as the Methodist movement in Britain, emerged precisely for the task of evangelizing those who no longer adhered to the West's cultural Christian heritage — and who were often neglected by traditional churches. It was appropriate to speak of such labors as "evangelistic," since they included many more forms of communication than "preaching" or "proclamation," which were still largely the protected reserve of ordained clergy.

The modern term "evangelism," therefore, picks up New Testament language that had long been neglected in the language of Christendom. The New Testament activity defined as "evangelizing" and "evangelization" focused on the communication of the gospel so that people might respond and become followers of Jesus Christ. Evangelists are bringers of good news, and evangelization is the process by which this news is brought.[6] This understanding has asserted itself again in the course of modern church history and continues to be the basic sense attached to the term "evangelism": it is "the initial proclamation to people, who have never believed or do not believe any longer, inviting them to make the decision for Christ."[7]

The language of evangelism was paralleled by the expanding vocabulary of "mission." Here again, the modern usage followed historical developments. Beginning in the eighteenth century, various organizations of Christians, with more or less support from the old established churches, began to engage in mission and at the same time found language to describe their vision and work. As noted earlier, before the modern period, the church had not commonly spoken of its ministry and expansion as mission. The sense of the church as commissioned by Christ, as "sent into the world," had been replaced by the imagery of the church as God's city built upon the foundation of Christ, the institution which represented Christ's rule and administered God's grace. If any biblical image defined Christian "mission" from Constantine onward, it was the Lukan injunction, "Go out into the roads and lanes, and compel people to come in, so that my house may be filled" (14:23).[8] As Westerners began to move across the cultural boundaries of Europe to non-Western, and thus non-Christian territories, they began to recover (however imperfectly) the New Testament emphasis upon the church's mission. Only then did the concluding verses of Matthew's gospel begin to be used as the "biblical mandate" for mission.[9]

The fundamental idea of the term "mission," based on its Latin root, is "sending" *(missio)*. For Western churches of modern Christendom from the seventeenth century on, the thrust of this sending was clear. Christendom sent its representatives, its Catholic and Protestant missionaries, to the non-Christian world, in order to evangelize non-Christian cultures. Believers went to pagans, the civilized to the barbarians, the sophisticated to the primitive, in order to evangelize them. The unquestioned assumption of Western Christians was that God in-

6. Barrett, *Evangelize,* pp. 11-18.

7. Emilio Castro and Gerhart Linn, "Evangelisation," *Evangelisches Kirchenlexikon* (Göttingen: Vandenhoeck & Ruprecht, 1986), pp. 1194ff.

8. Bosch, *Transforming Mission,* pp. 219, 236, 240, 339-41.

9. Bosch, *Transforming Mission,* pp. 339-41.

tended all people to become Christian and, in the process, become culturally Europeans. Historically, Western Christendom saw itself as the normative cultural form of gospel faith, was responsible for it, and now had the opportunity and obligation to spread its benefits abroad. European mission understood its sending as a proprietary enterprise; its task was to expand itself by establishing Christian churches and cultures that imitated Western Christianity. Christianity was intended to become "territorial" in the colonized areas of the world, just as it was in the West. Mission by diffusion was to continue.

Of course, there were many missionaries who opposed this kind of cultural imperialism. There were many who discovered in their encounters with other cultures that their way had been prepared for them. They found that in some sense Christ did have all authority in heaven and on earth, and that the God and Father of Jesus Christ could be known and served in cultural forms entirely foreign to the European patterns. There were, from the beginning of the modern mission period, critics of the diffusionist endeavor and advocates for the cultural translation of the gospel. It is, as Lamin Sanneh has frequently pointed out, necessary to correct one-sided versions of the modern missionary enterprise.[10] But, on the home front, very few were able to distinguish between the gospel and the Western culture of its representatives on the mission field. Support for Western missions, which was most generous, and enthusiastic commitment to go out in mission, which was most impressive, coalesced with a Western sense of obligation to "reach the world" for the betterment of those who were less privileged.

Thus, when the Presbyterian Church in the United States of America finally acknowledged the fact of mission in its confessional documents (at the beginning of the twentieth century), it added a paragraph to the Westminster Confession of Faith entitled "Of the Gospel of the Love of God and of Missions." Although the term "evangelism" does not occur in this statement, the passage clearly addresses the church's mandate to go out into the (non-Western) world and make disciples of all nations. The Christendom mindset is obvious when the Confession states that "believers" here at home "are . . . under obliga-

---

10. See, particularly, Sanneh, *Translating the Message*, passim, and also his "Christian Missions and the Western Guilt Complex," *Christian Century* 104, no. 11 (8 April 1987): 330-34.

tion to sustain the ordinances of the Christian religion where they are already established, and to contribute by their prayers, gifts, and personal efforts to the extension of the kingdom of Christ through the whole earth."[11] What was to be "extended" was the emerging kingdom of Christ which, in this Presbyterian view, was on the verge of arriving. Thus, in the optimism of Western culture and Christendom, the twentieth century opened with the expectation that soon this magnificent enterprise would realize God's kingdom on earth.

The Twentieth-Century Debate

The optimism of nineteenth-century Western culture and its worldwide mission ended abruptly in 1914. The First World War shocked the West's conception of itself. The spectacle of Christian nations conducting history's most devastating war against each other placed virtually every assumption of Western progressive civilization in question. The Christian legacy of the West was profoundly implicated in this shock. These lands and cultures that had sent missionaries around the world, proclaiming the love of God and the saving work of Christ, were now engaged in the wholesale denial of such love and salvation by their military adventure. On both sides of the front lines, Christian clergy prayed with the soldiers and blessed the weapons. Clearly a major crisis in Western civilization began to unfold; this culture of modernity, "the large intellectual environment of the Enlightenment in which we all have been nurtured,"[12] began a profound process of self-questioning. Indeed, by the end of this century, some analysts of Western culture describe this culture as "postmodern,"[13] and virtually all appear to agree that the crisis has deepened and widened, without any resolution in sight.

11. "Westminster Confession of Faith," ¶xxxv, Presbyterian Church (USA), *Book of Confessions,* 6.190; see also Lefferts Loetscher, *The Broadening Church: A Study of Theological Issues in the Presbyterian Church since 1869* (Philadelphia: University of Pennsylvania Press, 1954), especially chapter 10, "Revision Accomplished," pp. 83ff.

12. Walter Brueggeman, *Biblical Perspectives on Evangelism: Living in a Three-Storied Universe* (Nashville: Abingdon, 1993), p. 90.

13. See Stanley J. Grenz, *A Primer on Postmodernism* (Grand Rapids: Eerdmans, 1996).

As an integral element of this modern culture, the churches of Western Christendom have also struggled with their identity. This self-questioning has become a dominant issue of this century for the traditional churches. It had long been building. Intellectual skepticism about the foundational tenets of the Christian faith was at the heart of the Enlightenment, as I have pointed out. Academic theology, especially on the Continent, engaged this skepticism, and many of its most gifted practitioners embarked upon major redefinitions of Christian dogma which were revolutionary in scope.[14] The Bible itself became a battleground as scholars refined and expanded the newly developed tools of historical and literary criticism. For many, the results of their work profoundly threatened the church and the faith of the Christian population.[15] For a very long time, however, little of this intellectual enterprise actually seeped into the local life of the congregations. Nor did it have a profound impact upon the enthusiasm of the missionary movement. While nineteenth-century scholars like Strauss, Feuerbach, Wellhausen, Baur, and Schweitzer carried out their massive and erudite studies, thousands of young men and women responded to the plea for missionaries to go and save the world. In scholarly circles, growing uncertainty about the nature of the gospel and the person of Christ surfaced. But the missionary endeavor continued abroad and at home with unabated enthusiasm, little infected by such intellectual doubts.

In the early twentieth century, the tensions within Christendom were becoming apparent. The fundamentalist-modernist controversy in North America, with its resulting church schisms, began a continuing public debate about the truth and reliability of traditional Chris-

14. Karl Barth, *Protestant Theology in the Nineteenth Century: Its Background and History* (Valley Forge: Judson, 1973); Geoffrey W. Bromiley, *Historical Theology: An Introduction* (Grand Rapids: Eerdmans, 1978), pp. 305-450; William Hordern, *A Layman's Guide to Protestant Theology* (New York: Macmillan, 1967); Helmut Thielicke, *Modern Faith and Thought,* trans. G. W. Bromiley (Grand Rapids: Eerdmans, 1990); Otto Weber, *Foundations of Dogmatics,* vol. 1, trans. D. G. Guder (Grand Rapids: Eerdmans, 1981), pp. 128-66.

15. Peter Macky, *The Bible in Dialogue with Modern Man* (Waco: Word, 1970); Alan Richardson, *The Bible in the Age of Modern Science* (Philadelphia: Westminster, 1961); Jack B. Rogers and Donald K. McKim, *The Authority and Interpretation of the Bible: An Historical Approach* (San Francisco: Harper & Row, 1979), especially pp. 380ff; Claus Westermann, *Our Controversial Bible,* trans. D. H. Beekmann (Minneapolis: Augsburg, 1969).

tian faith. Critics of Christianity and Christians themselves also disputed the theme of missions. Representative of a growing skepticism about Western missions, as they had been conducted until then, was the Laymen's Foreign Missions Inquiry's report, *Re-Thinking Missions* (the "Hocking Report," 1932), which shook the mission world.[16] The theological assumptions of this report certainly merit the criticism they received.[17] For our purposes, it is important to see that this entire process revealed a growing awareness that all was not well with the Western churches' inherited understandings of mission and evangelism in this century.

There was a growing sense of the "cultural captivity" of the gospel and of the churches' compromises with their surrounding contexts. These questions emerged in more and more penetrating ways as the "daughter churches" became "sister churches" to Western Christianity, and Christians in non-Western cultures began to read their Bibles without Western lenses.[18] At the same time, a variety of critical approaches within its theological ranks reflected a growing disenchantment with the situation of Western Christendom. Karl Barth's publication of his commentary on Romans in 1919 provided a major example of the growing unease with the complacency, security, and captivity of Western Christendom. The commentary electrified the theological world with its emphasis upon human sin, the otherness of God, human dependence upon

16. John R. Fitzmier and Randall Balmer, "A Poultice for the Bite of the Cobra: The Hocking Report and Presbyterian Missions in the Middle Decades of the Twentieth Century," in Milton J Coalter, John M. Mulder, and Louis B. Weeks, eds., *The Diversity of Discipleship: Presbyterians and Twentieth Century Christian Witness* (Louisville: Westminster/ John Knox, 1991), pp. 105ff.

17. Looking back at the discussion of mission in the 1930s, which was dominated by the Hocking Report, Lesslie Newbigin succinctly captured the critical missiological issue at stake: "This report proposed a future for missions in which the name of Jesus would no longer have a central place, except as an illustration of a style of life to be commended to people everywhere. But that style of life was interpreted in such a way that it was hard to distinguish it from the broad ideals of contemporary liberal democratic capitalism. The business of missions was not to seek the conversion of people to Christ, but to assist all the religions to reconceive themselves around this picture of the human future." From "A Sermon Preached at the Thanksgiving Service for the Fiftieth Anniversary of the Tambaram Conference of the International Missionary Council," *International Review of Mission* 77, no. 307 (July 1988): 326-27.

18. Bible translation played a key role in this emancipatory process. See Sanneh, *Translating the Message,* passim.

God's grace in Jesus Christ, and its rejection of nineteenth-century liberal Christianity's cherished optimism about the human condition and the future of human civilization. Building on Kierkegaard, Barth's critique of religion can only be understood against the backdrop of cultural Christianity as it had evolved in Western Christendom.

This expanding turmoil directly affected both the thought and practice of mission and evangelism. As a result, the discussion of mission and evangelism grew into a major debate, or cluster of debates, carried on within denominations, among mission societies, and at the international level. The International Missionary Council, founded as a result of the Edinburgh Conference on World Mission (1910), charted this debate in the themes and discussions of its world conferences.[19] Out of these emerged a broad criticism of what Western churches had meant by "evangelism" and "mission" in the previous two to three centuries.

As we have seen, "mission" had basically meant the Western expansion of its own culturally conformed Christianity, carried out in a complex relationship with colonialism. Implicit in mission was the formation of the institutional church, an extension of the territory of Christendom. For Roman Catholic mission, this was often the most important dimension of their activity, since the *plantatio ecclesiae,* the planting of the church under the pope and his bishops, provided the means of grace to converts. Protestant mission took a variety of stances with regard to the institutional church, but the necessary result of their activity was invariably the formation of an institution, normally modeled on the church tradition of the missionaries.[20]

"Evangelism" became a central emphasis of mission, and the terms were often used synonymously. "Evangelism" stressed conversion, the salvation of the individual soul, the liberation of the individual from the fear of judgment, and the promise of heaven. Evangelism

19. Wolfgang Günther, *Von Edinburgh nach Mexiko City: Die ekklesiologischen Bemühungen der Weltmissionskonferenzen (1910-1963)* (Stuttgart: Evangelischer Missionsverlag, 1970); Bosch, *Transforming Mission,* pp. 369-72; Gerald H. Anderson, "The Theology of Mission among Protestants in the Twentieth Century," in Gerald A. Anderson, ed., *The Theology of the Christian Mission* (New York: McGraw-Hill, 1961), pp. 3-7.

20. For a more complete summary of these assumptions about mission, see David Bosch, "Mission and Evangelism: Clarifying the Concepts," *Zeitschrift für Missionswissenschaft und Religionswissenschaft,* 68. Jahrgang, 1/1984, Heft 1, pp. 161-66.

intended to produce the Christian, a person "who is distinguished from others by the address, reception, possession, use and enjoyment of the salvation of God given and revealed to the world by God in Jesus Christ."[21] The discussion of evangelism tended, therefore, to stress the methods and practices of evangelism. All assumed that the Western missionary brought the correct understanding of the gospel to the nonbelieving culture and needed only to figure out how to convey it accurately and persuasively. Within the Western churches, the meaning of evangelism varied depending upon the situation. In countries with established church traditions, "evangelization" involved the revival of inactive faith. In free or voluntary church situations (as in North America), "evangelism" referred to the proclamation of the salvation message with the linked goal of church member recruitment. Later in the twentieth century, "evangelism" was also used for programs of "new church development," or "church planting."[22]

These understandings began to be subjected to critical scrutiny as the twentieth-century debate proceeded. Many began to challenge the emphasis in mission upon "sending and receiving," with its cultural and institutional implications. Rather than seeing mission as merely a strategic expression of a self-expanding church, mission began to be viewed as an essential theological characteristic of God. Biblical scholars began to interpret the scriptural witness as a record of God's mission, God's sending. Karl Barth first proposed this idea in an address given at the Brandenburg Missionary Conference in 1932, and others soon took it up and began to reshape the conversation about mission.[23] Barth's influence has contributed importantly to the formation of missional theology.[24]

21. Karl Barth, *Church Dogmatics,* trans. G. W. Bromiley, IV, 3/2 (Edinburgh: T. & T. Clark, 1962), p. 561; Barth preserves this definition in order to criticize it, as we shall see in chapter 6.

22. For a helpful summary of the mission/evangelism/evangelization debate, see Wilbert R. Shenk, *Write the Vision: The Church Renewed* (Valley Forge, PA: Trinity Press International, 1995), pp. 30-76.

23. Karl Barth, "Die Theologie und die Mission in der Gegenwart," in *Theologische Fragen und Antworten,* vol. 3 (Zollikon-Zürich: Evangelischer Verlag), pp. 100-126 (first published in 1932); see Bosch, *Transforming Mission,* pp. 389-90.

24. P. J. Robinson, "Mission as Ethos/Ethos as Mission," *Missionalia* 18, no. 1 (April 1990): 157, summararizes the way that Barth, in *Church Dogmatics,* "treats the whole of theology as an aspect of mission."

This broadened understanding of the nature of mission has come to be referred to as *missio Dei* (mission of God), by which

> Mission (may be understood) as being derived from the very nature of God. It (is) thus put into the context of the doctrine of the Trinity, not of ecclesiology or soteriology. The classical doctrine on the *missio Dei* as God the Father sending the Son, and God the Father and the Son sending the Spirit (is) expanded to include yet another "movement": Father, Son, and Holy Spirit sending the church into the world. . . . mission is not primarily an activity of the church, but an attribute of God. God is a missionary God. . . . Mission is thereby seen as a movement from God to the world: the church is viewed as an instrument for that mission. . . . There is church because there is mission, not vice versa.[25]

Such an understanding of mission moves the subject far beyond the level of program or method. It disallows any understanding of mission that makes it a sub-topic of the church. The church's very nature is missionary. Thus, the discussion and understanding of mission must be dealt with when we consider God's actions, purposes, promises, and faithfulness.

Mission as *missio Dei* necessarily relativizes Western understandings and practices of mission. God cannot be restricted to what has been and is happening in Western cultural Christianity. God's work is universal in its intention and impact, and our task is to grapple theologically with that universality. Our categories for the discussion of mission will prove, again and again, to be too small over against the comprehensive nature of God's mission.

During the twentieth century, the essentially missionary nature of the church has become the dominant consensus of the worldwide community of Christian leaders and scholars whose common focus is Christian mission. For those involved in the ecumenical missiological discussion, the "theology of mission" has become "missionary theology."[26]

25. Bosch, *Transforming Mission,* p. 390, with reference to Anna Marie Aagaard, "Missio Dei in katholischer Sicht," *Evangelische Theologie* 34 (1974): 420-33; Johannes Aagaard, "Trends in Missiological Thinking During the Sixties," *International Review of Mission* 62 (1973): 8-25. See also Jürgen Moltmann, *The Church in the Power of the Spirit: A Contribution to Messianic Ecclesiology* (London: SCM, 1977), p. 64.

26. Bosch, *Transforming Mission,* pp. 492-96.

Although much of the theological guild within the Western church traditions remains to be persuaded, the new vocabulary of mission has established itself and its literature is expanding.[27] It is formally endorsed and expounded in official documents of the Roman Catholic Church (Vatican Council II: *Lumen Gentium* [Dogmatic Constitution on the Church], *Ad Gentes* [Decree on the Church's Missionary Activity], *Nostra Aetate* [Declaration on the Relation of the Church to Non-Christian Religions]).[28] A missiological definition of the church is the official position of the World Council of Churches, which is impressively documented in the document entitled "Mission and Evangelism: An Ecumenical Affirmation" (1982). In language representative of the present global consensus on missionary theology, "Mission and Evangelism" defines the church's mission in this way: "The church is sent into the world to call people and nations to repentance, to announce forgiveness of sin and a new beginning in relations with God and with neighbors through Jesus Christ. This evangelistic calling has a new urgency today."[29]

I have described how this relatively new word in the theological vocabulary, "mission," has become a major theological theme, energetically engaged by some theologians, ignored by many, rejected by others. In 1908, Martin Kähler stated somewhat prophetically, "Mission is the mother of theology."[30] Most of the academic theological establishment in the next decades did not rush to agree. In 1959, for example, Wilhelm Pauck commented that "with the possible exception of the early church, whose theology was decisively shaped by the missionary spirit,

27. See bibliographies in Anderson, *Theology of Mission*, pp. 315-36; Bosch, *Transforming Mission*, pp. 535-62; Gerald Anderson, *Bibliography of the Theology of Missions in the Twentieth Century*, 2nd ed. (New York: Mission Research Library, 1960); the regular bibliographies in every edition of the *International Review of Mission*, the publications of (for example) Orbis Books and the William Carey Library, and the major missiological journals: *International Bulletin of Missionary Research*, *Missionalia*, *Missiology*, *Mission Studies*, among others.

28. See Mary Motte, F.M.M., "Roman Catholic Missions," in James M. Phillips and Robert T. Coote, eds., *Toward the Twenty-first Century in Christian Mission* (Grand Rapids: Eerdmans, 1993), pp. 30-40; Louis J. Luzbetak, S.V.D., *The Church and Cultures: New Perspectives in Missiological Anthropology* (Maryknoll, NY: Orbis Books, 1988), pp. 109-32.

29. "Preface," World Council of Churches, *Mission and Evangelism: An Ecumenical Affirmation* (Geneva, 1982).

30. Martin Kähler, *Schriften zur Christologie und Mission* (Munich: Chr. Kaiser Verlag, [1908] 1971), p. 190, as quoted in Bosch, *Transforming Mission*, p. 16.

no part of Christendom has produced major theological responsibility and creativeness in connection with evangelistic endeavors"; and Gerald Anderson went on to report that "there is surprisingly little creative theological endeavor available for guidance," when we face the challenge "to rethink the motives, message, methods, and goals of [Christian] mission."[31] Almost forty years later, there is growing evidence that missiological theology is developing an expanding consensus.[32] By the time Pauck's dictum was written, one could point to the work of theologians such as Karl Barth, Hendrikus Berkhof, G. C. Berkouwer, and Emil Brunner as evidence of mission serving as the mother of theology. Kenneth Scott Latourette had redefined the study of the history of mission with his magisterial seven volumes, *A History of the Expansion of Christianity*.[33] In the latter half of the twentieth century, there are scholars in virtually every theological discipline who are probing the questions of mission.

Mission's own discipline, missiology, has developed into a major branch of scholarship and research.[34] It is a discipline integrated with all the theological areas. It must, of necessity, build on biblical foundations and foster a missional biblical theology. It must continue the historical analysis charted out by Latourette. It must approach all of the major doctrines in terms of their relevance to the church's mission. It must address the pastoral tasks of ministry, and move into the discussion among the practical-theological disciplines and the social and behavioral sciences. Thus, missiology can be seen from two overlapping perspectives: as the "systematic consideration of the nature of Christian mission," and as "the whole range of studies appropriate to the understanding of mission, its context and practical application."[35] Even if

31. Anderson, *Theology of Mission*, pp. 3-4, quoting Wilhelm Pauck, "Theology in the Life of Contemporary American Protestantism," in *Religion and Culture: Essays in Honor of Paul Tillich*, ed. Walter Leibrecht (New York: Harper and Brothers, 1959), p. 278.

32. See, for example, the essays in *Missiology* 24, no. 1 (January, 1996), under the theme "Mission Studies: Taking Stock, Charting the Course."

33. Kenneth Scott Latourette, *A History of the Expansion of Christianity*, 7 vols. (New York: Harper and Brothers, 1937-1945).

34. Bosch, "Mission as Theology," *Transforming Mission*, pp. 489-98; James A. Scherer, "Mission Theology," in Phillips and Coote, *Toward the Twenty-first Century*, pp. 193-202.

35. Andrew Walls, "Missiology," in *Dictionary of the Ecumenical Movement*, ed. Nicholas Lossky et al. (Geneva: WCC Publications/Grand Rapids: Eerdmans, 1991), p. 689.

it is still a marginal discipline to some Western theologians and theological institutions, missiology has nonetheless "arrived."

"Evangelism" as a Theological Task

The same kind of theological depth does not surround the twentieth-century usage of the second new term in the vocabulary of modern Christianity, "evangelism" or "evangelization." As previously noted, the missiological process in the twentieth century began with concerns for the "how" of mission. That discussion of mission has progressed over time and become a very substantive theological enterprise. In contrast, discussion and publications on evangelism have remained relatively superficial. They continue to focus upon methods, strategies, and programs. These methods and programs have become a major industry, reflected in the myriad publications, organizations, and training programs related to evangelism. David Barrett estimates that between 1850 and 1989, 9,280 (presumably Protestant) books on Christian evangelization appeared, 3,725 in English.[36] He further estimates that in the decade of the 1980s, at least 3,000 Roman Catholic books per year appeared on the subject, and from 1948 to 1987, 5,300 conferences on mission and evangelism had taken place.[37]

Whereas mission has become a central theme of theology, evangelism has continued to be an ambiguous term.[38] Secular dictionaries tend to define it as "announcing or preaching good news, and/or . . . winning or converting people." At the same time, virtually all Christian resource works, using biblical scholarship, emphasize that the root meaning of "evangelize" is gospel communication in the form of preaching, bringing, telling, proclaiming, announcing, and declaring. "In English, over 300 different definitions of the concept 'evangelize' have been proposed in print, using vastly different terminology and employing over 700 different terms or synonyms or near-synonyms or part-synonyms." Understandably, there are many voices which complain about the "bewildering

---

36. Barrett, *Evangelize*, p. 37.

37. Barrett, *Evangelize*, pp. 73-75.

38. The content of this paragraph is based on Barrett, *Evangelize*, especially the summary of his findings on pp. 77-79; quotations are taken from p. 77.

variety" of meanings and the "almost chaotic confusion" of the entire discussion of evangelism and evangelization.

Perhaps the most significant aspect of this confusion has to do with the relationship between "mission" and "evangelism." For many, the terms are synonymous. They have been used to describe, with a variety of nuances, the process of "winning souls for eternity" in the mission enterprise abroad or within the secularized West.[39] The specific understanding of soul-winning can range from "saving them from eternal damnation" with a rejection of all forms of social service, to a broad definition of salvation which includes social ministries. Whether or not evangelism must always refer to its results is controversial: for some, it must include the harvest, the bringing in of converts and the founding of churches, yet for others it is only a matter of sowing seed (98). Contrasted with these "evangelical" definitions of evangelism, there has been the tendency in "ecumenical" approaches to speak very broadly of all forms of Christian ministry as evangelism, or even to reduce its meaning to the call to humanitarianism, or to some this-worldly understanding of the kingdom of God (98).

Others have sought to define the terms "mission" and "evangelism" as distinct from each other. Some use "evangelism" for that particular ministry which seeks to reach those who are in a nominally Christian culture and are themselves no longer Christian. Thus, its usage is a response to the secularization of Christendom that has been a fundamental process of Western modernity (98-99). Others attempt to make one of the two terms the larger, overarching concept, with the other term fitting within it. Thus "evangelism" can describe "the entire manner in which the gospel becomes a reality in man's life" while "mission" provides the foundation and motive for it. More commonly, "mission" is understood as the broader concept, defining the mission and calling of the church (in the sense of *missio Dei*), and "evangelism" as the specific task of making known, witnessing to, and inviting response to the gospel (99). One of the recurring problems of these definitions concerns the question of Christian social and political action.

---

39. The discussion in this paragraph and the next is based on David Bosch, "Evangelism: Theological Currents and Cross-Currents Today," *International Bulletin of Missionary Research* 11, no. 3 (July 1987): 99-103; subsequent citations of this article will give page numbers parenthetically in the text. See also Bosch, "Mission and Evangelism," pp. 161-87.

The missionary enterprise of the church has almost invariably involved not only direct communication of the Christian message, but also educational, agricultural, medical, social, and even political ministries. Are these to be understood as part of the larger "mission," next to "evangelism"? Many attempt to resolve the problem in such a fashion: mission, then, is evangelism plus social action (99-100).

The entire discussion reveals that there is a great need for more biblical and theological discipline in our understanding, formulation, and practice of evangelism. Many of the distinctions currently in use are untenable. Lesslie Newbigin has rightly criticized the widespread distinction between "ecumenical" and "evangelical" as an "absurd and irrational dichotomy."[40] Similarly, the distinction between evangelism and justice, as found in the formulated goals of a typical mainline denomination like the Presbyterian Church (U.S.A.), is unacceptable.[41]

This book will seek to develop an understanding of evangelism that is rooted in the *missio Dei*, shaped by God's actions in history, faithful to the gospel, and at the heart of ministry. I will suggest that such an understanding can be symbolized by redefining what we have meant by "evangelism" with the term "evangelization." This term has at least four advantages to commend it. It is closer to the New Testament usage, with its emphasis upon the church's commission to evangelize *(euangelizein)*, that is, to communicate the gospel. It stresses the ongoing, dynamic, process character of the church's witness. It moves away from the reductionism of evangelism as method and program. And it confirms a common usage among Protestants and Roman Catholics, since it is already the preferred terminology of the Catholic world.

David Bosch correctly observes that "evangelism is the *core, heart,* or *center* of mission; it consists in the proclamation of salvation in Christ to nonbelievers, in announcing forgiveness of sins, in calling people to repentance and faith in Christ, inviting them to become living members of Christ's earthly community and to begin a life in the

40. Lesslie Newbigin, "Cross-currents in Ecumenical and Evangelical Understandings of Mission," *International Bulletin of Missionary Research* 6, no. 4 (October 1982): 146-51.

41. Darrell L. Guder, "Locating a Reformed Theology of Evangelism in a Pluralistic World," in Milton J Coalter and Virgil Cruz, eds., *How Shall We Witness? Faithful Evangelism in a Reformed Tradition* (Louisville: Westminster/John Knox, 1995), pp. 165-86, especially 174ff.

power of the Holy Spirit."[42] Further, it must be affirmed with the
World Council of Churches that there is an "inextricable relationship
between Christian unity and missionary calling, between ecumenism
and evangelization. 'Evangelization is the test of our ecumenical vocation.'"[43] But I intend for this term to signify more. If the Christian
community is to carry out its mission of gospel witness, then its
evangelization will be directed both to itself as well as to the world into
which it is sent. We need to free our language and our thinking from
the idea that evangelistic ministry is only directed to nonbelievers. The
New Testament is, as I have stressed, addressed to believers from beginning to end, and it evangelizes at every turning. Evangelizing churches
are churches that are being evangelized. For the sake of its evangelistic
vocation, the continuing conversion of the church is essential.

There is a small but growing conversation about the theology of
evangelization, that is, the serious grappling with the missiological understanding of evangelistic ministry, as compared with the methodological and strategic.[44] It is not an easy task. "Evangelism falls between
a rock and a hard place. The rock is the extraordinary silence on the

---

42. Bosch, "Evangelism: Theological Currents and Cross-currents Today," p. 100.
43. WCC, *Mission and Evangelism*, ¶1.
44. For example: William J. Abraham, *The Logic of Evangelism* (Grand Rapids: Eerdmans, 1989); Gerald H. Anderson and Thomas F. Stransky, eds., *Mission Trends No. 2:
Evangelization* (New York: Paulist; Grand Rapids: Eerdmans, 1975); Mortimer Arias, *Announcing the Reign of God: Evangelization and the Subversive Memory of Jesus* (Philadelphia:
Fortress, 1984); Richard S. Armstrong, *Service Evangelism* (Philadelphia: Westminster,
1979); Walter Arnold, *Evangelisation im ökumenischen Gespräch: Beiträge eines Symposiums
(Genf 1973)* (Erlangen: Verlag der Ev.-Luth. Mission, 1974); Orlando Costas, *Liberating
News: A Theology of Contextual Evangelization* (Grand Rapids: Eerdmans, 1989); Darrell
Guder, *Be My Witnesses: The Church's Mission, Message, and Messengers* (Grand Rapids: Eerd-
mans, 1985); Robert T. Henderson, *Joy to the World: An Introduction to Kingdom Evangelism*
(Atlanta: John Knox, 1980); W. J. Hollenweger, *Evangelisation gestern und heute* (Stuttgart:
J. F. Steinkopf Verlag, 1973); Ben Campbell Johnson, *Rethinking Evangelism: A Theological
Approach* (Philadelphia: Westminster, 1987); T. A. Kantonen, *The Theology of Evangelism*
(Philadelphia: Muhlenberg, 1954); Patrick R. Keifert, *Welcoming the Stranger: A Public The-
ology of Worship and Evangelism* (Minneapolis: Fortress, 1992); Vinay Samuel and Albrecht
Hauser, eds., *Proclaiming Christ in Christ's Way: Studies in Integral Evangelism* (Oxford:
Regnum Books, 1989); Walter Klaiber, *Call and Response: Biblical Foundations of a Theology
of Evangelism* trans. H. Perry-Trauthig and J. A. Dwyer (Nashville: Abingdon, 1997); see
also the April 1994 issue of *Interpretation*, for four major articles on dealing theologically
with the theme of evangelism.

part of systematic theologians on the subject of evangelism. The hard place is the inability of practical theology to reach any sustained measure of internal self-criticism."[45] Like its larger contextual discipline, missiology, evangelism must work integratively with all the disciples, especially biblical theology, systematic theology (ecclesiology), and practical theology.

It is my conviction that theological conversation about evangelism and evangelization must continue and deepen. Our theology of evangelistic ministry must be rooted in a biblical theology of mission and, above all, dominated and shaped by the gospel it seeks to proclaim. It must be open to learning from the history of Christian evangelization, as checkered as it is. Its method must be an expression of its content, its strategy an outworking of its discipleship. "The central task of a theology of evangelism is to provide a clear and credible account of the ministry of evangelism that will foster and illuminate responsible evangelistic practices by the Christian church and its agents in the modern world."[46] This work seeks to develop such an understanding of evangelistic ministry. As it proceeds, it will become clear that the only way that evangelization can truly be the heart of ministry will be through the continuing conversion of the church.

45. William J. Abraham, "A Theology of Evangelism: The Heart of the Matter," *Interpretation* 48, no. 2 (April 1994): 117.

46. Abraham, "A Theology of Evangelism," p. 117.

Chapter Two

God's Mission Is Good News

Our theology of evangelistic ministry must be rooted in a biblical theology of mission and, above all, dominated and shaped by the gospel it seeks to proclaim.

The Joyful News of God's Love

The fundamental certainty of biblical faith is the fact that there is good news about God. The "gospel of God" is the theme and content of the earliest Christian proclamation (1 Thess. 2:1, 8, 9; Rom. 1:1). The Gospel of Mark introduces Jesus' earthly ministry with this brief summary: "Jesus came to Galilee, proclaiming the good news of God, and saying, 'The time is fulfilled, and the kingdom of God has come near; repent, and believe in the good news'" (Mark 1:14-15). Mark calls his book a "gospel" (Mark 1:1): the whole story is good news. Eduard Schweizer translates it "joyful message" *(Freudenbotschaft)* in his commentary on Mark.[1]

The biblical witness to God does not argue about divine existence.

---

1. Eduard Schweizer, *Das Evangelium nach Markus,* NTD 1 (Göttingen: Vandenhoeck & Ruprecht, 1967), pp. 13ff on 1:1, pp. 23ff on 1:14; in the English translation, *The Good News According to Mark,* trans. E. H. Madvig (Atlanta: John Knox, 1970), *Freudenbotschaft* is translated "Good News" (pp. 28ff, 44ff).

It tells the story of God's actions in human history in the form of testimony. It testifies to God's goodness, a goodness which God has made known, has revealed, and which defines God's purposes. God's people have experienced this goodness; it has been Israel's gospel from the call of Abraham onward: "For the Lord is good; his steadfast love endures forever, and his faithfulness to all generations" (Ps. 100:5).

This good news about God is rooted in a particular history. Although the modern mind has been affronted by the biblical emphasis upon a particular, specific history as the event of God's self-disclosure, it is essential to the goodness of this news that it be historical: "precisely the historical character of biblical revelation is of essential significance for a biblical foundation for mission."[2] Israel's witness to the events of God's self-disclosure constitutes the missional nature of this "salvation history."[3] Through the particular encounter of God with Israel, the good news that God is loving and purposeful enters into human history and becomes knowable.

Apart from such a particular history, Christianity has no universal message to proclaim. The Bible is not a collection of universal ideas cloaked in a particular culture. Universal ideas cannot be the good news that the concrete testimony of a particular people at a particular time can well be, if their witness is credible. Such universal ideas are merely the product of human imagination and creativity. Christian witness is not the interpretation of philosophy but the continuation of the event of God's self-disclosure in human history. The historical experience of God is the surprising result of God's initiation, God's desire to speak and be heard. That surprise continues to define the concrete history of the world, and of the mission community within the world which is called to be the witness to God's goodness, the "gospel of

2. David Bosch, *Witness to the World* (London: Marshall, Morgan & Scott, 1980), p. 61; see the discussion of "God and History," ch. 6, pp. 58ff. See also John Howard Yoder's discussion of the historical particularity of the good news about God in "Why Ecclesiology is Social Ethics," in *The Royal Priesthood: Essays Ecclesiological and Ecumenical,* ed. Michael G. Cartwright (Grand Rapids: Eerdmans, 1994), pp. 113ff.

3. My use of this term should be understood missionally, especially as expounded by Johannes Blauw, *The Missionary Nature of the Church: A Survey of the Biblical Theology of Mission* (New York: McGraw-Hill, 1962), pp. 15ff; in the dynamic and eschatological way the term is developed there, it is worth reviving in spite of the justifiable criticisms of it in the last decades.

God." God's mission is good news because it is historical: it has been historical from the beginning and continues to be the history that defines our hope. We encounter God within that same history as God makes us part of salvation history for the sake of the world he loves.

As history, God's mission takes place within time. Because God's goodness is revealed within created time, there is liberating good news about our temporality. Time is not the impersonal structure that defines our existence, our beginnings and our endings. The "fulfilled time" of which Jesus spoke is not just the sequence of minutes, days, and years, countable time, the task of chronometers. It is rather time with a purpose, time as intentional movement initiated and guided by God, proceeding from a certain beginning to a promised conclusion — "to all generations." David Bosch describes the biblical term *kairos* as "decisive moment, fateful hour, extraordinary opportunity, turning-point in history."[4] Eduard Schweizer speaks of it as "the fulfillment of the special salvation-time which is distinguished from all other time."[5] God's purposefulness for creation gives time meaning, and that meaning grows as God's time moves toward its consummation. The world in its temporality is made by God and is the arena within which God pursues the *missio Dei*. This time can, therefore, fill until it overflows, until that point when the decisive event takes place. Jesus describes his own coming as <u>the</u> *kairos*, as the chosen time, "the filled present."[6] When Jesus says, "The time is fulfilled," he places his message about God's particular action now, in his coming, within the larger context of God's actions in history from creation onward to now and into the future. Jesus' coming and his message are good news, as it has always been good news when God makes God's self and purposes known.

Israel's testimony about God, over centuries of history, consistently emphasizes the goodness of the revealed news about God's self and purposes within temporal history. God's creation is good. God desires that all nations should experience blessing, and to make that happen, Israel and his seed will be blessed. God promises his people land and prosperity and confounds human expectations by providing heirs

---

4. Bosch, *Witness to the World,* pp. 64-66.

5. Schweizer, *Mark,* p. 45.

6. Bosch, *Witness to the World,* p. 64. See also Karl Barth's concept of "filled time" in *Church Dogmatics,* trans. G. W. Bromiley, IV, 3/2 (Edinburgh: T. & T. Clark, 1962), pp. 500ff.

when all hope is gone. God speaks so that his voice can be heard and the witness can testify, "God said!" God hears the pleas and the praise of his people and responds. "I have observed the misery of my people who are in Egypt; I have heard their cry" (Exod. 3:7). Over and over again, Israel experiences that God is victor, that no enemy can keep God from fulfilling his promises. The sea is parted, the pursuing armies overpowered, and the people liberated. God gives Israel the instructions they need in order to live under the divine blessing and to experience its goodness. God guides the people from captivity, through wilderness, to a good land of God's own choosing.

The fitting response to this continuing experience of God's goodness is celebration and thanksgiving. The Old Testament resounds with Israel's praise. The constant refrain of the Psalms is "praise the Lord!" The year is sorted out into regular times and festivals of celebration and praise, beginning with the Sabbath and culminating in the Passover. Israel looks back upon the "fulfilled times," the unique events of God's action in its midst, and continues to claim that presence and sovereignty now, making every experience of worship into a *kairos,* a time of God's choosing. Israel looks forward to the definitive *kairos,* when God will bring about the conclusively new thing: "The days are surely coming, says the Lord, when I will make a new covenant with the house of Israel and the house of Judah" (Jer. 31:31).

The good news of God in the history and experience of Israel centers upon the reality of God's love. God has always acted out of love, and that testimony is at the heart of Moses' great recounting of God's work in Israel, as framed by the Deuteronomist:

> "Because he *loved* your ancestors, he chose their descendants after them." (Deut. 4:37)

> "It was not because you were more numerous than any other people that the Lord set his heart on you and chose you — for you were the fewest of all peoples. It was because the Lord *loved* you and kept the oath he swore to your ancestors." (Deut. 7:7-8)

> "If you heed these ordinances, by diligently observing them, the Lord your God will maintain with you the covenant loyalty that he swore to your ancestors; he will *love* you, bless you, and multiply you." (Deut. 7:12-13)

"Although heaven and the heaven of heavens belong to the Lord your God, the earth with all that is in it, yet the Lord set his heart in *love* on your ancestors alone and chose you, their descendants after them, out of all the peoples, as it is today." (Deut. 10:14-15)

Therefore God's people may respond to his rule and actions with their love. This was and is a most unusual way to describe the relationship of the created to the creator: "Hear, O Israel: The Lord is our God, the Lord alone. You shall love the Lord your God with all your heart, and with all your soul, and with all your might" (Deut. 6:4-5). This response of love, of course, is possible because of the love of God that precedes and evokes it. God's actions reveal his love and goodness, which enable God's people to respond with love and live out that goodness. Israel thus receives and understands God's guidance for its life, the *torah,* as evidence of God's goodness, and therefore the source of human blessedness and the cause of thanksgiving and praise (Pss. 1; 119). To be sure, Israel's history, as told in the Old Testament, is marked more by breaches of this loving response than by faithfulness. But the character of God, beyond all chastisement and judgment, remains unchangingly compassionate: "Return, O Israel, to the Lord your God, for you have stumbled because of your iniquity. . . . I will heal their disloyalty; I will love them freely, for my anger has turned from them" (Hos. 14:1, 4).

God's Mission

The compassion of God is the motivating power of God's mission. Both God's act of creation and God's determination to heal his rebellious creation are the compelling reason for the salvation history which unfolds from Abraham onward.[7] God is revealed as "the One who . . . has compassion on the poor, the oppressed, the weak and the outcast" (50). When Israel praises God, the people sing of him as "the Father of

---

7. For the following discussion, see David Bosch, "God's Compassion," chap. 4, *Witness to the World,* pp. 50-57; subsequent references will give page numbers parenthetically in the text; see also Bosch, "Reflections on Biblical Models of Mission," in James M. Phillips and Robert T. Coote, eds., *Toward the Twenty-first Century in Christian Mission* (Grand Rapids: Eerdmans, 1993), pp. 175-92.

orphans and protector of widows. . . . God gives the desolate a home to live in; he leads out the prisoners to prosperity" (Ps. 68:4-6). Israel was also to honor and care for the stranger in her midst, as a further testimony to the compassionate character of the God who had chosen this people and made it his nation (Num. 9:14, 15:14; Josh. 20:9).

Congruent with the compassionate character of God, the act of Israel's election was itself rooted in God's gracious love. God chose Israel not for the people's merit but as an act of mercy (Deut. 7:7-8, cited above). That calling, however, was not for Israel's benefit alone. God's missional intention was that all the world should be blessed: "in you [Abraham and the posterity God will give him] all the families of the earth shall be blessed" (Gen. 12:3; see also 15:18). Israel's lack of faithfulness and tendency to reduce its call to the status of religious privilege were the reasons for constant prophetic admonition and divine punishment.

> The purpose of election was service and where this was withheld, election lost its meaning: "For you alone have I cared among all the nations of the world; therefore will I punish you for all your iniquities" (Amos 3:2). Election primarily conveyed neither privilege, nor favouritism, but rather responsibility. (52)

The story of Jonah, one of the few Old Testament episodes which appear to be missionary in nature, actually addresses God's summons to Israel to be a compassionate witness even over against such unworthy subjects as the Ninevites. Their conversion is not really the issue; Jonah preaches judgment to them and is surprised by their subsequent repentance. It is Jonah's problem which is the book's theme, "a 'missionary' without a missionary's heart" (53). The story calls "Israel to allow themselves to be converted to a compassion comparable to that of Yahweh" (53), so that God's mission can be carried out as God intends it to be.

The compassion of God for the lost and rebellious creation results in the sending of Jesus. The "gospel of God" is, for the New Testament witness, synonymous with the "gospel of Jesus Christ" (Mark 1:1; Rom. 1:9; 15:19, 29; 1 Cor. 9:12, 18; 2 Cor. 2:12; 9:13; 10:14; Gal. 1:7; Phil. 1:27; 1 Thess. 3:2). John's Gospel does not use the term "gospel," but it summarizes the New Testament consensus with words that emphasize the essential linkage between God's loving and God's sending or mission:

For God so loved the world that he gave his only Son, so that everyone who believes in him may not perish but may have eternal life. Indeed, God did not send the Son into the world to condemn the
world, but in order that the world might be saved through him. (John
3:16-17)

Jesus entered into his earthly ministry purposefully, carrying out
the implications of his Father's "divine affirmation": "You are my Son,
the Beloved; with you I am well pleased" (Mark 1:11).[8] Jesus accepted
his mission, God's sending of him, as he moved from Galilee to Jerusalem, from the countryside to the city, from the temple to the place of
the skull. He did so with the clear sense of who he was and why he was
sent. "Without seeing and acknowledging that the human Jesus already
laid claim to being the messianic Son of man whom God sent to Israel,
one cannot make sense historically of Jesus's ministry, or even the passion narrative."[9] He was now to carry out the public ministry for which
he came, which was "to call people, by [his] own authority, to repentance and to faith in the message of the impending dawn of the kingdom of God." This was his "messianic mission."[10]

Jesus' mission was God's mission, and it was characterized by the
same compassion that had been the central theme of Israel's experience
and testimony through the preceding centuries of salvation history. He
linked Israel's classical understanding of its faith response to God,
"you shall love the Lord your God," with the commandment to "love
your neighbor as yourself" (Mark 12:29-31).

For Jesus the twofold commandment of loving God and neighbor de-
termines the will of God in its entirety. If Jesus makes the commandment of love central, he does it on the basis that the one God, his Father, is a God of love and delights more in the repentance and life of the
poor, the godforsaken, and the sinners than in their destruction.[11]

Thus, he taught his disciples how to follow him by showing them
how God's compassion was to reach out into the world, precisely to

8. Peter Stuhlmacher, *Jesus of Nazareth — Christ of Faith,* trans. Siegfried S.
Schatzmann (Peabody, MA: Hendrickson, 1993), p. 23.
9. Stuhlmacher, *Jesus of Nazareth,* pp. 6-7.
10. Stuhlmacher, *Jesus of Nazareth,* pp. 15, 47-49 on "Jesus' Messianic Mission."
11. Stuhlmacher, *Jesus of Nazareth,* p. 16.

those who were on the margins of society — the rejected, the unclean, the poor, the imprisoned, and the sick. In carrying out this mission, he "radicalized the ethical demands of the *tôrâh* by focusing on the command to love, especially to love the enemy."[12] This radicalization meant that Jesus announced that God's compassion outweighs God's divine vengeance. Jesus ended his reading of Isaiah 61:1-2 in the synagogue at Nazareth by linking the "year of the Lord's favor" with the amazing claim that his own mission (sending) was in fact the "fulfilling of the *kairos*": "Today this scripture has been fulfilled in your hearing" (Luke 4:18-21).

His Jewish hearers, who understood this passage to be messianic, were outraged that he did not continue with the last phrase in Isaiah's text: "the day of vengeance of our God" (Isa. 61:2). As the messianic messenger, Jesus was empowered to proclaim that the kingdom of God, now coming about, was going to be very different from pious expectations. Such expectations would, justifiably, look for retribution for wrongs committed and vengeance for evils done. Jesus dares "to proclaim the dawn of the new era," claiming "the authority arbitrarily to truncate Scripture by omitting the reference to divine vengeance." His challenge is truly revolutionary: "Blessed is everyone who does not take offense at the fact that the era of salvation differs from what he has expected, that God's compassion on the poor and outcast has superseded divine vengeance!"[13] With this authoritative reinterpretation, Jesus already looked ahead to his own death as the event that once and for all demonstrated that God's mission is salvation, not vengeance.

God's Mission as the Coming Kingdom

Although the term itself does not occur until late Judaism, the kingdom of God was a major theme of Jewish expectation, a dominant line that can be traced through many levels and traditions of the Old Testa-

---

12. Bosch, *Witness to the World,* p. 54.

13. Bosch, *Witness to the World,* p. 56, with reference to both Jeremias's and Grundmann's emphasis on the major significance of Jesus' omission of Isaiah's reference to vengeance.

ment.[14] For Jesus, it represented the very heart of the good news he brought and embodied: "I must proclaim the good news of the kingdom of God" (Luke 4:43). Mark puts it in the summary sermon at the beginning of Jesus' ministry to underline its centrality: "The kingdom of God is drawing near" (Mark 1:15).

This theme inevitably evoked misunderstandings as Jesus' hearers put this language into their own framework of assumptions and hopes. The disciples gathered on the mount of the ascension asked Jesus, "Lord, is this the time when you will restore the kingdom to Israel?" (Acts 1:6). They used the word for counted or measured time (*chronos*), revealing their desire to restrict God's reign to their temporal categories. Jesus responds, "It is not for you to know the times or the seasons," referring both to measurable time and fulfilled time (*chronos* and *kairos*). Over against this constant temptation to define the kingdom of God in terms of our own human agenda and to fit it into our schedules, the disciples (and we) must learn to hear Jesus' message of the kingdom as the distinctively good news that he makes it to be.

Jesus proclaims that the kingdom is present and is also coming. He interprets his coming as fulfillment, as we just saw, and claims that his casting out of demons reveals that "the kingdom of God has come to you" (Luke 11:20). But then he teaches his disciples to pray, "Your kingdom come" (Luke 11:2; Matt. 6:10). This tension between the kingdom come and coming has always been difficult for the Christian tradition. As will be seen in the discussion of reductionism (chapter 5), the temptation has always been very strong to resolve this tension in favor of one of its poles, either the kingdom's present or future. It is, however, crucial to the mission of Jesus and his followers that the tension be maintained: "It is precisely in this creative tension that the reality of God's reign has significance for our contemporary mission."[15]

Clearly, something radically new has entered history with this

---

14. See John Bright, *The Kingdom of God: The Biblical Concept and Its Meaning for the Church* (Nashville: Abingdon, 1953), for an older but still very helpful overview of this theme; see also Herman N. Ridderbos, *The Coming of the Kingdom,* trans. H. de Jongste, ed. R. O. Zorn (Philadelphia: Presbyterian and Reformed, 1962).

15. David Bosch, *Transforming Mission: Paradigm Shifts in Theology of Mission* (Maryknoll, NY: Orbis Books, 1991), p. 32.

man, Jesus. "The kingdom is present in his words and deeds. The time of the good tidings has come."[16] This is taking place concretely in the event of the life and ministry of Jesus. It is the experience to which the Gospel records witness, but this kingdom in all its newness is not of human invention. Jesus affirms that this kingdom is a gift of God that must be received, with the simplicity and trustfulness of children. In fact, it is given precisely to those who have nothing to bring, no claim to make on God: "Blessed are the poor in spirit, for theirs is the kingdom of heaven" (Matt. 5:3).

God's reign is defined by the very character and action of God, which means that it cannot be reduced to simple definition nor made to serve human purposes.[17] It is God's concrete self-disclosure in human history making a new relationship with God possible and thus a new life with a new future. So the good news of the kingdom of God is always, at any particular moment, partial; it always emphasizes this or that dimension of the wonder beyond telling, which is God's reign in our midst. Jesus teaches about the kingdom by telling parables that illustrate its various dimensions and the many ways in which we can encounter it. Always, however, the message focuses upon the loving, gracious, inviting reality of God in our human history; it creates the radically new option of submission to God's rule and thus entry into God's kingdom. This submission to God's rule is, paradoxically, the liberation of the believer from all that separates from God. To enter into the kingdom means to experience the forgiveness of sins, the liberation from all the demons which possess us, the gift of new life, and the invitation to a new kind of community.

The message of the kingdom come and coming implies response, decision, on the part of those who hear its witness. That there is the option of entering the kingdom means, of course, that humans can choose to reject God's goodness and thus remain outside the kingdom. This has been true since Eden. Israel had always interpreted human reality as being *simul creatus et peccator* (simultaneously created and sinner), perhaps most vividly in its "prophecy turned backwards," the uni-

---

16. Mortimer Arias, *Announcing the Reign of God: Evangelization and the Subversive Memory of Jesus* (Philadelphia: Fortress, 1984), p. 15; the following discussion is based on pp. 13-25. See also Bosch, *Witness,* pp. 61ff.

17. Darrell L. Guder, ed., *Missional Church: A Vision for the Sending of the Church in North America* (Grand Rapids: Eerdmans, 1998), p. 90.

versal prehistory of Genesis 1 to 12.[18] There, the goodness of God's creation purposes is contrasted with the arrogant rebellion of the humans. The persistence of their sin is met by judgment and good news: God does not ignore or dismiss human sin, nor does he forsake the rebellious world. The divine promise and continuing presence accompany God's judgment over Adam and Eve; even after their joint act of rebellion, they can still hear God's voice. God still provides for their needs by clothing them. Cain is both punished and saved and continues to serve God's purposes. Abraham is God's servant even when he stoops to deceit and manifestly does not trust God to be faithful to all the promises. Joseph reveals to his brothers that what they intended for evil, God turned to good. The history that unfolds is the continuing demonstration of God's judgment and grace, always moving toward God's saving purposes for creation.

Whenever God's good news is made known, the bad news of our human reality is also revealed. As the kingdom approaches, "it launches an all-out attack on evil in all its manifestations."[19] The power of evil is never underestimated in the biblical witness; there is a fundamental conflict within creation rooted in the sinful rejection of God's gracious rule.[20] That conflict takes many forms, both individual and corporate. Jesus must grapple with Satan's arsenal of temptations before embarking upon his public ministry, and in that experience, he confronts both the personal and systemic dimensions of evil. Jesus challenges this evil in its individual and personal forms when he drives out demons, cures leprosy, heals sick children, overcomes hunger and doubt, and forgives sin. But he also combats corporate evil when he sits at table with publicans and sinners, makes fishermen and tax collectors into his disciples, demonstrates against the defiling of God's house, and challenges the hypocrisy of the religious establishment. There is no area of life outside God's reign, which means that the rule of God always opposes the other gods and powers which seek to enslave humans.

As Jesus demonstrated the character of the kingdom by all that he opposed and condemned, he revealed that the nearing of the kingdom

---

18. Johannes Blauw, *The Missionary Nature of the Church: A Survey of the Biblical Theology of Mission* (New York: McGraw-Hill, 1962), pp. 17-21.

19. Bosch, *Transforming Mission,* p. 32.

20. Walter Brueggemann, *Biblical Perspectives on Evangelism: Living in a Three-Storied Universe* (Nashville: Abingdon, 1993), pp. 19-25, on the "theological conflict."

entails suffering. Jesus' proclamation and demonstration of the coming of the kingdom, and of what it meant, made the lines of opposition clear and identified his enemies. Jesus healed on the Sabbath, kept company with notorious sinners, corrected sacrosanct understandings of the law, showed the dangers of wealth for true piety, allowed the payment of taxes to the hated occupying powers, and cleansed the corrupt marketplace of the temple. In all these sayings and actions, Jesus revealed the nature of God's reign and exposed the many ways in which that reign was resisted or diluted.[21] The gospel records constantly emphasize that there were many who did not welcome Jesus' signs of healing and restoration and who were enraged by his authority over the law and the traditions. One interpreter suggests that the difficult saying in Matthew 11:12 be rendered: "Since the times of John the Baptist the kingdom of God is forcing its way and demanding a powerful reaction."[22]

> The kingdom is in-breaking — forcing its way in through persons, institutions, and societies, attracting and repelling, being seized by faith, and being rejected by unfaith. The presence of the kingdom in Jesus Christ is opening its way among the people, forgiving sins, restoring life, creating community, but at the same time exacerbating the forces of the antikingdom that will take him finally to the cross. The presence of the in-breaking kingdom provokes a confrontation and demands an option.[23]

The Cross as the Center of the Gospel

While Jesus' disciples leave all to follow him and, as the students of a wandering rabbi, memorize his teachings, many others react to his message and actions with suspicion and finally radical rejection. How could the religious leaders respond to his demonstrative cleansing of the temple in any other way than with outrage? It was clear to them that his message directly challenged all that they held holy: "Even now the ax is lying at the root of the trees" (Luke 3:9). Jesus did not retreat

21. Stuhlmacher, *Jesus of Nazareth*, pp. 44-47.
22. Arias, *Announcing the Reign of God*, p. 44.
23. Arias, *Announcing the Reign of God*, p. 44. *Ibid.* See also Stuhlmacher, *Jesus of Nazareth*, pp. 48-49.

from this conflict. He set his face for Jerusalem, knowing that his enemies awaited him there. "Jesus is less concerned with protecting his own life than with his task to bring to bear the affirmation and claim of the one God who is present, whom he calls his 'Father.'"[24] The drama reaches its climax in the arrest and trial of Jesus, the passion story that is the essential core of all four Gospels.

> Thus Jesus is charged with messianic agitation and divine presumption. Because the Jewish court is not allowed to carry out a death sentence at the time of Jesus (cf. John 19:31), his Sadducean opponents must denounce Jesus as a messianic insurrectionist before Pilate the following morning and thereby urge the Roman prefect to take action against the suspect. Jesus also maintains his messianic confession before Pilate and does not attempt to defend himself (Mark 15:1-5). His confession earns him a scourging and death on the cross. Thus Jesus faces death with purpose and cognizance.[25]

"In fulfillment of his mission, Jesus died the death of atonement on the cross for his friends and his enemies."[26] At this point, the good news begins to be a problem for many modern people. A gospel of a loving, compassionate God is possibly still welcomed news. A gospel that speaks of new beginnings and envisions a radically different kind of world may gain a hearing, even if it uses the somewhat arcane language of "the kingdom of God." A gospel that is candid about the struggles, injustices, and cruelty of human existence will possibly be respected. But a gospel that unswervingly focuses on the New Testament's central emphasis, Jesus' death upon the cross, will encounter resistance. Paul spoke about the continuing experience of the church when he described the proclamation of Christ crucified as "a stumbling block to Jews and foolishness to Gentiles" (1 Cor. 1:22).

That same apostle may have defined the gospel in its most succinct form with the words, "Christ died for our sins in accordance with the scriptures" (1 Cor. 15:3). The early church may have defined its

---

24. Stuhlmacher, *Jesus of Nazareth*, p. 33.

25. Stuhlmacher, *Jesus of Nazareth*, pp. 32-33; see the entire discussion, pp. 29-35.

26. Peter Stuhlmacher, "Die Mitte der Schrift — biblisch-theologisch betrachtet," in *Wissenschaft und Kirche: Festschrift für Eduard Lohse,* ed. Kurt Aland and Siegfried Meurer (Bielefeld: Luther Verlag, 1989), p. 46.

faith clearly with these words from 1 Timothy: "For there is one God; there is also one mediator between God and humankind, Christ Jesus, himself human, who gave himself a ransom for all — this was attested at the right time" (1 Tim. 2:5-6; the word used is *kairos*). Modern or postmodern hearers, however, struggle with the apostolic assertion in 1 Corinthians that "Jesus' death for our sins and his resurrection by God constitute the center of the gospel of Christ."[27] They will certainly be uncomfortable with the insistence that "according to this text [1 Tim. 2:5-6] Jesus is the one God-appointed mediator between God and humans, who sealed his divine mission by means of delivering up his life for all and who established the witness of the gospel at the moment in time that God appointed."[28]

"The time that God appointed!" The Christian message states that the very heart of the good news that is God's mission is the death of Jesus on the cross. "The starting point of our proclamation is Christ and Christ crucified."[29] The goodness of this news must be sought in the transforming meaning of the death of Jesus. That meaning is rooted in Jesus' own sense of his mission, and especially in the Old Testament tradition in which he placed himself and his mission. He drew upon the writings of the prophet Isaiah to interpret his calling, beginning with the encounter in the Nazareth synagogue recorded by Luke (Luke 4:16-30). Especially important was the prophetic statement of Isaiah 43:4-5, in which God announces that he is going to provide a ransom for the people because of his love for them. This message is then expounded in the suffering servant passage of Isaiah 53. "God's servant is sent and commissioned by God to bear vicariously the punishment for the sin of the people and thereby to procure Israel's salvation. Jesus' voluntary path into suffering and death makes good sense if he understood himself to be called to take the way of the suffering servant of God."[30] We note that God's servant is sent for this purpose: here is the very heart of the gospel of God's mission (sending), demonstrating the depth and comprehensive character of God's love for the world — "For God so loved the world!"

27. Stuhlmacher, *Jesus of Nazareth*, p. 8.

28. Stuhlmacher, *Jesus of Nazareth*, p. 9.

29. World Council of Churches, *Mission and Evangelism: An Ecumenical Affirmation* (Geneva, 1982), ¶7.

30. Stuhlmacher, *Jesus of Nazareth*, p. 50.

It is clear that Jesus identified himself with the suffering servant when he said that "the Son of man did not come to be served but to serve and to give his life as a ransom for many" (Mark 10:45 par.). This self-interpretation was sealed, as it were, in the final supper with the disciples, where Jesus gave them the bread and the wine as gifts of his body and blood for them. In the parallel incident in John's Gospel, he demonstrates with the foot-washing that he was sent to serve his followers (John 13:1-20). It is germane to our understanding of the gospel of God's mission that this story is introduced with the words, "Having loved his own who were in the world, he loved them to the end" (v. 1). These sayings and actions, together with Jesus' prophetic words about his impending suffering, then enabled the apostolic community to recognize the gospel in the cross as they remembered them in the light of Easter.

That community proclaimed that Jesus died on the cross for our sins. Those rooted in Israel's faith pilgrimage, as witnessed to in the Old Testament, knew that the consequence of human sin was God's judgment. To be a sinner meant to be lost before God, for human sin is rebellion against the will of God, which results from human intention and leads to disobedient actions. It must result in death. Here the Old Testament is unequivocal and relentlessly clear: to rebel against God, to turn to other idols, to discount God's faithfulness is to deserve nothing more or less than God's judgment. Sinful humans experience that unavoidable judgment as the consequence of having turned their backs to God; God then "gives them up" to the implications of their decisions (Rom. 1:24, 26, 28), and they are lost. For them, as for all people, "sin exercises dominion in death" (Rom. 5:21, 6:23). When Jesus announced that "the Son of man came to seek and to save the lost" (Luke 19:10), he referred to that very state of lostness which must end in the death of the sinner. The hope of the sinner, for Israel, was never in what one might do to redress such sin. "An individual who is lost before God (as well as a nation in sin) has only one chance for salvation, according to Jewish belief — by God having mercy upon the offenders out of unconstrained love and sparing them from having to bear themselves the deadly consequences of their sin."[31] As an act of mercy, God gave Israel the sacrificial cult of

---

31. Stuhlmacher, *Jesus of Nazareth,* p. 51.

the atonement, in which life was given to save life. "But the life of the servant of God, too, can be a substitute for the ruined life of 'the many' according to Isaiah 53:10ff."[32] "Yet it was the will of the Lord to crush him with pain. When you make his life an offering for sin, he shall see his offspring and shall prolong his days. . . . The righteous one, my servant, shall make many righteous, and he shall bear their iniquities" (Isa. 53:10, 11b).

Jesus had proclaimed the message of the kingdom now near; he had gathered disciples to prepare them for the continuation of his ministry; he had demonstrated the nature of God's reign in his signs and sayings; he had revealed the character of the opposition to God's rule which now led to his arrest, trial, and verdict. Deliberately and compassionately, Jesus accepts the cup of crucifixion as the final step in God's mission for the saving of creation:

> Jesus decides to do the utmost he is capable of doing on earth: to offer himself to spare his friends and foes from the judgment of death. By means of his death Jesus does not appease a vengeful deity; rather, on his way of the cross he is the embodiment of the love of God, as sketched in Isaiah 43:3-4, 25. This love wants to spare the impenitent daughters and sons of Israel, as well as his feeble disciples, from having to perish because of their doubts about his mission and the consequences of their reserve toward Jesus' message. Even when he is nailed to the cross he does not curse his enemies but instead (like the servant of God) prays for them: "Father, forgive them, for they know not what they do" (Luke 23:34; cf. Isa. 53:12). Jesus keeps the commandment to love the enemy even on the cross. To his friends and mortal enemies alike he wants to open up the possibility of one day realizing and confessing with the community of Isaiah 53: "Because the punishment [for our sins] was upon him, we are saved; by his wounds we are healed" (Isa. 53:5).[33]

---

32. Stuhlmacher, *Jesus of Nazareth*, p. 51.
33. Stuhlmacher, *Jesus of Nazareth*, p. 52.

Jesus the Messenger and the Message, the Kingdom and the King

When God raised Jesus from the dead, the message and the messenger merged, the king and the kingdom came together.[34] "With his resurrection and ascension he has been totally confirmed by God in his mission. Jesus is thus the reconciler (= the atoner) and the Lord in one person, and his mission of the nearing rule of God cannot be separated from his exposition of the will of God."[35] The resurrection of the crucified Jesus became the foundational event, the supreme good news, which shaped the mission of the Christian church. This was the climax of Peter's first missionary sermon: "This Jesus God raised up, and of that all of us are witnesses. . . . Therefore let the entire house of Israel know with certainty that God has made him both Lord and Messiah, this Jesus whom you crucified" (Acts 2:32, 36). "In his resurrection, Christ becomes the good news in person, the personal embodiment of the gospel proclaimed by the apostles: 'We are here to give you the good news that God, who made the promise to the fathers, has fulfilled it for us their children by raising Jesus from the dead' (Acts 13:32-33)."[36] Thus, the entire New Testament is shaped not only by the certainty that Jesus was raised from the dead, but by the affirmation that in his resurrection Jesus has been shown to be both Messiah, the Christ, and Lord, the one who brings, incarnates, and rules the kingdom. To him has been given all authority in heaven and on earth (Matt. 28:18). God has put all things in subjection under his feet (1 Cor. 15:27). He is now the prince of peace who breaks down all walls of division (Eph. 2:15ff). He is the one upon whom we are now to wait, knowing that he "rescues us from the wrath that is coming" (1 Thess. 1:10).

Just as the psalms of Israel praise the mighty acts of God as the good news of God's compassion and victory, the doxologies of the New

---

34. Referring to C. H. Dodd's summary of the apostolic preaching, Albert Winn states, "We can see from this that the evangelion of Jesus has been largely replaced by an evangelion about Jesus. This is sometimes described in such as phrases as 'the proclaimer has become the proclaimed' or 'the messenger has become the message'" (Albert Winn, "What Is the Gospel?" in Coalter and Cruz, *How Shall We Witness?* pp. 6-7).

35. Stuhlmacher, "Die Mitte der Schrift," p. 46.

36. F. Durrwell, "Christian Witness: A Theological Study," *International Review of Mission* 69, no. 274 (April 1980): 124.

Testament community praise God for sending Jesus and raising him
from the dead:

> Christ Jesus, though he was in the form of God,
>> did not regard equality with God
>> as something to be exploited
> but emptied himself,
>> taking the form of a slave,
>> being born in human likeness.
> And being found in human form,
>> he humbled himself
>> and became obedient to the point of death —
>> even death on a cross.
> Therefore God also highly exalted him
>> and gave him the name
>> that is above every name,
> so that at the name of Jesus
>> every knee should bend,
>> in heaven and on earth and under the earth
> and every tongue should confess
>> that Jesus Christ is Lord,
>> to the glory of God the Father.
>
> (Phil. 2:6-11)

> There is one God;
>> there is also one mediator between God and humankind,
>> Christ Jesus, himself human, who gave himself a ransom for all.
>
> (1 Tim. 2:5-6)

> Blessed be the God and Father of
>> our Lord Jesus Christ
> who by his great mercy has given us new birth
>> into a living hope
>> through the resurrection of
>> Jesus Christ from the dead.
>
> (1 Pet. 1:3)

> The kingdom of the world has become the kingdom of our Lord
>> and of his Messiah,
> and he will reign forever and ever.
>
> (Rev. 11:15)

In the passion, death, and resurrection of Jesus Christ, God's salvation history reaches its climax.[37] God's mission has arrived at its decisive point in Jesus, the Christ, the One whom God sent. "One [can] say that by this means a new period in world history has dawned and a new creation has arisen around Christ. . . . Mission . . . is not only a *consequence* of Christ's dominion of the world, but it is also the *actualization* of it, [its manifestation]. The proclamation of the gospel is the *form* of the kingdom of God."[38]

We have arrived at a crucial threshold in the development of a theology for evangelistic ministry. Such ministry, "the proclamation of the gospel," is to be understood and practiced as "the form of the kingdom of God." This convergence of kingdom and king, mission and message, has profound implications for our theological task.

The gospel is the person and work of Jesus as the salvation event towards which God's mission has been moving and from which that mission now moves into the entire world on the way to its eschatological consummation when God fulfills all his promises. After Easter, the apostles modified the dominical instruction given in Luke 10 when the seventy were sent out. They were instructed then to announce, "The kingdom of God has come near to you" (Luke 10:9). "The content of their proclamation is no longer only the kingdom of God which has come near, but rather the proclamation of Jesus as the Messiah and returning Lord."[39] This risen Lord now sends his disciples into the world to carry out the *missio Dei* (mission of God) that was the purpose and content of his life, death, and resurrection. The mission of the Christian church is defined by the entire event of the life, teaching, proclamation, and passion of Jesus.

The church's mission looks with "living hope" (1 Pet. 1:3) toward the completion of the work God has begun in Jesus Christ, and this hope is firmly established in God raising Jesus from the dead.

37. Oscar Cullmann, *Christ and Time: The Primitive Christian Conception of Time and History,* trans. F. V. Filson (Philadelphia: Westminster, 1964), pp. 121-76, especially pp. 144ff: "The Present Stage of Redemptive History and Its Relation to the Christ-Event as the Mid-Point." See Blauw, *The Missionary Nature of the Church,* pp. 104ff.

38. Blauw, *The Missionary Nature of the Church,* p. 105 (my emendations of the ET are in brackets).

39. Peter Stuhlmacher, "Weg, Stil und Konsequenzen urchristlicher Mission," *Theologische Beiträge* 12. Jahrgang, 1981, p. 115.

Thus, the gospel is a witness both to fulfillment and to the initiation of expectation.

> The biblical story is the account of remembrance of encounters with God in real human history and expectations of future encounters. The Christ event is not an isolated occurrence of a totally different kind, but is rooted in God's history with Israel. . . . The significance of Jesus can therefore be grasped only on the basis of the Old Testament history of promise. His resurrection (in which the apostolic mission to the world has its origin) can only be understood within the framework of prophetic and apocalyptic expectation. . . . The proclamation of the reign of God does not introduce a new creed or cult but is the announcement of an event in history, an event to which people are challenged to respond by repenting and believing. In the coming of Jesus and in raising him from the dead, God's eschatological act has already been inaugurated. It is, however, as yet incomplete. Jesus' resurrection and exaltation signify just the beginning of the universal fulfillment still to come, of which the Spirit is a pledge. Only another future intervention by God will wipe out the contradiction of the present. Therefore, in Paul's Christology Christ is not so much the fulfillment of God's promises as the guarantee and confirmation of those promises (cf. Rom. 4:16; 16:8). Christ has not "fulfilled" the Old Testament, but "ratified" it. . . . The end is still to come.[40]

The *missio Dei* has always been the gospel, good news about God's goodness revealed in God's Word through Israel's experience, leading up to its climax and culmination in Jesus Christ. Throughout the biblical witness, God acts, initiates, and sends. God's compassion leads to his salvific action in human history. The Father sends the Son. This exclusive focus upon God as the subject of his mission is essential to the gospel, for it makes clear that humans, in their lostness, find hope in what God has done for them, not in what they might imagine they can do for themselves. Now, however, on the cross and at Easter, the salvation of the world was accomplished. God's mission now broadens to embrace the whole world for which Christ died. The gospel of God's love fulfilled in Christ is now to be made known to everyone. Because of

---

40. Bosch, *Transforming Mission*, p. 196.

the evangel, the call to evangelize is now heard. God's mission continues as that call takes shape in the apostolic community, the church.

A comprehensive understanding of the evangel must define our theological exposition of evangelism. "Our theology of evangelistic ministry must be rooted in a biblical theology of mission and, above all, dominated and shaped by the gospel it seeks to proclaim."[41] Such a theology is obviously Christocentric, if indeed Jesus Christ is both the message and the messenger, the good news himself.[42] Therefore, when we seek to work through the implications of Christian mission, or sentness, for evangelistic ministry, we can never move far from the One who is sent and who sends, the risen Lord. "Mission is . . . a predicate of Christology."[43] Jesus himself is "the primal missionary."[44]

41. See above, chapter 1, p. 27.

42. Such a Christocentric emphasis does not, under any circumstances, imply that missional theology should dilute its Trinitarian integrity. Rather, the Trinitarian basis of Christian theology is focused on the mission of God which is accomplished in Jesus Christ and his sending and empowering of the apostolic community through the Spirit. See Konrad Raiser's analysis and critique of "Christocentric universalism," in his *Ecumenism in Transition: A Paradigm Shift in the Ecumenical Movement?* (Geneva: WCC Publications, 1991), pp. 31-53. See also the interchange between Lesslie Newbigin and Konrad Raiser about the critique of Christocentric Universalism developed by Raiser: Lesslie Newbigin, "Ecumenical Amnesia," *International Bulletin of Missionary Research* 18, no. 1 (January 1994): 2-5; Konrad Raiser, "Is Ecumenical Apologetics Sufficient? A Response to Lesslie Newbigin's 'Ecumenical Amnesia,'" *International Bulletin of Missionary Research* 18, no. 2 (April 1994): 50-51; Lesslie Newbigin, "Reply to Konrad Raiser," *loc. cit.,* pp. 51-52. Newbigin's comment describes the understanding of Christocentricity which underlies my approach: "But a Trinitarian perspective can be only an enlargement and development of a Christocentric one and not an alternative set over against it, for the doctrine of the Trinity is the theological articulation of what it means to say that Jesus is the unique Word of God incarnate in world history" ("Ecumenical Amnesia," p. 2).

43. Bosch, *Witness to the World,* p. 82.

44. Martin Hengel, "The Origins of the Christian Mission," in *Between Jesus and Paul: Studies in the Earliest History of Christianity* (Philadelphia: Fortress, 1983), p. 63.

Chapter Three

Mission as Witness

The gospel is the person and work of Jesus as the salvation event toward which God's mission has been moving and from which that mission now moves into the entire world.

Formation of the Mission Community

What makes the gospel truly good news is the fact that the Jesus events are the outcome of God's loving decision to heal the broken creation. We have described this as God's mission. To demonstrate divine love, God brought about salvation for all creation in the death of Jesus on the cross. That joyful message is now to be made known to all the world. That is how God's mission now continues. The center or core of the *missio Dei* is evangelization: the communication of the gospel. Carrying the good news across all borders and into all the world is an essential part of the kingdom message which Jesus brought and embodied. Jesus Christ intended the mission of the apostolic faith community as the necessary consequence of God's redemptive work for all creation, which was accomplished in his life, death, and resurrection. "A clear line of connection can be drawn between the sending of Jesus and the sending of his disciples: as Jesus reflects in his actions the goodness and righteousness of his Father, who sent him into the world, so his disciples become witnesses and the image of Christ to those to whom Jesus sent them."[1]

Jesus selected and prepared the company of twelve disciples as the prefiguration of the people of God, the continuation and extension of Israel as God's witness to the nations.[2] The resurrected Lord encountered his confused disciples in Galilee and continued their formation into a "missionary community," a "sent out people," whose apostolic ministry would become possible when the Spirit came upon them, when the promised Paraclete entered into their midst. Their transition from discipleship to apostolate was Jesus' intention in his formation of the church as the community which was "to prolong the logic of his own ministry in an imaginative and creative way amid historical circumstances that were in many respects new and different."[3] This strong sense of Jesus' preparation of the early church for its mission pervades all four Gospels. It is clearly stated in the earliest Gospel when Jesus calls the twelve, "whom he also named apostles, to be with him, and to be sent out to proclaim the message, and to have authority to cast out demons" (Mark 3:13-14). It is the dominant theme of the latest Gospel: "As the Father hath sent me, so I send you" (John 20:21; "sending" = "mission").[4]

Pentecost has often been called "the birthday of the church." It may also be celebrated as the divine event which turned the people of God into a missionary people, opening their ranks to receive men and women of all nations, tongues, races, and classes; forming them into a new community; and empowering them to move out into all the world. In Pentecost, there is the continuing formation of God's people that was initiated with Abraham, as he received the blessing in order to bless the nations.

Foundational to an important strand in the tradition of Old Testament theology is the idea that God has selected a single people out of

---

1. Peter Stuhlmacher, "Weg, Stil, und Konsequenzen urchristlicher Mission," *Theologische Beiträge* 12. Jahrgang, 1981, pp. 107-35.

2. Gerhard Lohfink, *Jesus and Community: The Social Dimension of Christian Faith,* trans. J. P. Galvin (Philadelphia: Fortress, 1984), especially chapters 1 and 2, pp. 7-73.

3. David Bosch, "Towards a Hermeneutic for Biblical Studies and Mission," *Mission Studies* 3, no. 2 (1986): 76.

4. See Albert C. Winn, *A Sense of Mission: Guidance from the Gospel of John* (Philadelphia: Westminster, 1981).

all the nations of the world in order to make this people a sign of salvation. His interest in the other nations is in no way impeded by this. When the people of God shines as a sign among the nations . . . , the other nations will learn from God's people; they will come together in Israel in order to participate, in Israel and mediated through Israel, in God's glory. But all this can happen only when Israel really becomes recognizable as a *sign of salvation,* when God's salvation transforms his people recognizably, tangibly, even visibly.[5]

Thus the essential Jewishness of Jesus and the distinctive calling of Israel are not set aside at Easter and Pentecost, but are placed within the larger eschatological work of God, who continues to form his people as a sign and earnest of salvation. The resurrection witnesses announce that God's great work of salvation, longed for throughout the history of Israel, has now taken place in Christ. Linked with that continuity there is the discontinuity of the genuinely new that occurs at the cross and empty tomb. The suffering and death of Jesus, as has been said, form the very center of his messianic mission. Its newness is then emphasized and endorsed by the empowering presence of God's Spirit, who equips the apostolic community to become God's missionary people. The community spreads from Jerusalem to Judea to Samaria to the ends of the world, to make this good news known. From Pentecost on, the church must be understood primarily and centrally in terms of its mission as God's people. This is the reason it exists, and for this purpose the promised Holy Spirit is given to it.[6]

Jesus' own ministry with his disciples was his equipping of the future church for its mission. This is why they were to "be with him" (Mark 3:13), so that they could be formed for the mission they were to receive and to continue: Jesus' disciples were to become apostles. The Holy Spirit was given to the church to empower it for its apostolic mission (Acts 2). Then, that divine process of the equipping of the church for its mission continued and became concrete in the formation of the New Testament canon. When the early church acknowledged certain documents as apostolic, it in effect emphasized the missional character

5. Lohfink, *Jesus and Community,* p. 28.

6. Martin Hengel, "Origins of Christian Mission," in *Between Jesus and Paul: Studies in the Earliest History of Christianity* (Philadelphia: Fortress, 1983), pp. 48-64, 166-79; Stuhlmacher, "Weg, Stil, und Konsequenzen," p. 132ff.

of these writings. "Apostolicity" has primarily to do with faithfulness to the mission for which the apostles were equipped and sent out. That apostolic mission continues as the canonic scriptures continue to prepare the church for its service.

Recent New Testament scholarship has emphasized this perspective with the stimulating insight that "the New Testament has to be understood as a missionary document."[7] This approach is based on the actual character of the early church as reflected in the New Testament writings: "The early Christian movement that produced and canonized the New Testament was a movement with a specifically missionary character."[8] This missionary character defined the church from its very inception, long before the canonical record documented it. It has often been noted that the New Testament writings do not explicitly command the church to do mission — they assume that mission is what these communities were all about. Thus, we read the "Great Commission" incorrectly when we interpret it as an imperative intended to "launch the church on its missionary labors" and to "provide it with conscious motivation."[9] Rather, "in the reporting of Jesus' final words in the Gospels and Acts we should see not a command for the early churches to obey but an affirmation of what they found themselves doing. . . . [These texts] validate the experience of being in mission."[10]

"Witness" as Missional Vocation

The early Christian communities understood themselves to be witnesses to what God has done. The earliest evangelization was that done

7. David Bosch, *Transforming Mission: Paradigm Shifts in Theology of Mission* (Maryknoll, NY: Orbis Books, 1991), p. 54, see pp. 15-55. In the course of his argument, Bosch refers to the work of Fiorenza, Hengel, Kasting, Meyer, and Kähler; one might add Brown, Brownson, Cullmann, Goppelt, Hayes, Jeremias, Keck, Lohfink, Stuhlmacher, Riesenfeld, Riesner, Soards, and Wright to the growing list of scholars whose work supports a missiological interpretation of the New Testament.

8. James Brownson, "Speaking the Truth in Love: Elements of a Missional Hermeneutic," *International Review of Mission* 83, no. 330 (July 1994): 482.

9. George Hunsberger, "Is There Biblical Warrant for Evangelism?" *Interpretation* 48, no. 2 (April 1984): 135. See also Bosch's discussion of "Matthew: Mission as Disciple-Making," in *Transforming Mission*, pp. 56-83.

10. Hunsberger, "Biblical Warrant," p. 135.

by eyewitnesses, and they made their appeal for Jesus Christ based upon their experience of the events of his life, death, and resurrection. It is fundamental to the goodness of the "joyful message" that it can be witnessed, experienced, reported on, and passed on so that others may join in the experience. This conviction underlies the speeches in Acts,[11] Paul's defense of his apostolic missionary ministry (Gal. 1:11ff, 2 Cor. 10), and the Johannine understanding of witness (John 14–16, 1 John 1:1-4). The concept of witness, as we find it used in a variety of ways in the New Testament, describes the essence of the Christian experience from Easter onward. The New Testament cluster of terms based on the root for "witness" *(martyr-)*, in a broad diversity of forms and nuances, defines comprehensively the missional calling of the church in the New Testament. Mission is witness. In particular, evangelistic ministry, as the core of mission, is most appropriately defined and explained in terms of witness. The concept of witness provides a common missiological thread through all the New Testament language that expounds the church's mission. It serves as an overarching term drawing together proclamation *(kerygma)*, community *(koinonia)*, and service *(diakonia)*. These are all essential dimensions of the Spirit-enabled witness for which the Christian church is called and sent.[12]

When we place this emphasis upon witness as an overarching New Testament concept, we must be careful to avoid oversimplifying the diversity of themes and approaches in the New Testament. The canon does not "reflect a uniform view of mission but, rather, a variety of 'theologies of mission.'"[13] Thus, "the missional hermeneutic . . . begins by

---

11. Marion L. Soards, *The Speeches in Acts: Their Content, Context, and Concerns* (Louisville: Westminster/John Knox, 1994), passim, but especially pp. 192ff.

12. Selwyn's comment is germane: "I sometimes wonder whether the term KERYGMA has not been worked too hard, and whether the word MARTURIA and its cognates would not better describe the primitive and indispensable core of the Christian message. At any rate, if we examine the comparative occurrences in the New Testament of the two sets of terms, we find that the occurrences of the verbs alone which speak of 'witness' considerably outnumber the occurrences of KERUSSEIN, while the occurrences of the noun MARTURIA outnumber those of the noun KERYGMA by more than six to one"; E. G. Selwyn, "Eschatology in I Peter," in W. D. Davies and D. Daube, eds., *The Background of the New Testament and Its Eschatology* (Cambridge: Cambridge University Press, 1956), p. 395, quoted by Allison A. Trites, *The New Testament Concept of Witness* (Cambridge: Cambridge University Press, 1977), p. 1.

13. Bosch, *Transforming Mission*, p. 16.

affirming the reality and inevitability of plurality in interpretation."[14] At the same time, that plurality ("centered or focused diversity" might be a better term) can itself be understood as an aspect of the witness to the gospel. The gospel, as experienced and shared, necessarily is expressed with a great variety of images, metaphors, and theological formulations. They are all, in effect, forms of witness. The various New Testament strands, traditions, and faith communities in all their diversity are witnesses to the same gospel. Paul and Peter, when they differ, are still witnesses to the same Christ, carrying out the same mission. Four Gospels, rather than a harmonized account like the *Diatesseron* offered by Tatian and ultimately rejected by the church, provide a witness to the history of Jesus enriched by the differences among them. This broad and diverse spectrum of witness is truly catholic in the essential sense of that term: "that which is according to the whole — *kath'holon*. . . . The canon is catholic, not because it has extended its power over all the world as a sort of universal rule, but because it makes room for the multiform witness to the Gospel from the various perspectives of four different evangelists."[15]

Thus, to focus upon witness as the overarching definition of mission means that there is in this concept a commonality which does not lessen the significance of other New Testament images and metaphors but focuses them missiologically. It is not an imposition of a false harmonization of the various strands of New Testament teaching to find "the missionary character of witness" reflected throughout the literature: "Whatever the specific content of witness in the NT, its purpose is to induce faith. . . . Bearing witness is in the NT a missionary activity, a quality which distinguishes it from the OT usage."[16] We are using a

14. Brownson, "Speaking the Truth in Love," p. 483.

15. Justo González, "Ecumenical Tensions of the Church in the West: A North American Perspective," unpublished manuscript of lecture delivered in Paris, January 1996, pp. 3ff, 6.

16. Martin Walton, *Witness in Biblical Scholarship: A Survey of Recent Studies, 1956-1980,* IIMO Research Pamphlet No. 15 (Leiden/Utrecht: Interuniversitair Instituut voor Missiologie en Oecumenica, 1986), p. 23. The problems and possibilities of a terminological study are demonstrated by the International Association for Mission Studies' project on Biblical Studies and Missiology (BISAM) in the 1980s, in which it took "witness" as a theme. See Marc Spindler, "Visa for Witness: A New Focus on the Theology of Mission and Ecumenism," *Mission Studies* 3, no. 1 (1986): 52; Bosch's critique of the project is summarized in his "Towards a Hermeneutic for Biblical Studies and Mission"

missiological hermeneutic when we read the New Testament as the testimony (witness) of witnesses, equipping other witnesses for the common mission of the church.

What does it mean, then, to understand mission as witness? What is the missiological import of the usage of witness and its cognates, if in fact this language does "describe the primitive and indispensable core of the Christian message"?[17] How, in particular, does the "witness" word family assist us in developing "an understanding of evangelism which is rooted in the *missio Dei*, shaped by God's actions in history, faithful to the gospel, and at the heart of ministry"?[18]

The Concept of Witness in the New Testament

It is missiologically provocative that this word family includes terms for the person who is the witness (*martys*, mainly in Acts), the testimony rendered by the witness (*martyria, martyrion*), and the process of giving or bearing witness (*matyrein, diamartyresthai*). This cluster of meanings indicates that Christian witness defines the identity of the Christian (thus, Karl Barth speaks of "the Christian as witness"), the impact of such persons within human experience (their testimony), and the dynamic process of living out witness.[19] Although the predominant meaning of witness has to do with oral communication,[20] there is ample reason to understand witness in a much more comprehensive sense, as defining the entire Christian life, both individually and corporately. By the same token, "evangelization" as the core of mission must be seen

(cited above) but then softened in "The Scope of the 'BISAM' Project," *Mission Studies* 6, no. 1 (1989): 61-69. For the broader context, see also Bosch's discussion of "Common Witness," in *Transforming Mission*, pp. 457-67.

17. See note 12, Selwyn quote.

18. See above, p. 25. The following discussion is based on Karl Barth's discussion of the "witness" word family in *Church Dogmatics*, trans. G. W. Bromiley, IV, 3/2 (Edinburgh: T. & T. Clark, 1962), pp. 610-14; Lesslie Newbigin, "Witness in a Biblical Perspective," *Mission Studies* 3, no. 2 (1986): 80-84; Trites, *Concept of Witness;* Walton, *Witness in Biblical Scholarship*.

19. Barth, *Church Dogmatics*, IV, 3/2, pp. 554-614, especially pp. 608-10.

20. Walton, *Witness in Biblical Scholarship*, pp. 23ff; the major role of the speeches in Acts also underlines the central character of oral communication as witness, cf. Soards, *Speeches in Acts*.

in a much more comprehensive fashion: "to think of evangelism in terms of mere proclamation fosters the practice of disconnecting evangelism from the life of the local church."[21]

This is certainly true of Luke-Acts, where Jesus defines the task and identity of the mission community with the statement, "You shall *be* my witnesses" (Acts 1:8). These final words of Jesus to the disciples on the mount of the ascension set the theme for the ministry of the early church. The operative term is "witness," as a comprehensive definition of Christian persons and communities. The author uses this concept to build the theological bridge between his Gospel and the story of the first church,[22] and it then serves as the leitmotif for the expanding ministry of the apostolic church.[23]

The missional task of the witness in Luke-Acts and in John is to present the eyewitness evidence to Jesus so that people might "believe the claims of Christ and enter into a personal experience of his salvation. For both writers the significance of witness lies in its ability to induce faith."[24] God used the witnesses' personal experience of Jesus before and after his death and resurrection to draw others into the relationship of faith in Jesus Christ. God makes that possible through the gift of the Holy Spirit, which grants to the witnesses' testimony its persuasive and inviting power.

Thus God's Spirit employs the evidence presented by the eyewitnesses to induce faith in the risen Christ as God's Messiah and to draw people into the community of witness as Christ's servants. The major emphases of the Lukan witness are developed in the speeches that play such a prominent role in the book: "the speeches unify the Acts ac-

21. William Abraham, "A Theology of Evangelism: The Heart of the Matter," *Interpretation* 48, no. 2 (April 1994): 125.

22. Soards, *Speeches in Acts,* p. 197, discussing the relationship between Luke 21:11-13; 24:44-49, and Acts 1:8. Soards's discussion of the "witness" word family is on pp. 192-200.

23. "[T]he apostles declare that their obedience to God is both the gift and demand of their being Spirit-empowered witnesses to God's work in and through Jesus Christ" (Soards, *Speeches in Acts,* p. 189).

24. Trites, *Concept of Witness,* p. 128. The term "witness" in this sentence illustrates the importance of the ambiguity in English when using the term: it can and should be understood to refer both to the person as witness, and to the activity of witness, testimony.

count and through them Luke advances his theme of divinely commissioned unified witness to the ends of the earth."[25] The transforming power of God's action in Jesus Christ is now extended, through the community's witness, to the whole world for which this good news is intended.[26]

In Johannine usage, "witness" enjoys two complementary points of emphasis. It refers to the disciples' reliable testimony to the facts of Jesus' life and message — "what we heard, what we have seen with our eyes, what we have looked at and touched with our hands" (1 John 1:1). At the same time, the apostles witness to the transforming truth of this message as it changes their lives — "By this everyone will know that you are my disciples, if you have love for one another" (John 13:35).[27] The linkage of his emphasis upon "belief and unbelief" with the "testimonial and evidential character of this Gospel" demonstrates that in John it is the role of the witness to "convince people that Jesus is the Christ, the Son of God."[28] Their witness is not neutral: they are advocates who make their witness out of their experience with Christ and their continuing relationship to him. This emphasis upon their intimate personal union with Christ, which is basic to their identity as Christ's witnesses, is underlined in the image of the vine and the branches in the final discourse (John 15) as well as in Jesus' prayer for his followers in John 17. The Paraclete will come to those who have received the gift of eternal life and whose faith makes them into Jesus' witnesses in order to enable their pleading the cause of Christ (John 14:15ff; 16:4bff). Jesus summarized the central missional understanding of the witnesses' calling in his post-Easter appearance to the disciples: "Peace be with you. As the Father has sent me, so I send you. . . . Receive the Holy Spirit" (John 20:21-22; see 17:18).

Paul emphasizes the calling and formation of the Christian church as a community of witness, but he does not use the "witness" terminology with the same emphasis as do Luke-Acts and the Johannine litera-

---

25. Soards, *Speeches in Acts,* p. 15; see also Trites, *Concept of Witness,* pp. 139ff.

26. "[T]he plan of God is grounded or rooted in God's actions relative to Jesus Christ, so that the plan continues to be realized by divine necessity in the obedient witness of the apostles — and, as Acts shows, the other members of the early church. Thus, one should understand that the decisive activity of God in relation to Jesus Christ inaugurated the ongoing testimony to God's saving work" (Soards, *Speeches in Acts,* p. 189).

27. Trites, *Concept of Witness,* pp. 84ff, 114-16.

28. Trites, *Concept of Witness,* p. 81.

ture.[29] In his epistles, Paul teaches the early Christian communities to "practice a missionary lifestyle," to "be a community of those who glorify God by showing forth his nature and works and by making manifest the reconciliation and redemption God has wrought through the death, resurrection, and reign of Christ.... [The church] is involved with the world, which means that it is missionary."[30] The focus of the Pauline letters is the formation of Christian communities "to lead a life worthy of the calling to which you have been called" (Eph. 4:1; see 1 Thess. 2:12; Col. 1:10; Rom. 12:1). These writings "should be read as instruments of community formation," expressing Paul's confidence that "God is at work through the Spirit to create communities that prefigure and embody the reconciliation and healing of the world."[31] These communities are more than the assemblage of individual Christians. Their corporate life is essential to their witness — the "you" in Eph. 4:1 is plural. Thus the apostle must be concerned (as in 1 Corinthians) with any aspect of their corporate life which would invalidate their witness. "The community, in its corporate life, is called to embody an alternative order that stands as a sign of God's redemptive purposes in the world."[32] As a sign, a witness, the church for Paul is "not the ultimate aim of mission. The life and work of the Christian community are intimately bound up with the God's cosmic-historical plan for the redemption of the world."[33]

The other synoptic Gospels, Matthew and Mark, also equip and instruct the Christian communities for their mission. Perhaps some of the most stimulating biblical work of late has been in the missiological interpretation of the Gospels; but there is much important work still needed.[34] The concept of witness does not dominate the synoptics as it does John, but the calling to mission as witness is implied throughout,

29. Trites, *Concept of Witness,* pp. 199ff.

30. Bosch, *Transforming Mission,* pp. 137, 168.

31. Richard B. Hayes, "Ecclesiology and Ethics in I Corinthians," *Ex Auditu,* 1994, p. 2.

32. Hayes, "Ecclesiology and Ethics," p. 5.

33. Bosch, *Transforming Mission,* p. 178.

34. See, among others, Mortimer Arias and Alan Johnson, *The Great Commission: Biblical Models for Evangelism* (Nashville: Abingdon, 1992); Bosch, *Transforming Mission,* pp. 15-122; Ferdinand Hahn, *Mission in the New Testament,* trans. F. Clarke (London: SCM, 1965); Lucien LeGrand, *Unity and Plurality: Mission in the Bible,* trans. R. R. Barr (Maryknoll, NY: Orbis Books, 1990); Donald Senior and Carroll Stuhlmueller, *The Biblical Foundations for Mission* (Maryknoll, NY: Orbis Books, 1983).

especially in the formation of the disciples for their approaching apostolate.

> To be a disciple is to be part of a new community, a new polity, which is formed on Jesus' obedience to the cross. The constitutions of this new polity are the Gospels. The Gospels are not just the depiction of a man, but they are manuals for the training necessary to be part of the new community. To be a disciple means to share Christ's story, to participate in the reality of Christ's rule.[35]

Missio Dei and Its Witness

The way that the Bible talks about witness and witnesses is framed in the larger context of Scripture itself as the written witness to God's self-disclosure. This dynamic understanding of Scripture and its authority rests on the foundational biblical claim that God discloses God's self in human history, and that this self-disclosure within human history has been and continues to be reliably witnessed. "God is not only active, but we can also know and confess him in his activity."[36] The Word of God is first of all God's self-disclosure as event and message; Otto Weber speaks of this as "Word happened."[37] The "Word happened" is, by virtue of God's enabling grace, immediately and necessarily "the Word witnessed." God's intention in revelation is that there be response, that God be recognized and submitted to and served: "Be still and know that I am God." By virtue of the loving character of God, God seeks and finds the beloved creature and restores the broken relationship between it and the creator. Thus, the uniqueness of God's salvation event, of the Word of God as "Word happened," is that it does not become merely a past and concluded event, but rather continues present and ef-

---

35. Stanley Hauerwas, *A Community of Character: Toward a Constructive Christian Social Ethic* (Notre Dame and London: University of Notre Dame Press, 1981), p. 49.

36. Arnold A. van Ruler, "A Theology of Mission," in *Calvinistic Trinitarianism and Theocentric Politics: Essays Toward a Public Theology*, trans. J. Belt (Lewiston: Edwin Mellon, 1989), p. 220.

37. Our discussion is based upon the survey and interpretation of the tripartite theology of the Word offered by Karl Barth, in Otto Weber, *Foundations of Dogmatics*, trans. D. L. Guder, 2 vols. (Grand Rapids: Eerdmans), 1:178ff. The discussion of the "Word witnessed" begins on p. 185.

fective, as the Word witnessed and, ultimately, as the Word proclaimed. The biblical witness derives its authority from the action and Word of God to which it witnesses.

> Thus the biblical witness is always a report, the making known of history which has happened. . . . The Word witnessed to is not the Word by virtue of the religious powers of the witness . . . , but by virtue of the confrontation of the witnesses with the Word-event which is made known in their testimony. The authority of the witnesses consists of their having no independent authority and not wanting to have any.[38]

The essence of witness, then, is the gracious action of God that produces such witnesses and their testimony. Those called to the mission of witness experience God's grace and healing. That is fundamental to their witness: "It is here that we catch a glimpse of the fact that their vocation does actually include their personal blessing, [renewal] and endowment. . . ." However, the purpose of their calling is not to be reduced only to their own salvation — I am anticipating here the discussion of "gospel reductionism" in chapters 5 and 6. Rather, this experience of grace is to be understood as "something secondary and accessory, which certainly will not pass them by, but which remains linked with the primary and proper element in their status and [has] its own power and constancy [only] in this relationship." Their "status" is, of course, their calling to be Christ's witness.[39]

By defining the character of the call to witness in this way, we emphasize that in the strictest sense, the commission to be witness is granted by God independently of any causes or motivations in our human existence. We present no abilities or needs or desires that would justify the granting of this commission; there is no form of human creativity or virtue that is a necessary prerequisite for this calling. It comes from outside ourselves and is, in fact, a constant surprise for us. It is the result of God's initiation of God's mission.[40]

---

38. Weber, *Foundations of Dogmatics,* 1:186, 189.

39. Barth, *Church Dogmatics,* IV, 3/2, p. 575. (Brackets indicate my emendations of the translation.)

40. As a result of God's initiating *missio Dei,* the people of witness "with their whole being, action, inaction and conduct, and then by word and speech, . . . have to

What is true of the original witnesses, preserved in the canonic record, continues true of witness thereafter from generation to generation. God's people are called to carry forward this unique witness, to
translate it into every new situation of history, so that the Word happened continues to be the Word witnessed, heard, responded to, and
obeyed. All witness is defined by calling and mission. "It is common to
all the biblical accounts of calling that to be called means being given a
task."[41] The very existence of the Christian as witness is "existence in
the execution of this task." Such a calling necessarily means a complete
transformation of the lives of these witnesses, individually and corporately. They are to become an "alternative colony" or "resident aliens"
because "as they no longer belong to themselves, they no longer belong
to human society," although they do not cease to be a part of it. Their
commission stands not at the end of their religious search for meaning,
but results from their encounter with God in Christ. The community
of faith is called to become God's witness, and "He Himself legitimates,
authorises, instructs and nourishes them."[42]

The Comprehensive Character of Missional Witness

In the church traditions of the Reformation, the theology of the Word
as happened and witnessed focused upon its proclamation. The
Protestant movement seeks to bring the Word event into the actual life
and experience of the church through preaching.[43] Because of this emphasis upon the proclaimed Word, the central place of witness has been
understood to be the corporate worship of the faith community.[44]
"Proclamation" as the primary form of witness has tended to narrow
the understanding of witness to that which is oral, that which is said in

---

make a definite declaration to other men, [they have a particular message to communi-
cate]. The essence of their vocation is that God makes them His *witnesses*" (Barth, *Church
Dogmatics*, IV, 3/2, p. 575; brackets indicate my emendations of the translation).

41. Barth, *Church Dogmatics*, IV, 3/2, p. 573.
42. Barth, *Church Dogmatics*, IV, 3/2, p. 574.
43. Weber, *Foundations*, 1:190-95, for the discussion of the "word proclaimed."
44. "The witness which Holy Scripture contains is essentially the proclamation of
what has happened once and for all so that it will be accepted and believed as the event
which is once and for all" (Weber, *Foundations*, 1:186.)

a particular place (churches) by particular people (preachers or priests) at particular times (formal services of worship).

For our purposes, it would be more helpful to develop our understanding of God's Word and its witness as, first of all, the event or the revelatory history; second, its authoritative witness found in the canonic Scriptures; and finally, the witness of the people of God resulting and continued, as they hear and respond to God's joyful news communicated in Scripture and empowered by God's Spirit. It is important to insist upon the unique authority of the revelatory events and their primary witness, the scriptural record. What follows in the history of mission, as God's people make this joyful message known, is continuation, result, dependent consequences. But it is, at the same time, the Spirit-empowered witness that is *far more* than particular oral messages. It is the demonstration in the life and activity of God's people of the tangible fact that God's rule is breaking in among the disciples of Jesus Christ.

If we understand mission as witness and seek to be guided by the biblical language of witness, the missiologically structured theology of evangelism will have to include these emphases:

Witness is *theocentric:* God's saving activity in Christ constitutes the gospel and its continuing witness.

Witness is *Christocentric:* The gospel is the event of the incarnation, death, resurrection, and ascension of Christ.

Witness is *pneumatological:* The Holy Spirit is God's initiating action to evoke faith, enable response, and empower mission.

Witness is *historical:* The truth and power of witness are based on unique and particular events that have universal importance as history continues.

Witness is *eschatological:* The missionary message is that the kingdom of God is near, breaking in, present and active in Jesus Christ, and yet to come in all its fullness.

Witness is *ecclesiological:* God's people are called and equipped for witness as particular communities whose lives and actions are a continuing demonstration of their message.

Witness is *multicultural and ecumenical:* Witness is spread throughout the world as the mission community translates the gospel into every culture.

1. Witness Is Theocentric

God's saving activity in Christ constitutes the gospel, and God continues that redemptive work by calling and enabling the witness to this joyful message by forming his people. Witness is therefore always response, always secondary, always in reference to that which is witnessed, which is God's initiation and action.

All biblical language plainly stresses the distinction that must be made between the witness (as person and as testimony) on the one hand, and that which is witnessed to.[45] The very existence of the witness is dependent upon the event, the person, the message which evokes the witness: the gospel of Jesus Christ as God's mission carried out in Jesus' life, ministry, death, resurrection, and ascension. The relationship of the witness to its theme or content is secondary; it follows after and is dependent upon what one witnesses to. No witness articulates an original word or creates the message. Instead the witness experiences, observes, receives, passes on, and authenticates. God is the author, the subject, the initiator of the events to which then Christian witness is given. "It is God himself who elicits the testimony and evangelizes, for it is he who begets his Son in the world, raises him from the dead, and sends him as the risen Lord to his brothers and sisters."[46]

Witness is theocentric as it confesses that God, the Father of Jesus Christ, the Son, has acted ultimately and conclusively in the incarnation of Christ to establish God's gracious reign in human history. It is the "gospel of God" which is the content of Christian witness (1 Thess. 2:2, 8, 9), and thus the human word of witness is, in fact, the word of God: "when you received the word of God that you heard from us, you accepted it not as a human word but as what it really is, God's word, which is also at work in you believers" (1 Thess. 2:13). This "gospel of God" is the joyful news that in Jesus Christ, God's kingdom has drawn near, and those who are called may receive it, enter it, and become its witnesses. "[T]the coming of Jesus has introduced into history an event in which the reign of God is made known under the form of weakness and foolishness

45. Barth, *Church Dogmatics*, IV, 3/2, pp. 607ff.
46. F. Durrwell, "Christian Witness: A Theological Study," *International Review of Mission* 69, no. 274 (April 1980): 129.

to those to whom God has chosen to make it known, and . . . it is made known to them so it may be proclaimed to all."[47]

2. Witness Is Christocentric

The gospel is the event of the incarnation, death, resurrection, and ascension of Christ. In this event God's work of salvation is carried out, and those who encounter this risen Christ are called and empowered to be his witnesses. Witness is therefore Christocentric.

Witness emerges from the encounter with the risen Christ. The New Testament witnesses are not advancing ideas but are reporting on experience and the meaning of that experience. "The idea of witness as related to Christ and his gospel plays an essential and highly important part in the New Testament writings and in the Christian faith and life universally. Not only in the primitive preaching, but also in all effectual preaching throughout the history of the Church, the gospel is conceived not as a speculative system, but as a witness to Jesus Christ as being Himself God's Witness to the world."[48] What Allison Trites says with regard to the testimony of Acts may be generalized for all sections of the New Testament: "the content of the apostolic testimony is thoroughly Christocentric."[49]

Lesslie Newbigin surveyed "witness in a biblical perspective" and found that the Christocentricity of this witness was its most emphasized characteristic:

> God himself bears witness to Jesus. He does this: (a) in the prophets and others of the Old Testament; (b) in the ministry of John the Baptist; (c) in the ministry of Jesus himself by the "signs" which he is enabled to accomplish; (d) in the ministry of those chosen as witnesses, since they are given the gift of the Holy Spirit, who is God himself in action.[50]

47. Lesslie Newbigin, *The Open Secret: Sketches for a Missionary Theology* (Grand Rapids: Eerdmans, 1978; 2nd ed., 1995), p. 40.

48. J. R. van Pelt, "Witness," in *Dictionary of Christ and the Gospels,* ed. J. Hastings, 2 vols. (Edinburgh, 1908), 2:830, quoted in Trites, *Concept of Witness,* p. 223.

49. Trites, *Concept of Witness,* p. 143. See also, Durrwell, "Christian Witness," pp. 121-23: "The Christian witness bears witness to a person."

50. Newbigin, "Witness in a Biblical Perspective," p. 84.

3. Witness Is Pneumatological

The Holy Spirit is God's initiating action to evoke faith, enable response, and empower the mission of witness. To be, to do, and to say witness is only possible through the empowering gift of the Holy Spirit.

The promise of Jesus on the mount of the ascension was fulfilled at Pentecost, when the Spirit entered into the waiting community and enabled them to communicate the gospel with power and conviction. The witnesses do not chose their commission, nor do they bring qualifications that entitle them to become witnesses. It is the work of the Spirit which makes one into a witness. "It is as anointed with His Spirit that they are bearers of His commission, and in no other way. . . . Indeed, . . . the Holy Spirit is Himself the primary and essential witness, and it is only His presence in the disciples which makes it possible for them truly to witness to Him."[51]

To understand witness as pneumatological is to stress its dependence upon God, both in its initiation and its continuation. Witness is an essential form of spirituality: in and through witness to the gospel, the Holy Spirit is experienced as the enabler and encourager.

4. Witness Is Historical

The gospel happened, and its historical happenedness is essential to its truth and power; therefore, its witness must emphasize the distinctively historical and particular character of the gospel.

Christian witness always asserts that particular events have universal importance.[52] Although this particularity is offensive for the Western heirs of the Enlightenment as much as for the Buddhist or Hindu,[53] faithful witness must continue to make known that God's

---

51. Lesslie Newbigin, *The Household of God: Lectures on the Nature of the Church* (London: SCM: 1953), p. 95, quoted in Trites, *Concept of Witness*, pp. 116-17. "Certainly the initial qualification of a witness is based upon what he has seen and heard," Weber, *Foundations*, 1:187.

52. See John Howard Yoder, "'But We Do See Jesus': The Particularity of Incarnation and the Universality of Truth," in *The Priestly Kingdom: Social Ethics as Gospel* (Notre Dame: University of Notre Dame Press, 1984), pp. 46-62. especially pp. 54ff.

53. Newbigin, *Open Secret*, pp. 56ff.

particular actions in this one man, Jesus the Christ, are cosmic in their intention and impact. This can only be demonstrated by the witnesses, rather than proven. That has always been true: Jesus did not leave written documents or other artifacts to serve as evidence of the truthfulness of his message and claims. Rather, he equipped and sent out witnesses. Their witness to this particular story, translated into their particular stories, is the way the Holy Spirit continues the event character of God's actions into every generation and age. The historical character of witness is evidenced, in particular, in the institutional structure of the church, and in the personal and corporate behavior of the Christian community. Historical witness makes ethics into an evangelistic concern of high priority.

5. Witness Is Eschatological

As Christocentric witness, mission announces that the kingdom of God is near, breaking in, present and active in Jesus Christ, and still coming. The witness to the reign of God takes place in the tension between the "already" that God has begun in Christ and the "not yet" of Christian hope. That hope is the expression of Christian realism, rooted in what God has already done (raised Jesus Christ from the dead; 1 Pet. 1:3) and confident that God will be faithful and complete the work of salvation (1 Pet. 1:10, 13).

Jesus both announces the kingdom and is the king.[54] The coming of the kingdom is experienced in submission to the Lord, the *kyrios*, in obedient discipleship, and the coming of the kingdom is anticipated as the mission community carries its cross in faithful discipleship. The community of witness is called to demonstrate the presence of Christ through its life, service, sacrifice, suffering, and hope. This demonstration is possible because "all power has been given to Christ in heaven and on earth" and he has promised to be with this followers "always, to the end of the age."

It is essential for mission as witness that the reality of the kingdom become tangible in the church — not that the church is the king-

---

54. See Newbigin, *Open Secret*, for his discussion of "Sharing the Life of the Son: Mission as Love in Action," pp. 44-61.

dom, but that the church demonstrates the nearness of the kingdom, the first fruits of its coming. The ethics of Christian community are the primary context of kingdom witness, and within that context, the spoken witness, the proclamation of the gospel, can take place.[55] This is demonstrated, as noted above in the discussion of Paul's writings, in the parenetic or exhortatory sections of every epistle: there, the concern is for the integrity of Christian witness on the part of the entire community. In their praxis of Christian witness, the missional communities demonstrate that Jesus Christ is truly Lord, and that the kingdom is breaking in.

6. Witness Is Ecclesiological

The witness to Jesus Christ is made by the community called and equipped for that purpose, and it entails inviting others to become part of that community to join in the obedience of witness. The gathering of God's people for witness throughout the earth is a fulfillment of Old Testament anticipation and the earnest of the consummation of God's salvation.

Since the definition of Christian calling as witness constantly stresses the secondary, dependent, functional role of the church, the church is not the priority of witness, but its means. This is, of course, the missiological definition of the church which has emerged within the concept of *missio Dei*, as discussed in chapter 1: "mission is not primarily an activity of the church, but an attribute of God."[56] The church as witness does not regard itself as its own purpose, but rather as God's Spirit-empowered means to God's end. "It is not the church that has a mission of salvation to fulfil to the world; it is the mission of the Son and the Spirit through the Father that includes the church."[57] The Benedictines have taken St. John the Baptist as their patron and portray him as always pointing away from himself to Christ. This image

55. Thus, it is important to explore the ethics of Christian community as do, for example, Gerhard Lohfink in *Jesus and Community,* Stanley Hauerwas in *Community of Character,* and John Howard Yoder in virtually all of his writings.

56. Bosch, *Transforming Mission,* p. 390.

57. Jürgen Moltmann, *The Church in the Power of the Spirit: A Contribution to Messianic Ecclesiology* (London: SCM, 1977), p. 64.

captures the character of Christian witness as developed in John's Gospel and emphasizes the secondary nature of witness common to the New Testament.[58]

The invitation to respond to the gospel, however, must necessarily lead to incorporation into the community of witness.[59] It is clear from the New Testament that God's Spirit forms a community for mission. God's call has always formed a people, a community, within which God was known, worshiped, made known, and served. "God has selected a single people out of all the nations of the world in order to make this people a [visible] sign of salvation."[60] Jesus continued this process with the formation of the disciples into a mission community. "[T]he eschatological gathering of Israel, initiated by Jesus, was continued by the post-Easter community of disciples in faithfulness to Jesus."[61] Individual Christian existence is only possible and meaningful within such a community. The life of the community is the primary form of its witness, and it is also the equipper and supporter of each individual Christian in the practice of his or her vocation as witnesses for Christ. This community is, as ecclesia, called out and set apart for public witness, for demonstration before the world of the presence and power of Jesus the king. We must grapple with the problems presented by the institutional church, but there can be no biblically based theology of mission and witness which does not emphasize the centrality of the "called out people" for that mission.

7. Witness Is Multicultural and Ecumenical

Witness to the gospel is to go out into all the world. The Holy Spirit enabled everyone present at Pentecost to hear the good news in his or her own language. The gospel is to be translated into every language and culture on the earth. The people of God can be shaped by God's Spirit in every culture and tongue, although no one culture or tongue may

58. Barth, *Church Dogmatics*, IV, 3/2, pp. 604ff.

59. Jesus' calling together of the people of God as expounded by Lohfink, in *Jesus and Community*, helpfully expands my understanding of "the community of witness," although he tends to understate the essentially missional thrust of the people of God.

60. Lohfink, *Jesus and Community*, p. 28.

61. Lohfink, *Jesus and Community*, p. 76 (italicized in the original German).

claim to be normatively that people. The gathering of the people of God from all the earth is an eschatological sign of the inbreaking kingdom. Within every culture, the people of God are to be gathered as the witness to that culture and as a witness to the unifying power of the gospel which supersedes all cultural divisions.

The New Testament community, beginning with the circle of the twelve disciples, was a radically multicultural community that found its unity in Christ and in its common calling to witness. An essential aspect of the joyful message was the powerful love that breaks down human barriers and creates a community beyond ordinary imagination. Thus, among the twelve there is a tax collector and a Zealot; the community in Acts is made up of Palestinian and Hellenistic Jews who are being made into one people; Peter must learn that the gospel is intended for all, even Roman centurions. The transforming work of the Prince of Peace is to create a community that would not be humanly possible, where there is neither Jew nor Greek, male nor female, slave owner nor slave, as the tangible evidence of the inbreaking kingdom.

Thus, no particular culture, not even the traditional Jewish culture, may now be regarded as normative for the gospel community. The gospel may be translated into every language and lived out in every culture.[62] Every human culture is thus both honored by the gospel witness as well as challenged by it. Mission is to be a continuing process of translation and witness, whereby the evangelist and the mission community will be confronted again and again by the gospel as it is translated, heard, and responded to, and will thus experience ongoing conversion while serving as witness. The multicultural diversity of Christian experience is, however, never to be absolutized. It is not an end in itself, just as the church is not. The multicultural diversity of the church demonstrates that the gospel is going to the ends of the earth, and thus, in their diversity, the churches are constantly summoned by the gospel to confess their oneness in Christ. The church's ecumenical calling is essential to its witness: "There is a growing awareness among the churches today of the inextricable relationship between Christian unity and missionary calling, between

62. Lamin Sanneh, *Translating the Message: The Missionary Impact on Culture* (Maryknoll, NY: Orbis Books, 1991), pp. 28ff.

ecumenism and evangelization. 'Evangelization is the test of our ecumenical vocation.'"[63]

A final word with regard to mission as witness: The depth of meaning in the Greek *mart-* word family is lost in English translation when we find ourselves unable to maintain the common unity of the *mart* root in English and must render the original with both "witness" and "testify/testimony" and their various meanings. "Translations are seldom consistent or concordant."[64] However, the ambiguity is also helpful, since it constantly reminds us that witness in the biblical sense is multidimensional, a comprehensive definition of Christian existence. To approach the biblical breadth of the understanding of witness, one needs to consider, as I have suggested, the witness as person (the *being* of witness), the witness as action (the *doing* of witness), and witness as communication (the *saying* of witness).[65] In other words, there is a profoundly ethical dimension to the biblical understanding of witness, as it describes the church's whole sense of its being, doing, and saying: "the most important social task of Christians is to be nothing less than a community capable of forming people with virtues sufficient to witness to God's truth in the world."[66]

---

63. World Council of Churches, *Mission and Evangelism: An Ecumenical Affirmation* (Geneva, 1982), ¶1.

64. Walton, *Witness in Biblical Scholarship*, p. 6.

65. Darrell Guder, *Be My Witnesses: The Church's Mission, Message, and Messengers* (Grand Rapids: Eerdmans, 1985), especially chapters 5-9.

66. Hauerwas, *Community of Character*, pp. 105-6.

PART II

Challenges: The Church's Need for Conversion

We turn now to the challenges that confront the church today when it seeks to be faithful to its missional vocation. That vocation emerges out of God's saving action in Jesus Christ. There is good news about the reign of God, now breaking into human history through the lordship and saviorhood of Jesus Christ. The church has been formed by God's Spirit to be the witness to that good news and the first fruits of the inbreaking kingdom. I have, therefore, argued that evangelization is the core of mission and the heart of the church's ministry. This is rooted in the mission of God. The evangel must be made known. The good news is to be shared. Disciples are to become apostles. Witness to the gospel defines the identity, the activity, and the communication which are the calling of the church since Pentecost.

One might expect that we could move from the foundations just laid to their implications for the practice of evangelistic ministry today. The pilgrimage of the church since Pentecost makes that step impossible. We must examine what has happened to this gospel and the church in the intervening generations of Christian witness, particularly in the Western church. If we are to be translators of the gospel today, we need to understand the risks and opportunities of the translation that has passed the gospel "once delivered to the saints" through all these years to us. In that process, there has been a "reductionism of the gospel" which we must confront if we are to become a truly missional church.

Our need for continuing conversion is linked directly with the reductionism of the gospel that has become pervasive in our traditions and churches.

I approach this difficult theme with great respect for all the saints who precede us. The challenges we face today have, in some way, always faced the church. Wherever Christian witness has effectively planted the church in a particular culture, the problem of cultural compromise has surfaced. Our faithful witness can only happen when we learn to see and repent of our conformities. These conformities must be addresed when we examine the issue of gospel reductionism and open ourselves to our own continuing conversion.

Chapter Four

Translation in Mission

Mission is to be a continuing process of translation and witness, whereby the evangelist and the mission community will discover again and again that they will be confronted by the gospel as it is translated, heard, and responded to, and will thus experience ongoing conversion while serving as witness.

This statement from the previous chapter focuses our attention on the actual historical process of evangelization and mission. I am not concerned here to write a history of evangelization;[1] however, a theology of the church's evangelistic ministry must be informed by the history which precedes us. If the challenge of evangelization is a problem for the Christian churches on both sides of the Atlantic — and there would be little difficulty in demonstrating how problematic it is — then we need to look at the historical process that has produced the problem. This history reveals over and over again that the *missio Dei,* as God works it out, is fraught with risk. This risk, I suggest, is the necessary

1. See, for example, David Bosch, "Historical Paradigms of Mission," in *Transforming Mission: Paradigm Shifts in Theology of Mission* (Maryknoll, NY: Orbis Books, 1991), pp. 181-345; Michael Green, *Evangelism in the Early Church* (Grand Rapids: Eerdmans, 1970); Milton L. Rudnick, *Speaking the Gospel Through the Ages: A History of Evangelism* (St. Louis: Concordia, 1984); John M. Terry, *Evangelism: A Concise History* (Nashville: Broadman, 1994).

companion of the love that God translates into reality in the life, death, and resurrection of Jesus Christ. This love is the content and motive of Christian mission.

The Context of God's Loving Risk: Sin as Control

I have already discussed the candid way in which Scripture describes human reality in its ambiguity. Humans exist as *simul creatus et peccator* (simultaneously created and sinner) — that is how the stories of Genesis 1 to 11 describe human reality. The continuing crisis of their humanness is their constant rebellion against God.[2] God's willingness to enter into human experience in order to heal this rebellious creation, what we have called the *missio Dei*, has always been surrounded by risk. It has always been possible for humans to encounter God's Word and work in history and to ignore it, to reject it, to distort it, or to manipulate it for selfish ends. Inherent in God's grace is his willingness to take this risk for the sake of the faith response of the people of God, who are set apart to serve the divine purposes. God respects the freedom of the creation but mercifully does not treat us the way we treat him. God's grace continues to surround all creation, so that our rebellion never leads us so far away from God that we cannot hear his voice calling us to him. Nor does our disobedience ever totally obliterate the goodness of God's creation and the image of God that marks his human creatures. "Since Eden God is busy protecting people from what they have coming."[3]

The biblical record makes abundantly clear that the people to whom God speaks and reveals God's self are just as sinful as all the rest of creation. There are no special qualifications or virtues that set apart Abraham, Moses, David, or the prophets and make them more appropriate recipients of the divine self-disclosure. The fallibility of the disciples is documented in all the Gospels, as well as in Acts and the epistles. In fact, the sinfulness of God's witnesses is a major theme

2. See chapter 2, pp. 37-39.

3. John Howard Yoder, "To Serve Our God and to Rule the World," in *The Royal Priesthood: Essays Ecclesiological and Ecumenical,* ed. Michael G. Cartwright (Grand Rapids: Eerdmans, 1994), p. 138. What I am describing as God's gracious risk has been discussed for centuries under themes such as the *condescension of God,* or *God's accommodation.*

of the scriptural witness, both in the Old and New Testaments. All of the biblical witnesses could testify with Isaiah, "I am lost, for I am a man of unclean lips, and I live among a people of unclean lips; yet my eyes have seen the King, the Lord of hosts!" (Isa. 6:5). That Isaiah was unworthy was not an obstacle to the gracious self-disclosure of God, who called Isaiah into his service. In spite of his uncleanness, Isaiah could confess with that important "yet" that he had seen God. The "yet" is so important because it documents God's gracious willingness to risk communicating his love to creatures who may reject it. That loving risk is what makes the history of salvation and the living hope of faith possible.

In the process of collecting the Scriptures, there was never an attempt to retouch the record, to make the very human instruments of God's revelation into superhuman heroes of faith. Rather, we encounter in the Bible people like us. Perhaps the most compelling example of this relentless realism in the biblical witness is the story of David. He is portrayed in all the ambiguity of human existence: God's anointed, uniquely gifted, profoundly fallible, proud and penitent, a human being like us. We should be grateful for and encouraged by that realism. For it makes it clear that God's self-disclosure is always an act of his unmerited favor, an expression of the "yet." This realism about the human frailty of God's people defines God's grace and love as God's action that makes the response of faith possible but does not coerce it.

From Genesis 3 on, human existence is described and defined as *simul creatus et peccator*, simultaneously created and sinner. But it continues to be existence defined in Genesis 1 as created in the image of God *(imago Dei)*. This means that, even in human sinfulness, the human can hear and respond to God's address. We need never regard that sinfulness as a barrier to God's gracious action. Within the mysterious sovereignty of God's compassionate grace, God can turn even our rebellion so that it serves his purposes while it violates the divine will. We are never robots, and God is never a tyrant. God's judgment is always surrounded and shaped by his love: the crucifixion of Christ is the supreme manifestation of that sovereign love in action on behalf of sinners. As noted in chapter 2, this act of supreme human cruelty and rebellion is, under God's sovereign and gracious rule, the event which brings about the reconciliation of the lost creation. Therefore, our theology of the church's mission, and especially of its evangelistic ministry, must always deal realistically with the sinfulness of the believing community, because God's grace and love make that realism possible.

The Germans have a saying: "Trust is good, but control is better." Although undoubtedly cynical, it conveys a profound truth about the nature of the human rebellion. One can interpret the biblical teaching about human sin as the constant attempt to bring under human control what we are not qualified to control. Its most radical form, of course, is the attempt to bring God under human control. This is the very essence of the Fall. In that foundational story in Genesis 3, we see the human creatures doubting God's Word and seeking to move beyond the boundaries of human existence, to wield powers which are reserved for God.

> In Genesis 3 the basic temptation for man is set forth as the temptation for man to exceed the bounds that have been set for him, which are precisely the bounds that indicate his humanity! He is so near to God as creature and yet not content to act as privileged creature. Instead, there is a (willingly accepted) suggestion that this privilege of being created as man in communication with and dependent upon God is not man's *treasure* but his *deficiency*. In the story of the serpent we are confronted with the temptation of man to bring God and himself to one common denominator.[4]

The nature of sin as control is documented throughout Scripture. Idolatry is such a mechanism of control, as it reduces the divine to the level of a product of human craft and ingenuity, the "one common denominator" of which Blauw wrote. "The Prophets unmasked man's religiosity as being not just a desire for God, but a desire to *have* a god, to possess him, to have him for their own, at their disposal."[5] When Israel reinterpreted its election as its own spiritual privilege, then it was seeking to control its status before God and all the other nations of the earth. The great rites of atonement and forgiveness could be reshaped by the priests of Israel into a control system that brought God's favor and human restitution under religious management.

Sin as control continues to challenge the integrity of Christian

---

4. Johannes Blauw, "The Biblical View of Man in His Religion," in *The Theology of the Christian Mission*, ed. Gerald H. Anderson (New York: McGraw-Hill, 1961), p. 33.

5. Blauw, "Biblical View of Man," p. 35.

witness. The New Testament documents this. The desire of the disciples to share Christ's throne (Mark 10:35-45) or to know the time the kingdom will be restored (Acts 1:6) betrayed common motifs of control which constantly bedevil the Christian church. Indeed, the gospel's insistence that conversion must be linked with repentance is a clear indictment of the human urge to control. To acknowledge one's need for forgiveness is to renounce the human demand to control one's own life and fate. Arne Rasmusson, commenting on Stanley Hauerwas's discussion of sin as control, states:

> [I]t is more difficult to accept forgiveness than to give it. It is so because to accept forgiveness means giving up the control of one's own life and consequently to trust someone else. In the classical Christian way [Hauerwas] says that it is through accepting the forgiveness of God one can receive the capacity to give up this control and acknowledge that one's life also is in other hands. Christians must therefore be a people that risk trusting others and not fear the new, the different, and the surprising.[6]

If we accept Karl Barth's distinction between the Christian faith and religion, then the human desire to exercise control would certainly be one of the major characteristics of all religious systems. These systems can be very pious and impressive. But, in one way or another, they are ultimately expressions of "the hidden desire of the human heart . . . to use God merely to serve [one's] human purposes." When God reveals the divine name to Moses, he is asserting in Exodus 3 what was rejected in the human sin of Genesis 3: the unlimited and uncontrollable sovereignty of God. "The name of God is in itself a protest against man's mastery of God for human purposes. . . . Serving God in your own way is serving God for your own purposes, and that is the same as original sin."[7]

6. Arne Rasmusson, *The Church as* Polis: *From Political Theology to Theological Politics as Exemplified by Jürgen Moltmann and Stanley Hauerwas* (Notre Dame: University of Notre Dame Press, 1995), p. 195.

7. Blauw, "Biblical View of Man," p. 35.

The Risk of Translation

God's loving desire to restore all creation to God's self resulted in the joyful event and message of Jesus. The incarnation translates and embodies God's love for creation. That translation of God's love into human history, commencing with Abraham and climaxing in Jesus, is the great and gracious risk of the mission of God. That risk of translation became global as the gospel of Jesus became the missionary message of the early church. The church was empowered and directed to cross boundaries and to take this message to the ends of the earth.

For Israel, the movement of human response to God's claims had a geographical magnetic point: the holy land, the holy city, the holy building, the holy of holies. The faithful gathered in Jerusalem to experience the fullness of God's presence. They were gathered for that reason on the occasion of the first Pentecost, as narrated in Acts 2. The outpouring of God's Spirit, empowering the first Christian community to become Christ's witnesses, exploded the geographical orientation of God's work in history in all directions, into all the world. Rather than coming together in one place, God's people were to scatter themselves across the world, as salt, leaven, and light, "in Jerusalem, in all Judea and Samaria, and to the ends of the earth" (Acts 1:8b). To document that intention, the Spirit empowered the first witnesses to make the joyful message known in all the languages represented in that multicultural Jewish festival in Jerusalem. "Each one heard them speaking in the native language of each" (Acts 2:6b). This event, which we celebrate as the birthday of the church, demonstrated paradigmatically the fundamental translatability of the gospel.

The translatability of the gospel is a basic theme of missiological thought and practice.[8] Although revealed in all its power at Pentecost, it is germane to the entire sweep of the biblical history of redemption as the *missio Dei*. The covenant with Abraham had, as its ultimate intention, the blessing of all the nations. The psalmists and the prophets, especially Second Isaiah, often referred to that worldwide scope of God's saving purposes. Jonah is a polemic against the Jewish control of its

---

8. This discussion of translatability is based, with gratitude, on Lamin Sanneh, *Translating the Message: The Missionary Impact on Culture* (Maryknoll, NY: Orbis Books, 1991), pp. 1-129.

faith tradition that ruled out the proclamation of good news to the Gentiles. Jesus came first to his own people to call them into the service of God's kingdom for all peoples. In his interpretation of the law, his critique of the religious leaders of the day, and his actions toward the marginal and the non-Jewish, he demonstrated the universal scope of the kingdom drawing near. He challenged the very heart of the restrictive view of God's saving work when he cleansed the temple and asked the question: "Is it not written, 'My house shall be called a house of prayer for all the nations'?" (Mark 11:17). He taught his disciples to pray for the coming of the kingdom "on earth" and not just in Judea, and he sent them out "to make disciples of the nations."

Like the birth, the death, the resurrection, and the ascension of Jesus, Pentecost is an event that happened once and yet continues to become real history in the faith community as God's Spirit makes this story into the history of his people. In this event, like all events in the history of redemption, God is the initiator and carries out his mission through empowered recipients of the message, witnesses of the happening. The signs of wind, fire, and tongues all underline the initiation and sovereign action of God in giving the Spirit for the church's missionary obedience.[9]

It has often been suggested that Pentecost reversed the confusion of human tongues at Babel. But the history of salvation is not cyclical; it does not move backward but forward to the "new" which God has promised and brings about. Thus the confusion of tongues at Babel was not reversed by the creation of one tongue. Instead, the Holy Spirit made translation into *all* tongues possible. In the gracious economy of God, the joyful message was intended from the very outset to be infinitely translatable and multicultural; it is to be conveyed into every language and culture of the world. In the book of Acts, this is then demonstrated paradigmatically in the evangelization of the Ethiopian eunuch, the mission to the Samaritans, the conversion of Cornelius, and Paul's missionary movement into the Gentile world. The full confession of God's grace and glory can only take place through the assembled choirs of all human tongues and cultures. We catch something of

---

9. See my discussion of "the vision of the church in Acts," in *Be My Witnesses: The Church's Mission, Message, and Messengers* (Grand Rapids: Eerdmans, 1985), pp. 35-54, especially 3.3, "The Enabling Event of Pentecost," pp. 44ff.

this sense of massed multicultural choirs praising God in the heavenly anthems that we find in the visions of the Revelation.

Confession of faith in all languages is possible because of the distinctive character of God's action, as it leads to faith. God's self-communication takes the form of incarnation in history, events in which God encounters us and enables us to recognize that it is God who is speaking and acting. These events lead toward and find their climax and ultimate purpose in the Word that became flesh, the "Son of man." He announces the inbreaking of the kingdom of God, teaches what that kingdom is in his words and actions, and calls people to follow him and become his witnesses, "fishers of people" (Mark 1:17 pars.). Through the continuing witness to this One and all that he said and did, successive generations of people become witnesses to Jesus Christ, to his life, death, resurrection, and present sovereignty in human history. As such witnesses, they experience and pass on the good news of God's healing love granted in Jesus Christ. Thus, they become part of God's continuing mission.

Because this incarnation in history could be witnessed, it could be reported and be put into words. Yet, there are no particular sacred words in a sacred language that must always be learned and used in order to encounter the divine. The witness does not create an arcane language or cultus that must be appropriated and practiced in order to know God. Rather, the person and the event were witnessed and that witness (*martyrion*) was passed on by the witnesses (*martyrioi*, the apostolic community) to become the scriptural witness assembled in the Bible. As these witnesses made their testimony known, many came to believe and join the missionary community that was the early Christian church. Their purpose was the continuing transmission and translation of the joyful news wherever God sent them and the Spirit opened doors for them. In that transmission and translation, the salvation events, the gospel itself, continued and continue to have their unique impact as individuals respond and individual lives are transformed or converted. This joyful news becomes, as the Spirit empowers its witness, each new Christian's story and self-definition. The basic pattern of witness as translation was demonstrated by Paul: "For I received from the Lord what I also handed on to you" (1 Cor. 11:23); "For I handed on to you as of first importance what I in turn had received" (1 Cor. 15:3).

By the gift of God's Spirit, this witness may be translated into every human setting, since Jesus may be met and known in every human setting. The particularity of Jesus, a man in the first-century Jewish culture of Palestine, can be translated into the particularity of every other culture and place.[10] It is events and human discourse, not ideas, which can be translated and continue to work as historical encounter in every human setting. The Word continues to become flesh as it is witnessed to. This is possible because he, this particular man Jesus, is risen and alive, and "all authority in heaven and on earth has been given to [him]" (Matt. 28:18). The early church's experience is to be repeated by every person who responds to Christ: "And the Word became flesh and lived among us, and we have seen his glory" (John 1:14). The gospel is rooted in the distinctive history of God's saving actions and words, and in its life-changing impact upon those who respond and submit to Christ as his followers and learn all that he taught (Matt. 28:20). Therefore, because the joyful news is about God's mission, God's loving intentions for all creation, it is fundamentally missionary in nature, universal in scope, and, necessarily, translatable into the particular.

From the outset of the Christian pilgrimage, the translatability of the gospel has been a challenge and a risk for the church. It has not been easy to grasp how inclusive God's love truly is and how universal the missionary apostolate is to be. The book of Acts documents the struggle of the early church with the translatability of the gospel. The events of Pentecost establish the framework within which the church began its pilgrimage of continuing conversion. Empowered by the Holy Spirit to be Christ's witness, the community will discover over time the fullness of God's missionary power and the breadth and depth of the mission mandate. As it makes that discovery, it encounters Christ in ways that broaden and deepen its understanding of the gospel. The issue in Acts that most profoundly shows this was the mission to the Gentiles. As the early church struggled with this challenge, it began to discover the evangelical meaning of "all the world" and "all nations" and "the ends of the earth." The church's continuing conversion today

10. For a stimulating discussion of the particularity of the incarnation, see John Howard Yoder, "'But We Do See Jesus': The Particularity of Incarnation and the Universality of Truth," in *The Priestly Kingdom: Social Ethics as Gospel* (Notre Dame: University of Notre Dame Press, 1984), pp. 46-62.

is always, in some way, related to the comprehensiveness of its missionary calling. We are still discovering the meaning of "all the world" today.

Translation as Cultural Formation and Transformation

It becomes clear in this struggle that the issue is not just a question of language, but rather of all that languages signify and embody, that fullness of specific human experience which we describe with the term "culture." The gospel witness is not just any narrative or story: it is reporting of happenings that are of life-changing significance, news that everyone needs to know. It is not the text which saves, nor the ideas, metaphors, and images conveyed by the text, but Jesus, his story and his message, as witnessed to both by the scriptural record and the confessing tradition of the missionary church. Translation is therefore not just a question of retelling a narrative as literally as possible in another language. It is the challenge, which the Spirit empowers Christian witnesses to meet, to report the history of Christ and present him as the present Lord and Savior, calling people to faith, hope, and love in a new life which, as Jesus told Nicodemus, is "born from above." This challenge always means calling people to receive God's gift of salvation and to become the witnesses to the kingdom that is present and coming under Christ.[11]

The difficult question of circumcision in the early experience of the church illustrates the difference between literal translation and cultural translation. Is the task of the witness merely to move the narrative from one language to another? Or is it to articulate the witness in a different cultural setting in such a way that the joyful news of Jesus is heard and responded to? Does the translation of the gospel from one culture to another mean the translation of a religious and cultural rite in one receiving culture (Judaism) into another receiving culture (Hellenism)? Did Greeks have to become culturally and religiously Jews, after

---

11. For a full discussion of the theme of this section, see Louis J. Luzbetak, S.V.D., *The Church and Cultures: New Perspectives in Missiological Anthropology* (Maryknoll, NY: Orbis Books, 1988).

the pattern of Moses, in order to encounter Christ? Many of the Jerusalem believers assumed that there were limits to the translatability of the gospel. For them, translation had to mean the acceptance of circumcision (as the symbol of the legal distinctiveness of Jewishness) and other particularly important practices of the Jewish faith community. But the translatability of the gospel meant for Paul that discipleship in the receiving culture will be formed in new ways. This did not necessarily mean the literal translation of every practice from the evangelist's culture to the receiving culture. Rather, it meant the creation of corresponding practices in the receiving culture which demonstrated the "circumcision of the heart" (Rom. 2:29). In some way, the fact that Christians belong to God body and soul must find tangible expression in every culture.

The translation was more than mere literal language conversion: it was witness to Christ as expressed by persons of the receiving culture. It was the event of faith, the experienced relationship of faith, becoming event and relationship in a new cultural context. This faith response is always to the same event: God's self-disclosure in Jesus Christ. The salvation events do not change, nor does their meaning become relativized. Rather, the events are translated in such a way that Jesus is recognized as Lord and Savior, his call to discipleship is followed, his teaching received and implemented, and the apostolic witness extended. This must happen so that God's mission may continue in Christ's witnesses to the ends of the earth: the Word must become flesh in each successive evangelized culture so that its witness may go out within that culture and then beyond it, in order to move across future frontiers of witness.

To put it in other words: It was not merely God's intention that the message, as disembodied language, be translated from one language to another. The gospel is not merely a set of words grammatically related, or a system of ideas arranged in a philosophically informed structure. It is history that makes history. That is, it is history that becomes every Christian's history as the Spirit draws followers to Christ and molds them into his Body. So, it was God's intention that the call of Christ be articulated and the concrete practice of discipleship and apostolate be shaped in each culture as a Spirit-empowered response, as Christ's lordship prepares and empowers this translation to happen.

Translatability is not merely a linguistic passage, limited to words, but a cultural appropriation for which the language becomes the primary medium and symbol, and the practices of faith become the tangible demonstration. The result of the process of translation was the formation of a mission community, a people of God in a particular place, sent and empowered by God to be gospel witnesses in that cultural context. The appeal to them was "to lead lives worthy of the calling to which you have been called" (Eph. 4:1). The missional purpose of the formation of new faith communities must be stressed. As the New Testament epistles reveal, the apostolic evangelists continued to instruct the newly formed communities so that their witness to their surrounding mission fields would have integrity and serve God faithfully.

The translatability of the gospel event and its meaning are, in fact, a concrete expression of God's loving purpose for the world. God loves the world and wants it to experience that love in Christ in such a way that it can respond to it and share it. This means, then, that no particular culture is privileged in the missionary enterprise, and no culture is rejected. All human cultures, marked as they are by the tension of being *simul creatus et peccator* (simultaneously created and sinful), are honored by God as potential receivers of Christ and his calling. Jesus demonstrated this radical translatability and cultural openness of the gospel by choosing disciples from such disparate and unlikely backgrounds, by socializing with publicans and prostitutes, by praising the faith of pagan military officers, by talking with and using Samaritans as teaching examples, and by initiating his ministry in Galilee rather than Judea.[12] All cultures may become missionary cultures, receiving and passing on God's love in Christ. Within every culture, God's missionary people can be formed. The representatives of all cultures are potentially evangelizers, even though they all are weak, frail, and subject to conversion. In Lamin Sanneh's language, all cultures are destigmatized and relativized.

The process of gospel translation is profoundly interactive, however. That means that as the gospel is heard within a culture, and as a missionary people is formed within it, that culture will also be challenged. To destigmatize and relativize cultures does not mean to sanc-

---

12. On the importance of the Galilean origins of Jesus' ministry, see Orlando Costas, *Liberating News: A Theology of Contextual Evangelization* (Grand Rapids: Eerdmans, 1989), pp. 49ff.

tify them. All cultures bear the marks of human sinfulness. Therefore, the impact of the gospel will be both affirming and critical of all cultures. The missionary people formed within a culture will also be a transforming force. This transforming impact is what the biblical images of salt, leaven, and light are all about. I referred above to the ethical witness of the gospel within cultures, and shall return to discuss this witness in greater detail later. For now, I underline that one of the most significant missiological implications of translation is the transformative power of the gospel to shape a community for its evangelistic ministry in its context.

This engagement necessarily must be a confrontation. Every culture, as it receives the gospel, is placed in question by it. If the gospel is faithfully translated, then it continues to work as a two-edged sword. That transformative witness will hallow some elements of the culture, adapt others, and reject others. The receiving culture cannot be any more normative than the culture of the evangelizing witnesses. The desire to control constantly asserts itself here. Cultures try to bring the gospel under their control, attempting to fit the person and work of Christ into their patterns of accepted religious practice. Translation is a risk, and thus the process must be one of continuing conversion. The first stage of translation must be succeeded in any culture by successive re-translations, corrections and expansions, as the converting power of the gospel reviews human reductions of the gospel and challenges the Christian community to greater faithfulness and a more obedient response to God's love.

As Christianity became the established religion of expanding European culture, the problem of control constantly presented itself. Following the disintegration of the Roman Empire, as various cultures migrated and changed the cultural map of Europe, Christian mission was remarkably effective. These cultures rapidly became integrated into the Christian civilization over which the Latin pope exercised authority. Although originally Germanic, these various cultures (Franks, Saxons, Suevians, Allemanians, etc.) accepted (or had imposed on them) the Roman culture of established Christendom. Acknowledged as the spiritual authority in the western half of the empire, the Latin papacy claimed that it could define the doctrinal *and* cultural shape of faith as Christendom expanded its boundaries and absorbed more and more cultural groupings.

One of the forms of control that emerged early in the Middle Ages involved the languages of the Christian faith. The established church began to assert that it was God's will that the faith be expressed in Hebrew, Greek, or Latin, and only these. It was argued that Pilate placed these languages over the head of Jesus on the cross. But this so-called trilinguistic theory was contested. A synod convened in Frankfurt during 794 promulgated, in Canon 52, this basic principle of gospel translatability: "It is not to be believed that God is only to be worshiped in the three languages. Because God is worshiped in all languages, man is heard if he strives in pursuing the right."[13]

The missional purpose of all faith communities, Christ's definition of the church as his witnesses, must guide the formation of every Christian church in every culture. When other criteria and interests replace this priority of God's mission, then gospel reductionism is at work.

The implications of gospel translatability are obviously profound for our understanding and practice of biblical interpretation.[14] James Brownson has commented that "a missional hermeneutic begins with the assumption that the mode in which God is present among the faithful is irreducibly multicultural." His exposition of the non-normative character of all cultures with reference to biblical hermeneutics summarizes the understanding of translation that I have advanced thus far:

> The reality of God's presence is at least potentially available through the symbolic world projected by any specific culture. Though each culture is called to repentance, its specific contours are not obliterated. . . . [A] missional hermeneutic includes the awareness that the reality of God is not exhausted by any particular culture's ways of naming and worshiping God. . . . [E]ach culture's apprehension of God in Scripture may be accurate but is always provisional, and . . . God is most fully known and glorified through a diversity of cultures and cultural perspectives. . . . A missional hermeneutic presupposes one God, one scripture, and one sacred story. At the same time, how-

13. See Francis Dvornik, *Byzantine Missions among the Slavs: SS. Constantine-Cyril and Methodius* (New Brunswick: Rutgers University Press, 1970), p. 367, note 29, p. 115; English translation by Sanneh, *Translating the Message,* pp. 73-74.

14. See chapter 3, pp. 51-55, especially notes 7 to 11.

ever, this sacred story does not serve to promote or sanction a monocultural religious perspective, but rather a multicultural one. God's presence is irreducibly multicultural. . . . [T]he God whose presence calls forth a distinctive form of doxology in [one] culture is the same God whose mercy calls forth grateful praise as well from other cultures, in other forms.[15]

Translation as Continuing Conversion of the Church

The church's first translation passage was from the Palestinian/Jewish context of the first community of witnesses to the various Hellenistic settings of the first-century Mediterranean world.[16] The study of that process equips us better to understand the continuing task of translation today. These passages (Bosch speaks of them as "paradigm shifts") teach us what it means to take the risk of translation. They teach us much about faithful witness. Our learning is always a process of grateful reception and modest criticism of what has gone before us. Nevertheless, through every "paradigm shift" we see the human striving to control the gospel. Again and again, we perceive the faithfulness of God asserting his gracious love in spite of the church's ambiguous and even unfaithful witness. We also see the continuing conversion of the church as each translation reveals dimensions of the gospel that had not been fully seen before.

The task of translation always begins with God's self-revelation to Israel. The Jewish tradition must be clearly acknowledged as the historical vessel into which God's message had been translated for centuries. But it was no longer to make that claim as an exclusive one. Rather, in the fulfillment of the promises made to Israel, the nations would now be brought into the promise, joined to the covenant, and made part of the expanding and ever more diverse new Israel in Christ. This had always been the intention of God's call to Israel: to be a blessing to the nations. Now, that calling was entering fulfillment, not as a rejection of

15. James Brownson, "Speaking the Truth in Love: Elements of a Missional Hermeneutic," *International Review of Mission* 83, no. 330 (July 1994): 485f.

16. Sanneh, "The Birth of Mission: The Jewish-Gentile Frontier," *Translating the Message*, pp. 9-49; Bosch, "The Missionary Paradigm of the Eastern Church," in *Transforming Mission*, pp. 190-213.

Israel but an expansion of the good news that had always been the heart of Israel's experience of God.

> The other thing we cannot say about this new communication move is that it leaves Judaism behind. That would be anachronism again; the writers of these texts and the singers of the hymn in Philippians were all Jews. They were proclaiming the pertinence and the priority of the meaning-frame of messianic Judaism, with all its concentration upon empirical community, particular history, synagogue worship, and particular lifestyle, over against the speculative and skeptical defenses of its cultured despisers. Instead of requesting free speech and room for one more stand in the Athenian marketplace of ideas for a new variant of already widely respected diaspora Judaism, their claim was that now the Hebrew story had widened out to include everyone; that, with the inbreaking of the messianic era, the Jewish hope in process of fulfillment was wide enough to receive all the nations and their riches.[17]

The Christian communities in all cultures now share as one of their most important bonds their common rootage in Israel. They acknowledge their indebtedness to Israel and their gratitude that God has chosen to let them become "engrafted branches" on the root of Israel (Rom. 11:17). They glory in the particularity of God's election of Israel, because it sets the pattern for God's continuing particularity in calling forth faith communities in all the particular cultures of the world. They receive the translation of God's Word from the cultural setting of Israel in the Old and New Testaments and praise God for the Spirit-empowered continuation of that witness in their tongues and experience.

Therefore, they must battle and reject the heresy of anti-Semitism, wherever it breaks out, as a profound denial of the gospel itself. Where they do not battle such heresy, they become guilty themselves of profound distortions and reductions of the gospel. For the Christian traditions of the post-Constantinian era, one of the most important aspects of faithful witness is contrite admission of complicity in the heresy of anti-Semitism. Christian witness to Jewish brothers and sisters stands on the common foundation of God's salvation history. For both

17. Yoder, "'But We Do See Jesus,'" p. 54.

Christians and Jews, the completion of God's mission is as yet before us: we share the same hope that God will be faithful to all his promises to all the called-out people. Only within that commonalty of roots and future hope can Christians faithfully represent God's love in Christ to their Jewish brothers and sisters.

Translation from the particular culture of the biblical communities into the receiving cultures across the globe is itself a faith venture in which the lordship of Christ is experienced and affirmed. The missionary translators, beginning with the New Testament apostles and continuing to today, constantly encounter the preparatory work of God's Spirit when they enter into a new place. They do not bring the gospel: Christ, as Lord over heaven and earth, is already there. Christ brings his witnesses across frontiers into new areas of mission. They then witness to the reality of Christ as they find words, experiences, images, and metaphors in another language for the testimony of faith — we think of Paul's address on the Areopagus. At the same time, they translate the gospel into practices that demonstrate the meaning of God's love in Christ. The verbal witness is accompanied by the ethical witness. Therefore, Paul speaks so often of the life-changes that his Christian readers could look back upon: "These are the ways you also once followed, where you were living that life. But now you must get rid of all such things" (Col. 3:7-8; see also Gal. 4:8ff; Eph. 5:3ff; 1 Thess. 4:1-12).

Missionary translation always includes the continuing conversion of the translator-evangelists. The Spirit, in wonderful ways, makes their telling and showing into their own hearing and responding. Peter experienced this in his encounter with Cornelius, following his unsettling vision of the unclean animals he was commanded to eat. As he discovered that "God shows no partiality" (Acts 10:34), his own encounter with Christ was deepened, and his own sense of the scope of the gospel was revised — and expanded. Even the disciple of Jesus who was eyewitness to the salvation events needed continuing conversion.

One can make this point with the language of New Testament eschatology. Translation opens up ever more dimensions of the one gospel. The meaning of God's healing work is constantly revealed in the overcoming of walls of separation between Jews and Greeks, slave owners and slaves, men and women, rich and poor, black and white and brown and yellow. As we pray in all languages, we learn that we are praying in the name of the same Lord Jesus and that we are invoking the will of God who desires that we all be one even as the Father and the Son are one (John 17). The future tense of faith is anticipated and experienced in the translation of the gospel and in the formation of faith communities whose discipleship often reveals dimensions of the gospel we had not yet grasped. In their adventure of faith, the kingdom of God comes nearer, and we are drawn into it more fully as we share that experience.

This is perhaps the most profound reason for ecumenical exchange: the continuing mutual conversion of Christian communities in diverse cultures. Every particular culture's translation of the gospel contributes a witness that corrects, expands, and challenges all other forms of witness in the worldwide church. We are experiencing very concrete examples of this powerful spiritual movement when we encounter the base Christian communities of Central and South America, China's house churches, and the indigenous churches of Africa and Asia. Western Christianity is only beginning to discover the great resources of evangelical witness which have developed in Eastern Orthodoxy through its centuries of translating the gospel into cultures stretching from eastern Europe across Asia to the Pacific Ocean.

The translatability of the gospel is a challenge, even a shock for rebellious humans. As beings who are so concerned about control, we find the cultural openness of the gospel offensive. A translatable gospel is fundamentally not controllable. It unsettles us to discover that faithfulness to Christ can, in cultures different from ours, look different from the patterns we have evolved. We build up a certain security in our cultural faith traditions, as did Israel in its faith. When important components of our tradition (circumcision, dietary laws, patterns of church administration and polity, creedal formulations) are not essential to the translation of the gospel in order for Christian witnesses in another culture to be faithful in their obedience, we feel relativized and often threatened. Like Peter, every particular Christian community within its culture must constantly have visions of "unclean animals"; it must confront its own limitations of the gospel and be converted by God's revolutionary love as it breaks down human boundaries.

This is happening today in many ways as the churches founded in the non-Western world have come of age and become full partners with the older churches who sent out the missionary evangelists. Many of these newer churches are highly critical of their North Atlantic sister churches. They denounce "Eurocentric theology and paternalism," often for very good reasons. "Eurocentric" North Atlantic Christians may find this hard and painful. Sometimes they react with even more sweeping condemnations of their own mission history, and even go so far as to call for an end to cross-cultural missionary activity.[18] The present discussion of Christian mission history must deal with the realities, the ambiguities, and the dynamics of gospel translation across cultures with missiological sensitivity. Neither condemning the generations of missionaries who preceded us nor making them into infallible heroes is appropriate. Rather, we see in our most recent history the continuation of the church's conversion begun in Acts.

To be sure, the history of modern missions is marked by innumerable painful instances of missionary arbitrariness. Many could not envision the freedom of God's Spirit to form the faith community in a new culture in different ways. The result has been untranslated components of Christian cultures that are anachronisms today: Gothic churches in Africa, British colleges in India, American standards of success in Korea. It is necessary that we struggle with the resentments and bitterness among many Christians in the "newer churches" which resulted from our uncritical Western persuasion that our version of the gospel was final and ultimate. We in the West really (if perhaps naively) believed that gospel translatability had reached its climax in European Christendom. For decades, we went about the business of the "evangelization of the world in this generation," persuaded that we should share the gospel in an indissoluble linkage with the "benefits of Western civilization."

In many churches of the non-Western world, this legacy is questioned and often reshaped, if not rejected. From this episode, we are learning that the glory of gospel translatability is its powerful testimony to God's sovereignty within human affairs. We are learning to acknowledge gratefully the work of God's Spirit in teaching us how to name the name of Christ in all our cultures (including the old Western ones), and at the same time, we are learning to repent of the limitations we have imposed upon that translation process. As we grasp that, we can truly begin to join Paul in his great doxology at the end of his struggle with the issues of multicultural mission in Romans 9–11: "O the

18. See chapter 1, note 10.

depth of the riches and wisdom and knowledge of God! How unsearchable are his judgments and how inscrutable his ways!" (Rom. 11:33).

Missional Implications of Translation

Gospel translation is empowered by the Holy Spirit but takes place in the ambiguity of human frailty and cultural limitations. This is the risk that God, in his compassion for his creation, constantly takes. The Scriptures are a continuing attestation of God's faithfulness in and through the very human ways in which his witnesses testify to his actions and words. That ambiguity produces what may be described as "gospel reductionism." I turn now to the critical examination of this constant dimension of Christian mission.

To summarize what we have observed, mission as translation means that the apostolic ministry of witness takes place in a plurality of cultural forms. None of them is normative for the others. But they are all essential to each other as mutual affirmation, correction, and challenge. They are all complementary in that they all respond to the same story, proclaim the same Christ, and pursue the implications of the same gospel in their various particular settings. No particular cultural rendering of the gospel may claim greater validity than any other, and all cultural formulations of the faith are subject to continuing conversion as the gospel challenges them. That challenge often happens in the ecumenical interaction of Christian communities, whose commonalty in Christ makes it possible for them to be witnesses to each other of the gospel, which is greater than any particular version of it. In other words, all cultural formations of Christian discipleship are both authentic and sinful. They are shaped by God's grace and deformed by our desire to control that grace. They are imperfect but subject to God's continuing work of perfecting. God's grace continues to be the source and force of salvation; human work never saves.

This means that all forms of nationalism and ethnicity are relativized. No national church, no ethnic Christian tradition possesses absolute truth or permanent validity. The particular problem of Western Christianity is this: it has assumed that it represented the cultural perfection of the gospel. Therefore, its mission could take place in the process described by Sanneh as "diffusion": the gospel spread itself in its Western cultural form and replaced the cultures it conquered. This was largely how European medieval mission took place, although the interaction of cultures was stronger than this generalization implies. Mission by diffusion finds it difficult to deal with the many ways in which the gospel continues to challenge one's culture, especially cultures which self-confidently describe themselves as "Christian" (e.g., the "Christian West," the "Judeo-Christian tradition," and "Christian America or Germany or Britain"). It assumes that one's culture has already reached the status of Christianity that is the goal of the gospel. That assumption forms the basic mentality of the civilization we call Christendom, or the *corpus Christianum*. Within that framework, mission always mixes or conflates gospel translation and cultural imperialism. This fateful mixture is a part of the Western missionary movement. Its influence can never be denied, although we can (as do many) overstate its significance. Moreover, while the external structures of the Christendom system have been collapsing for four centuries, this mentality remains very influential.

The gospel freely enters all cultures and places all cultures in question. It is translatable as the witness and message of Jesus, who may be known, confessed, and followed in every human setting. The Lord's Prayer may be prayed in every language. The call to discipleship may be shaped in every culture and will always be both a blessing and a scandal in that culture — if it is faithful to Christ. The risk of translatability is that sinful humans are its agents. The witnesses are always very ambiguous saints. They (we) never divorce themselves from the desire to bring this powerful and radical gospel under control. Thus, in the process of translation, complex forms of reduction take place. Such reduction is a necessary aspect of translation, but under certain circumstances it can jeopardize the church's missional faithfulness.

The translatability of the gospel is not to be understood solely in terms of translating the Bible into other languages, as important as that is. Cultures do not stand still. They evolve and change, and so must the work of translating. As our Western cultures move beyond the forms of Christendom, new translation hurdles arise. The language, attitudes, values, and expectations of secularized populations in Western societies constitute new challenges for gospel translation. Youth cultures, young adult cultures, inner-city cultures, recreation and leisure time cultures, media cultures, as subsets of our cultural systems, are mission fields into which the gospel can and must be translated.

Lesslie Newbigin speaks of the need for Christian communities to be culturally bilingual.[19] He refers here to the fundamental missionary task of Christian communities. As followers of Christ, they are being formed into distinctive communities speaking the language of faith rooted in and informed by Scripture. Therefore, they share with all Christian communities the cross-cultural commonalty that is the presence and rule of Jesus Christ. As they follow Christ, their language makes them, in many ways, distinctive within their communities. They are, as they learn Christ, more and more "strangers and aliens" (1 Peter), "resident aliens" and "colonies" (Hauerwas and Willimon), "contrast societies" (Lohfink).

This distinctiveness lies at the heart of their calling to be Christ's witnesses. To follow Christ one must leave some things behind. But, they do not leave the societies behind, for they are called to be missionary communities where they are. If they are to be such missionary communities, then they must constantly translate the gospel into and among the cultures into which they are sent. They do this as "light, salt, and leaven" among the people and societies in which they live. Their presence should be a blessing, replacing darkness with light, bringing savor to life while quietly shaping God's presence within a particular place. Like the early Christians in Jerusalem, they "praise God and have the good will of all the people" (Acts 2:47). They experience what Paul described when he told the Corinthians that through them God "spreads in every place the fragrance that comes from knowing him" (2 Cor. 3:14). If they are truly missional, they may not become separated strangers and aliens, exclusive resident aliens, ghettoized colonies, judgmental contrast societies. Rather, they practice the continuation of Pentecost: they witness to the gospel so that all may hear in his or her own language.

This hearing is the result of what Newbigin describes as the "cultural bilinguality" of the Christian community. The Christian witness can and must be translated into the myriad subcultures that are in-

19. Lesslie Newbigin, *The Gospel in a Pluralist Society* (Grand Rapids: Eerdmans, 1989), pp. 55-65.

creasingly the hallmark of Western urbanized societies. Missionaries are called and gifted by God's Spirit for that mission. This is what it means to say that the West has become again a mission field. The translation task is ever new and ever before us.

The radically changed situation in central and eastern Europe provides a remarkable example of this challenge. In Rumania, Hungary, the Czech Republic, Slovakia, the former East Germany, and the states of the former Soviet Union, Christianity once was the dominant cultural and religious force. Its monuments still stand, and church towers still ornament the skylines. But the outward form of this culture has lost its critical mass and its rootedness in the sensibilities of the people. As has often been remarked since the revolutions of 1989-1990, in the former communist empire, communism lost but atheism won. With the exception of Poland, the active Christian population has become a minority. Most of the people in these countries are religiously ignorant. Most of them have never been inside a church. They do not know the most familiar Bible stories. They cannot interpret the most common symbols of the Christian faith in the old buildings in their towns and cities. Their cultures have become secularized, although some of the outward trappings of their Christian history remain. The challenge facing the Christian churches in these countries is missiological: Can they perceive the nature and task of these new secular cultures and address them missionally? Can they find out how to translate the gospel? Can they learn the language, the interior shape of these cultures and become, within them, culturally bilingual? Can they become, again, light, salt, and leaven in their contexts?

The danger in that part of the world, as throughout the North Atlantic societies, is that we shall continue to function as though our inherited cultural shapes are still normative. We may delude ourselves into believing that we can do today what we did before the dramatic events of this century. We ring our bells, conduct our worship services, provide the traditional pastoral services when called upon at the thresholds of life (baptism, confirmation, wedding, funeral), and wait for this very different world to come to us. We mount pulpits and preach sermons as we have done for centuries, before this new culture emerged. We pursue our internal arguments about doctrine and order as though nothing outside had changed. In effect, we continue to speak church Latin, expecting our immediate mission field, our world, to learn it and respond in our language.

But much has changed. The people are not coming back to the churches simply because they now have the freedom to do so. When they walk into our buildings, they do so as curious tourists, ignorant of their Christian legacy. They do not expect the traditional churches to say anything relevant or even understandable for them.

The missionary task in this changed situation is, as it always has been, Pentecostal translation: learning to speak the languages of the cultures in which we find ourselves, risking translation, and moving in trust toward the shape of the church which is to come. What we have been is not normative. No culturally evolved shape of the church is normative. What we have received from our traditions must be empowered by God's Spirit so that it can be "passed on" (*traducere* — tradition), and we are to be the agents of that translation. This becomes very concrete: the language we use, the forms of communication we adopt, the music and symbolism, the liturgies — all of this can and must be translated for the sake of the witness we are to be and to do. Our worship services are to be missionary events, invitations to follow Christ. This may mean that they must be substantially changed in many settings in our world.

Where continuity with the past is maintained, it must be done so very sensitively and creatively, so that the uninformed secular participant is invited to discover that past as his or her own history. Our link to our past is a matter of Christian witness, a testimony to the faithfulness of God. When it degenerates into mere aesthetic or historicist fascination with days and customs gone by, then it is no longer missionary translation. The transforming power of the gospel must address, first and foremost, the traditional ways we have communicated the gospel. From there, it will move into our larger contexts and illumine where Christian witness may say "yes" and must say "no." As in every other culture in the world, Christian witness engages Western culture in diverse ways: accepting, adapting, changing, and rejecting. This means, among other things, that the culturally bilingual church must expect to change and be changed, must expect its own continuing conversion, as it encounters Christ the Lord in the cultures into which it now is sent as his witnesses.

Chapter Five

The Challenge of Reductionism

The risk of translatability is that sinful humans are its agents. The witnesses are always very ambiguous saints. They (we) never divorce themselves from the desire to bring this powerful and radical gospel under control. That means that in the process of translation, complex forms of reduction also take place.

Translation and Reduction

In this approach to a theology of evangelistic ministry, I have defined the church's mission mandate in terms of witness. Then, I have stressed that this witness happens through the Holy Spirit's continuing empowering of the mission community to translate the gospel across all cultural boundaries. This ministry of witness is carried out by frail and forgiven humans, whom God chooses, forms into missional communities, and sends. Their sinfulness expresses itself in a constant, and often subtle, process: while adapting the gospel to the cultural context, which is essential to faithful witness, there is always the temptation to bring the gospel under control, to make it manageable. Thus, the task of witness as translation makes the continuing conversion of the Christian community necessary as it interacts with its culture. This continuing conversion comes about as the Christian community discovers that the claims of Christ and his gospel confront its sinfulness, reveal its drive to control the gospel, and uncover its compromises with its environment.

We need to explore this complex process of reductionism further, because I am convinced that this is the precise point of challenge to Western churches if they are to become faithfully missional in our changing world.

The church reduces the gospel as it translates it in its witness — this is the place where we must focus our thinking. As we proceed, I must emphasize again that this sober view of the humanity of the church is not to be understood as arrogant criticism of Christians in other situations and eras. When Paul wrote to the Corinthians, he thanked God for their witness, and then moved from one problem to another in their understanding and practice of their mission. Similarly, we need always to relate to our Christian tradition as both grateful and critical heirs. That is what I will seek to do as I grapple with the problematic aspects of translation and reduction. We must do so if we want to be open to the continuing conversion that is God's essential and empowering work, making us fitter for our missionary vocation.

Gospel reduction is as unavoidable as the reduction that occurs in the translating of texts from one language to another. God's willingness to risk translation reveals God's willingness to risk that reduction. Translation is a powerful process. It can uncover dimensions of a message which have not been recognized in quite the same way in previous translation processes. But, it also can, and usually does, reduce in some way or another that which it translates. This is true of translation in the narrower sense, from one language to another, and in the broader sense, from one culture to another. It is never possible to translate a text so that it adequately and completely conveys every nuance, every hidden or assumed dimension of the original. This is not so much a problem to lament as it is a definition of translation as a continuing task. The work of translation is ongoing.

This is well illustrated by the dynamic history of Bible translation. Usually such translations are now done by groups of scholars, who struggle together toward the goal to produce an accurate and nonreductionist translation. Once published, a translation is continually subjected to learned critique. Trained readers go back to the original Hebrew and Greek to weigh the merits of a particular modern translation and propose improvements. The findings of archeology throw light on ancient terms and practices and thus change the way translations must be made. Articles are written and published, texts discussed in seminary classrooms, interpretations and corrections offered in sermons and Bible studies. A generation later, that discussion often is reflected in a new translation.

The biblical witnesses are profoundly aware of the risk of reduction in the translation of God's Word into their situations. They know that their words never fully capture the wonder and truth of God's personhood and work. They are aware of their own unworthiness, as was Isaiah when confronted by the vision of God (Isa. 6:5), and of God's majestic greatness beyond human explanations, as profoundly explored in Job. The truly amazing thing about the scriptural record is the witnesses' confidence that they were hearing and passing on God's Word, even though they were its unworthy vessels and their renderings of it were in some way a reduction. Even though Moses stood on holy ground when God encountered him in the burning bush, and even though God's self-revelation included the holy mystery of God's name, the story was reported and ultimately written down. All the biblical witnesses of God's words and actions were confident that God had spoken and acted and this could be testified to and the witness preserved. Further, they were confident that God would continue to speak and act as their witness was passed on orally and in written form to subsequent generations. Thus, the reduction inherent in all human witness and translation is overcome by the power of God whose work of self-disclosure continues as this witnessed Word is read, proclaimed, responded to, and struggled with. It is the continuing work of the Holy Spirit, as the Reformers emphasized, which empowers the translating, the proclaiming, and the hearing of the biblical witness as God's Word. That same Spirit also empowers the response of faith — and calls the faithful to continuing conversion.

Thus, Christian witnesses may be aware of their reduction of the gospel, but they need not fear that their witness is thus rendered irrelevant, or that relativism reigns. These options are often posed as the only available ones, especially when dealing with the question of biblical authority and interpretation. Here, as elsewhere, caution is advisable when anyone proposes that there are only two options in a difficult issue. Such an assertion obviously reduces the power of the Holy Spirit to act. When discussing the meaning of "paradigm shift in missiology" and the accu-

sation that such an interpretive approach must foster the belief that
"there really are no ultimate norms or values," David Bosch counters:

> [T]he real point here is that one should in all research, whether in
> theology or the natural or social sciences, never think in mutually ex-
> clusive categories of "absolute" and "relative." Our theologies are
> partial, and they are culturally and socially biased. They may never
> claim to be absolutes. Yet this does not make them relativistic, as
> though one suggests that in theology — since we really cannot ever
> know "absolutely" — anything goes. It is true that we see only in part,
> but we do see. . . . We are committed to our understanding of revela-
> tion, yet we also maintain a critical distance to that understanding.
> In other words, we are in principle open to other views, an attitude
> which does not, however, militate against complete commitment to
> our own understanding of truth. . . . It is misleading to believe that
> commitment and a self-critical attitude are mutually exclusive.[1]

Reduction + Control = Reduction*ism*

Reduction, as a necessary aspect of our humanness, is thus not necessarily a problem for biblical faithfulness, until the sinful human desire
to control begins to do its work. The message is committed to earthen
vessels (2 Cor. 4:7). The gospel can be reduced by these vessels in a great
diversity of ways. The danger rests in our desire to "control God" which
leads us to regard our unavoidable reductions of the gospel as validated
absolutes. We are constantly tempted to assert that our way of understanding the Christian faith is a final version of Christian truth. We
tend to enshrine one cultural articulation of the gospel as the normative statement for all cultures. This may happen when we regard one
creed or tradition as canonical, making its authority co-equal with
Scripture. It may happen when we make a particular institution the unquestioned agency of God's work and even equate it with God's kingdom. This may happen when we insist that a certain spiritual experience or practice of piety must be a requirement for authentic Christian
existence. However it happens, we cut, shape, and fit the gospel into a

---

1. David Bosch, *Transforming Mission: Paradigm Shifts in Theology of Mission* (Maryknoll, NY: Orbis Books, 1991), pp. 186-87.

cultural setting to serve all kinds of alien purposes. When such reductions, which inevitably occur, are made absolute and then defended as normative truth, then we confront the problem I call "reduction*ism*."

Reductionism is at work when we as human witnesses are no longer aware of our own reductions of the gospel. It is present when we argue a supreme authority or rightness or a finality to our formulations. A reductionist view assigns an authority to a reduction that ends up making it into a distortion.

The call to follow Jesus, to be his witnesses, and to make known the presence and future of his kingdom, challenges the human drive for control. The person and work of Jesus, as history with a future (eschatology), defies the control mechanisms with which we seek to reduce them to manageable proportions. The favored way to accomplish this over the centuries has been to diminish the historical particularity of Jesus by reducing him and his message to a set of ideas, an intellectual system, often connected with a codified ethic, and managed thematically within the church's rites and celebrations. John Howard Yoder has argued that this "thrust against particularity" is the "much older and more natural concern to shun the risk of particular allegiance itself, especially to avoid the specified risk of having that allegiance bound to the crucified Jesus and the cost of following his way."[2]

This concern was obviously already expressed in Corinth where the message of the crucified cross was a "stumbling block to Jews and foolishness to Gentiles" (1 Cor. 1:23). The mechanism of human control over God's word has, ever since Eden, insinuated that for various obvious reasons one cannot take God at his word: "Did God [*really*] say, You shall not eat from any tree in the garden?" (Gen. 3:1). Jesus' own teaching, as the equipping of the church for its missional vocation, quickly encountered the same fate. As David Bosch commented, "Through the ages . . . Christians have usually found ways around the clear meaning of the Sermon on the Mount."[3] We can, thus, read the history of Christian theology as the story of our various ways of reducing the gospel, especially in its par-

---

2. John Howard Yoder, "Why Ecclesiology Is Social Ethics," in *The Royal Priesthood: Essays Ecclesiological and Ecumenical*, ed. Michael G. Cartwright (Grand Rapids: Eerdmans, 1994), p. 111. See also Yoder, "'But We Do See Jesus': The Particularity of Incarnation and the Universality of Truth," in *The Priestly Kingdom: Social Ethics as Gospel* (Notre Dame: University of Notre Dame Press, 1984).

3. Bosch, *Transforming Mission*, p. 69.

ticularity and specificity, to make it more compatible to our world and palatable for ourselves. Yoder is perceptively and painfully on target when he comments that the classical Christian arguments against the particularity of the gospel are attractive because they "provide respectable grounds to relativize [i.e., bring under control] the real claims of Christ."[4] The real and sinful purpose of reductionism is to

> back away from the call of Jesus, who has always admitted that if we entrust our life to him and his cause, we will never be proven right until beyond the end of this story and cannot count on being positively reinforced along all of the way. What is thus stated in the form of a general rejection of all particularity in favor of a vision of universal validity is, when more deeply seen, more particular and more negative; namely, a specific pattern of avoidance of the particular claims of Christian loyalty in its continuing risk and uncertainty.[5]

My thesis is that our particular Western reductionisms are the great challenge that the North Atlantic churches face when they seek to develop a theology of evangelistic ministry. We are not simply dealing with the need for continuing translation because of the inevitable reductions that occur in that process. Our challenge is far broader. It is a question of the church's radical conversion from a deeply engrained reductionism whose result is a gospel that is too small.

The reductionisms of Western Christianity are very deeply rooted in a long history. They are, by now, largely unconscious. They define the air we breathe as Western Christians. We have taken them with us into the modern missionary enterprise and left them as a dubious legacy with the churches we have founded. The problem is not simply an issue of gospel translation any more. The reductionism we struggle with is related to our attempts to reduce the gospel, to bring it under control, to render it intellectually respectable, or to make it serve another agenda than God's purposes.[6] Therefore, we cannot move constructively towards the formu-

---

4. Yoder, *Royal Priesthood,* p. 112.

5. Yoder, *Royal Priesthood,* pp. 112-13.

6. A very similar analysis has been recently published by Donald McCullough, *The Trivialization of God: The Dangerous Illusion of a Manageable Deity* (Colorado Springs: NavPress, 1995). His approach to reductionism focuses upon the holiness of God, which in every way is a complementary approach to mine, which emphasizes the understanding and interpretation of the gospel of salvation.

lation of a theology of evangelistic ministry without addressing critically and candidly this reductionism of the gospel. To be faithful witnesses, we in the Western traditions must also be penitent witnesses, receiving the gift of conversion from God's Spirit.

The Early Shape of Reductionism

As part of the risk of God's self-disclosure, and as a continuing challenge to all translation, our reductionism has deep roots. The effect of sin as control, as discussed above, has consistently been intentionally reductionistic. When we read the prophetic messages of the Old Testament and Jesus' polemics against the religious leaders of his day, we are hearing attacks on ancient reductionisms. Our history is a sequence of absolutized reductions that call for our own conversion as we recognize them and repent of them. When we look closely at many of the renewal movements in the church, we recognize that they often were reacting to various forms of reductionism as they called the church to greater faithfulness to the gospel.

Many scholars have explored the reduction of the gospel and the New Testament message of the kingdom over the course of history. Not a few have regarded this reduction as a necessary and positive step for the maintenance and success of the church as a movement in history. Ernst Troeltsch, for instance, described the primitive Christian community as a "sect" which started "from the teaching and life of Jesus," while the later "church" type was rooted in the emphasis upon "the Exalted Christ and Redeemer." He contrasted the "sect" with its emphasis upon "the lordship of Christ and discipleship, and therefore also the life and message of Jesus," with the institutional church which became "an established type of organization that is conservative, accepts secular order, dominates the masses, has universal claims, and therefore uses . . . the state and the ruling classes to sustain and expand its domination and to stabilize and determine the social order."[7] Over the long

---

7. Arne Rasmusson, *The Church as* Polis: *From Political Theology to Theological Politics as Exemplified by Jürgen Moltmann and Stanley Hauerwas* (Notre Dame: University of Notre Dame Press, 1995), p. 234, discussing Troeltsch, *The Social Teaching of the Christian Churches,* 2 vols. (London, 1931), pp. 328-43.

haul, Troeltsch found the established church type superior, although he candidly admitted that "it cannot be denied that this does mean a modification of Christian thought in order to *bring it down to the average level, to the level of practical possibility,* [my italics] and it is a principle of far-reaching adjustment and compromise."[8] This process is undoubtedly far-reaching and creates the situation today for which the continuing conversion of the church is the only faithful option.

For the purposes of my argument, I will follow David Bosch's able survey of the reductionism of the gospel that began at a remarkably early stage of the church's development. He locates this fundamental predilection for gospel reductionism (although he does not use this term) in the early church, when he describes "where the early church failed."[9] He speaks of three fundamental reductionisms which, in his view, were especially important to the development of Christian mission from the outset.

First, the early church reduced its understanding of its own calling and allowed itself to become one more religion within the multiplicity of religions present in the first century. This was not Jesus' intent.

> Those who followed him were given no name to distinguish them from other groups, no creed of their own, no rite which revealed their distinctive group character, no geographical center from which they would operate. . . . The twelve were to be the vanguard of all Israel and, beyond Israel, by implication, of the whole ecumene. The community around Jesus was to function as a kind of *pars pro toto,* a community for the sake of all others, a model for others to emulate and be challenged by. Never, however, was this community to sever itself from the others.[10]

The early Christian community evidenced the desire to assume control by reducing this "high level of calling" and becoming preoccupied with what distinguished it from others. "Their survival as a sepa-

---

8. Rasmusson, *Church as Polis,* p. 237, n. 28, referring to p. 1007 in Troeltsch.

9. Bosch, *Transforming Mission,* pp. 50-52.

10. Bosch, *Transforming Mission,* p. 50. A similar argument is presented by Gerhard Lohfink in *Jesus and Community: The Social Dimension of Christian Faith,* trans. J. P. Galvin (Philadelphia: Fortress, 1984).

rate religious group, rather than their commitment to the reign of God, began to preoccupy them." Second, this fundamental reduction was linked with the church's transition from a movement to an institution. This process was sociologically necessary if the church were not to be an imaginary, non-incarnational, docetic spirituality. But it also motivated reductionistic tendencies that ultimately were fateful for the church's missionary mandate. Third, the growing antipathy between Christians and Jews resulted in the tragic inability of the Christian community "to make Jews feel at home."[11] This chasm between the Christian and Jewish faith communities has resulted in a pervasive reductionism of the gospel with regard to our rootedness in Israel and the Old Covenant, and the importance of the Jewishness of Jesus and the early church. "[T]he domestication of the biblical witness meant relegating to unimportance the specificity of the Jewishness . . . of Jesus."[12]

The reductions that arose from the paradigm shifts of the church's history have affected all areas of the church's life and practice. From the perspective of missiology, the most fateful of these early reductionisms for our understanding of evangelistic ministry concerned the gospel itself, the meaning of salvation. In very subtle ways, salvation became more and more focused upon the individual, and the cosmic thrust of the gospel shifted into a concern for the person's life after death. This would have wide-reaching implications for the church in every dimension of its mission, implications that shape the church today. Although this separation was already present in the church's gospel proclamation before Constantine, the process was solidified when the Christian church became the formal, legally established and protected religion of the Roman Empire. The continuing conversion of the church must deal, thus, with the legacy of Constantine.

11. Bosch, *Transforming Mission*, pp. 50f.
12. Yoder, *Royal Priesthood*, p. 111. "Domestication" is an additional way of describing what I mean by reduction*ism*.

The Reductionist Gospel of the Constantinian Church

I have already noted that the first major cross-cultural translation of the gospel was from the Palestinian and Jewish world of the early church into the diverse world of Hellenistic culture. This was an enormously complex and risky undertaking. It was thoroughly missional in its motivation, symbolized by Paul's response to the Macedonian vision. It was also, from a historical and institutional point of view, incredibly successful. Three hundred years after the Christian movement's inception, it entered into the cultural passage we call "Constantinianization" in which Christianity became the official and protected religion of the European and Mediterranean worlds. The implications of that shift, however, raise a number of questions about the reductionism that accompanied it.

In the encounter with the Hellenistic world, Christian witnesses to the gospel sought, in a variety of ways, to translate the joyful message into the new context. While rejecting the pagan religions they encountered in every town and marketplace in the Mediterranean world, the early Christian witnesses found much in Hellenistic philosophy that was helpful in the translation of the gospel. The outcome of this process, which is too complex to be reviewed here, had profound implications for the Christian understanding of the gospel.[13]

Gradually the focus of the emerging Christian theology shifted from the event character of the gospel to the formulation of a defined faith system.[14] In the New Testament and early apostolic communities, the emphasis had been upon the witness to Jesus Christ as the ruling and reigning Lord whose kingdom was coming and was yet to come. Now, in the development of classical Christian thought, the gospel became more and more a truth system, borrowing heavily from the meta-

---

13. For excellent surveys of this process, see Jaroslav Pelikan, *The Emergence of the Catholic Tradition (100-600),* vol. 1, *The Christian Tradition: A History of the Development of Doctrine* (Chicago and London: University of Chicago Press, 1971); J. N. D. Kelley, *Early Christian Thought* (New York: Harper & Row, 1968); Robert D. Sider, *The Gospel and Its Proclamation,* vol. 10, *Message of the Fathers of the Church* (Wilmington: Michael Glazier, 1983); Justo L. González, *Christian Thought Revisited* (Nashville: Abingdon, 1989; reissue, Maryknoll, NY: Orbis Books, 1999).

14. Bosch, *Transforming Mission,* pp. 194ff, and Lamin Sanneh, *Translating the Message: The Missionary Impact on Culture* (Maryknoll, NY: Orbis Books, 1991), pp. 50ff.

physical categories and definitions of Hellenistic philosophies. The abstract idea, as taught by Plato, was taken to be more authentic than the actual historical event and the mere experience of it. These were actually parables or symbols of the truth behind them. Meaning came before relationship; metaphor replaced experience; truth became an idea that was more than a person, even one who said, "I am the truth." Events were of interest as symbols of meanings that transcended them.

For some Christian witnesses, this meant that the truth of Christianity was to be argued with the tools of logic and rhetoric. The goal was to define and explicate the meanings behind the events, the "system" of authentic truth symbolized by the history (or story). "Systematic theology" began to emerge. For others, borrowing from a range of influential philosophical and religious options, the Christian faith was best understood as a distinctive and mysterious *gnosis* (knowledge) which could be gained through secret rites and ceremonies. These various approaches and translation attempts battled with each other. Issues of orthodoxy and heresy became urgent concerns of the church. Synods and councils met to iron out the difficulties and create a doctrinal consensus for the church. Out of this broad and fascinating process emerged the language and terminology of both Western Catholic and Eastern Orthodox theology. "God's revelation was no longer understood as God's self-communication in events, but as the communication of truths about the being of God in three *hypostases* and the *one person* of Christ in two *natures*. . . . 'The message became doctrine, the doctrine dogma, and this dogma was expounded in precepts which were expertly strung together.'"[15]

The movement from event to system was closely linked with the tendency in patristic Christian thought to reduce the gospel of salvation by redefining its eschatology. "There is probably no area in which the Hellenistic church differed so profoundly from primitive Jewish Christianity as that of its eschatology and understanding of history."[16]

---

15. Bosch, *Transforming Mission*, p. 195. The second quotation is Bosch's translation of A. J. van der Aalst, *Aantekeningen bij de hellenisering van het christendom* (Nijmegen: Dekker & van de Vegt, 1974), p. 138.

16. Bosch, *Transforming Mission*, p. 196. See also J. Pelikan, "The Apocalyptic Vision and Its Transformation," in *Emergence of the Catholic Tradition*, pp. 123-32: "If the teachings of the early church and of Jesus could simply be described as consistent eschatology, we could then trace the decline of such an eschatology as the primary factor in the establish-

In chapter 2 I discussed the essentially historical character of God's work of salvation in Christ, and I have emphasized the importance of that historicity for Christian witness in chapter 3.[17] These emphases merge in the strongly eschatological focus of the New Testament message: "As Christocentric witness, mission announces that the kingdom of God is near, breaking in, present and active in Jesus Christ, and still coming."[18]

Whereas Jesus was experienced and proclaimed as the bringer, founder, and incarnation of the kingdom which is coming and will come, the doctrinal development tended to reduce that historical dynamism to a universally true religion, asserting its validity for all humanity. Salvation was anticipated eagerly in the New Testament witness as the "outcome of your faith" (1 Pet. 1:9). Over time, it becomes the possession of the Christian, as administered by the church. "At whatever point it occurred, it was certain that Christians acquired an unshakable conviction that Jesus was the present Savior, the Savior-come rather than the Savior-coming, and that the victory was already won."[19]

There is a range of missional implications to this shift away from the eschatological openness of the New Testament gospel, as it was synthesized by the evolution of Christian dogma. More and more, the future tense of God's kingdom came to be understood as the eternity that awaited the Christian after death. "The church . . . is the body of believers scattered throughout the world, who are to be gathered into the (eschatological) kingdom of God."[20] The tension of Christian witness between the "already" and "not yet" of the king and the kingdom was replaced by the call to believe in the "already consummated eternal

---

ment both of ecclesiastical structures and of dogmatic norms. . . . It was nothing less than the decisive shift from the categories of cosmic drama to those of being, from the Revelation of St. John the Divine to the creed of the Council of Nicea" (p. 131).

17. See especially pp. 59-66.

18. See above, p. 66.

19. Sanneh, *Translating the Message*, p. 57.

20. Reinhold Seeberg, *History of the Doctrines in the Early Church, Text-Book of the History of Doctrines,* vol. 1, trans. C. E. Hay (Grand Rapids: Baker, 1977), p. 74, summarizing the *Didache;* similarly in the *Homily of Clement,* p. 77: "If man has thus fulfilled the will of God, or Christ, striven against his evil passion, and done good, he receives from God eternal life in the Kingdom of God (eschatologically conceived) as the reward for his works."

kingdom of Christ," represented on earth by the church and its sacraments, and awaiting the believer in its perfect form in heaven. "The kingdom of God, or the supreme good, is, in accord with the whole tendency of the prevailing religious conceptions, regarded as a purely future entity."[21] The resurrection had already taken place, making it possible for the believer to be given a redeemed soul. The immortality of that soul became now the substance of Christian hope, as the church taught that saved souls entered paradise upon death. The future hope of the resurrection of all believers subsided over against the parallel vision of earthly existence (time) and heavenly existence (eternity), and a vertical relationship between them. "People's expectations came to be focused on heaven rather than on this world and God's involvement in history; instead of looking forward to the future they looked up to eternity."[22]

The service of God, as the ministration of love, continued but was often linked with the conviction that such service compiled merit which would assist the sinner upon death to pass on to a blessed reward. This emphasis upon eternity would become more and more influential as, in the Middles Ages, earthly existence tended to be seen as a "vale of tears," a time of testing preparing for a heavenly life awaiting us all at death. The struggle to gain and keep salvation became the overriding concern, replacing the biblical understanding of calling to witness and mission.[23] In the process, the message of salvation was almost entirely separated from the witness to the kingdom of God, with the fateful result that, over the centuries, "the kingdom-of God theme has practically disappeared from evangelistic preaching and has been ignored by traditional 'evangelism.'"[24] Long before

21. Seeberg, *History of the Doctrines in the Early Church*, p. 81, summarizing his survey of the apostolic fathers.

22. Bosch, *Transforming Mission*, p. 197.

23. I have already referred to the concept of "mission as diffusion," developed by Lamin Sanneh. This model emerged in the Middle Ages, where mission was based on the assumption that the Christian religion imposed by the expanding empire was a truth system under the control of the church (and its state partner). It was the moral responsibility of Christian Europe to expand its boundaries to guarantee the salvation of all those pagans beyond its boundaries. See Sanneh, *Translating the Message*, pp. 9-87.

24. Mortimer Arias, *Announcing the Reign of God: Evangelization and the Subversive Memory of Jesus* (Philadelphia: Fortress, 1984), p. xv. The theme of the Kingdom of God does not receive significant attention in any of the doctrinal surveys listed in note 13 nor

the anthropocentricism of modernity asserted itself, the focus of Christendom's religion was upon the experience and salvation of the individual.

These shifts in emphasis were based on profound alterations of the church's understanding of Jesus Christ's person and work. The formulation of the gospel records reveals how important for the early church's missionary witness were the reports of the life, words, and actions of the man Jesus. The incarnation was significant precisely because of its emphasis upon Jesus' humanness and its demonstration of what faithful witness to God is to be as taught and demonstrated by Jesus. In the doctrinal and systematic process of emerging Western Christianity, the emphasis shifted from the humanity of Jesus to his cosmic and divine significance. Concern for the question of Jesus' origins replaced the church's anticipation of Christ's coming.[25] The theological issues of the preexistence of Christ, the two natures, the relationships among the persons of the Trinity, and the perfection of Christ were debated and theologically defined. As the tradition moved in to the Middle Ages, the missional importance of the life and teaching of Jesus as the schooling for all who are his witnesses was largely lost. To be sure, the incarnational character of the Christian life was preserved or re-visioned by various monastic orders in waves of spiritual renewal. Many medieval monks followed the incarnational model of Jesus in the way they went about their mission. But even for the monastic orders, the imitation of Christ came to be seen more as those disciplines which prepared the individual for eternal bliss, rather than as the equipping of witnesses to become "fishers of people." The essential character of the incarnation as the definition

---

in Seeberg's textbook, *History of the Doctrines in the Early Church*. Pelikan's survey of the "Meaning of Salvation" in his discussion of "The Faith of the Church Catholic" in *Emergence of the Catholic Tradition* never mentions the kingdom or reign of God; see pages 141ff.

25. The case can be made, and often is, that this process was a reaction to the fact that Jesus' return did not take place as quickly as expected. One may ask if such a reaction is not also a form of reductionism on the part of early Christians, indicated by the disciples' question on the mount of the ascension (Acts 1:6): "Lord, is this the time when you will restore the kingdom to Israel?" Jesus' response, instructing them (and us) that we are not to know either "the times or periods" (the *chronos* or *kairos*) of God's action, is an admonition to resist human attempts to bring the reign of God under our control. The problem was present from the inception of the church.

of Christian existence was largely diluted for the majority of Christendom.[26]

I have stressed that the concrete presence and action of Christians in the world was their witness, their way of carrying out God's mission by demonstrating what the gospel was. Now, Christian activity was gradually being recast as the disciplines of Christian behavior that would prepare one for heaven. Rather than reading the canonic Scriptures as equipping for mission, the church began to understand them as sacred texts that provided guidance for spiritual improvement and perfection. Their orientation was, then, the completion of the saints' salvation rather than the missional witness for which purpose they were called and being saved. God's victory in history with its implications for all of human life, although never questioned and always affirmed, was subordinated to the greater issue of God's promise of eternal rewards in heaven for virtue and endurance on earth. Whereas discipleship was understood by the first- and second-century faith communities as the practice of Christian witness, it became more and more the fulfillment of the ethical, moral, and liturgical requirements which would guarantee entry into heaven.

This indicates that the understanding of the nature of salvation was also being reduced — or perhaps, more accurately, was not carried forward from the biblical period in all its fullness. In the first six centuries of the church's history, "the saving work of Christ remained dogmatically undefined,"[27] although it was always central to the liturgical

---

26. Although my analysis of this process is largely critical, because of its reductionistic impact upon the church's understanding of the gospel and its mission, I must acknowledge with Bosch that "it is to the Greeks that we owe the *intellectual discipline of theology* and the classical formulations of the faith." Further, "this paradigm shift was unavoidable and had a very positive side to it. The Greeks provided theology worldwide with the array of concepts which were necessary for the unfolding of a more critical, systematic, and intellectually honest approach in matters of faith" (p. 206). One can even see, in the early centuries of this development, its missional energy as it engaged the dominant philosophical schools of the day and sought to state the gospel in terms understandable to them. The reductions became a reduction*ism* when, over time, this "[o]rthodoxy . . . became increasingly inflexible, tended to puts its dogma . . . on a par with biblical truth" (p. 206). For an appreciation of the distinctive contributions of the Eastern Orthodox tradition to missional thought and practice, see Bosch, *Transforming Mission,* pp. 206-10.

27. Pelikan, *Emergence of the Catholic Tradition,* p. 141.

practice and the evangelistic preaching of the patristic church. Pelikan's survey of the various ways in which salvation was understood identifies three basic categories to interpret what Christ's work of salvation effected: "the revelation of truth, the forgiveness of sins and justification, immortality and deification."[28] These categories imply that the salvation of the world proclaimed by Jesus and the apostles was becoming progressively a highly individualized issue: the salvation of each person, and everything that had to be done to initiate it, guarantee it, and preserve it. Salvation became, in effect, a property or status that gradually was determined, at least in part, by human actions — the assertion again of the human desire to exercise control. In the long history of Christendom, the argument tended to focus upon who controls an individual's salvation, the church or the individual, rather than upon the dubious reductionism of salvation itself.

To reduce salvation to a controllable religious factor, it was necessary to "reify" it, that is, to make it into a manageable thing (res). Very gradually, in a process that lasted centuries and was never unopposed, salvation came to be understood as a commodity which the Christian had, or owned, or could gain, or could lose, and one that the church mediated. There is a great diversity of ways in which this reductionism works itself out, ranging from the Pelagian emphasis upon human efforts to maintain one's savedness to the redefinition of transubstantiated bread and wine as salvation "things" which actually make certain aspects of salvation happen.[29] The sacraments were understood to convey salvation, as these liturgical rites themselves gradually acquired reifying powers. In baptism and eucharist, grace was conveyed like a commodity moving from one bank account to another, or a quantifiable amount of grace transferring from a divine treasury to an individual. Thus, over time, the sacraments became essential to one's salvation and a very powerful weapon in the hands of the medieval Christian church as it "managed" and "administered" salvation. Salvation is predicated on the work of God in Christ, to be sure, but there was a growing sense of human co-responsibility for its

28. Pelikan, *Emergence of the Catholic Tradition,* p. 152.

29. Speaking of the development of the "means of grace" between 100 and 600 (long before the idea of transubstantiation entered the debate), Pelikan points out that "it was possible to emphasize the sacraments as something which a man did, at the expense of grace as something which God gave"; *Emergence of the Catholic Tradition,* p. 156.

maintenance, which centuries later became the passionate issue of the Reformation.

This spectrum of reductions, which we may associate with the Constantinianization of the church, profoundly altered the organizational form of the church. As partner of the state and divine administrator of God's grace through its hierarchy, sacraments, indulgences, pilgrimages, and crusades, the church wielded enormous power. Rasmusson summarizes Jürgen Moltmann's criticism of the "Constantinian turn" aptly for us:

> As Christianity became the state religion of the Roman empire it acquired the functions of civil religion, i.e., it became society's administrator of the system of religious meaning. The church now had a similar organizational structure as the civil society. The result was that the visible Christian communities were replaced by geographical division, with the consequences that the offices of bishop and priest became part of the power structures of the empire and that priesthood and laity were sharply separated from each other. Faith was then practiced primarily as participation in church arrangements. Evangelization was replaced by forced christianizing, and the fellowship in the church by fellowship with the church. Its community acts became official sacramental acts.[30]

That the church's primary business is the management and distribution of salvation is a continuing pattern up to today, when the church often describes its ministry in terms of needs to be met, religious products to be supplied.

Gospel Reductionism, Reformation, and Modernity

One way to interpret the Reformation struggle is to look upon Luther's spiritual and theological process as the rejection of significant aspects of medieval gospel reductionism and the renewal of a biblical view of salvation, especially that of Paul. Justification by faith alone became the programmatic key which Luther and his followers used to re-form both the church's doctrine and its practice. Consequently,

---

30. Rasmusson, *Church as* Polis, p. 78.

any sense of human co-responsibility for one's salvation was replaced by a massive emphasis upon God's grace and our total dependence upon it. "The starting point of the Reformers was not what people could and ought to do for their salvation but what God had already done in Christ."[31] The sovereign and initiating action of God was stressed even more passionately by Calvin as he wrote what was to become the major systematic work of the Reformation, *The Institutes of the Christian Religion*.

For the Lutheran and Reformed Reformers, however, the issue was centrally and dynamically the question of personal salvation, how one became sure of it, what one did about it, and how the church related to God's work of salvation. The "individualization" and "ecclesiasticization" of salvation, which medieval Roman Catholicism had worked into an impressive system,[32] was not fundamentally questioned. Luther's question, "How do I get a God who is gracious?" focused upon the faith struggle of the individual. The concern for individual salvation which was so deeply rooted in Western Christianity emerged out of this struggle as the dominant understanding of the church's mission. The definition of the church which emphasized the preaching of the Word and the administration of the sacraments corrected the reification of earlier centuries. But it maintained the Christendom focus upon the management of each soul's salvation on earth in preparation for heaven. Thus, Moltmann is probably right when he "does not think that the Reformation succeeded in changing these patterns" inherited from the "Constantinian turn."[33]

In general, the context of Christendom continued as the guarantor and protector of Christianity as the dominant religious force in society. To be sure, the brave voices of the Radical Reformation challenged the continuing partnerships between church and states, but they were prophetic for their age and persecuted for their convictions.[34]

---

31. Bosch, *Transforming Mission*, p. 241.

32. Bosch, *Transforming Mission*, p. 215-20.

33. Rasmusson, *Church as* Polis, p. 78.

34. This important tradition is well represented in the many books and essays of John Howard Yoder. See, for a succinct summary of the argument with regard to what the Reformation did and did not accomplish, "Christ, the Hope of the World," in *Royal Priesthood,* pp. 194-218, especially 198ff, and "The Disavowal of Constantine: An Alternative Perspective on Interfaith Dialogue," pp. 243-61 in the same volume.

With the exception of one brief allusion in the Heidelberg Catechism to "winning one's neighbors,"[35] the confessional documents of the Reformation traditions largely focus upon soteriological issues and their implications for the doctrines of the church, the Scripture, and the Christian life. There is virtually no mention of the church's mission, nor is there any sense in which individual salvation is related to one's calling to be Christ's witness.

Just as the first two centuries of the Reformation era produced no significant mission effort in the Reforming churches,[36] there is little in the theology and practice of Reformation Christianity, as long as it is largely defined as Christendom, which would directly inform a theology of evangelistic ministry in a post-Christendom world. To be sure, there are significant elements of Calvin's theology and practice which would ultimately shape evangelistic ministry in Europe and which have the potential to do so today.[37] The course of Reformed Christianity, however, reveals that its addiction to the Christendom patterns of interdependence between church and state very often diluted whatever evangelistic energy was there.

This reductionistic focus upon the individual's salvation assumes new levels of meaning as the Western churches enter into the

---

35. "Q. 86. Since we are redeemed from our sin and its wretched consequences by grace through Christ without any merit of our own, why must we do good works?

"A. Because just as Christ has redeemed us with his blood he also renews us through his Holy Spirit according to his own image, so that with our whole life we may show ourselves grateful to God for his goodness and that he may be glorified through us; and further, so that we ourselves may be assured of our faith by its fruits and by our reverent behavior may win our neighbors to Christ." *Book of Confessions; Presbyterian Church in the U.S.A.* (Louisville: Office of the General Assembly, 1994), 4.086. The North American Presbyterians finally addressed "foreign" mission when they added a paragraph on this theme to the Westminster Confession early in the twentieth century; see *Book of Confessions,* 6.187-6.190.

36. Bosch, *Transforming Mission,* pp. 243ff: "The Reformers were indifferent, if not hostile to mission"! More recent scholarship has raised some questions about this sweeping judgment, but in general it does hold. See Catherine Gunsalus González, "'Converted and Always Converting': Evangelism in the Early Reformed Tradition," in Milton J Coalter and Virgil Cruz, eds., *How Shall We Witness? Faithful Evangelism in a Reformed Tradition* (Louisville: Westminster/John Knox, 1995), pp. 73-91.

37. Merwyn Johnson, "Calvin's Significance for Evangelism Today," in *Calvin Studies: Papers Presented to the Davidson Colloquium on Calvin Studies,* ed. John Leith (Richmond: n.p., 1990).

modern period. As the Enlightenment stressed the autonomy of human reason and the educability of the human person, it contributed in its own way to the reduction of the gospel. The human problem was not so much sin as it was ignorance and the failure to develop one's innate reasonableness. Morality was possible; natural goodness was assumed; therefore, rigorous moral and mental training were the answer to the human problem. The road to salvation was thus the schooling of the mind and the formation of the moral person. The goal was, as hallowed in our public traditions, "the pursuit of happiness." The Enlightenment defined the norms and expectations of this brave new world with a humanism "which presupposed that intrinsic evil did not exist, nor did man have any higher task than the attainment of his own happiness."[38]

Using the newly developed understandings of the scientific method, the rational human mind was able to function as a knowing subject, probing and manipulating nature as its object, and bringing about scientific and technological advances which were truly amazing — I have discussed this in chapter 1. The philosophical assumption which accompanied this positive view of human reason and its capacity was the certainty of progress — thus, every discovery was an "advance." New worlds opened for exploration across the seas and under the microscopes, and rational humans uncovered the order and system of all things, making them accessible to human manipulation toward good and desirable ends. Progress was, however, the unfolding of the already innate goodness and reasonableness of creation. The assumption that all things were determined by their causes replaced the profound evangelical conviction that history and life were defined by God's purposes, which God would certainly bring about. With the loss of philosophical teleology as a dominant view, the reduction of Christian eschatology, already so significant, proceeded further. It survived for the most part as the marginal preoccupation of enthusiastic groups whose interest in charts, timelines, and approaching cataclysmic events could only earn the scorn of enlightened Christians. They, for their part, pursued the study of the Christian faith as redefined by modernity. The theological disciplines were profoundly re-

38. Stanley Hauerwas, *Community of Character: Toward a Constructive Christian Social Ethic* (Notre Dame and London: University of Notre Dame Press, 1981), p. 76.

shaped by the intellectual environment that adopted and adapted the scientific method as authoritative.

The growing confidence in the human ability to assess causes and thus determine results also had a reductionistic impact upon mission and evangelism. The individualized gospel that modern Western Christianity inherited fit well with the growing preoccupation with the methods that would bring about the state of salvation. These methods could be emotional and psychological, or logical and persuasive. One could be convinced of the universal truths of religion, as rational deists sought to demonstrate. Or one could be convicted of sin and drawn to repentance under the emotional impact of revivalist preaching. All along the spectrum of religious experience, the gospel itself and its implications for the individual were reductionistic. Contemporary approaches to evangelism, with their emphasis upon method, program, results, and measurement, are a further consequence of the victory of Enlightenment thinking, even in those parts of the church which disavow Enlightened theology.[39]

The evangelistic gospel of contemporary postmodern, post-Constantinian, North Atlantic Christianity is thus largely individualized. As a result of the historical process of the separation of church and state, and the progressive disestablishment of religion, the Christian presence has also been privatized. Faith commitments are looked upon as inappropriate themes for public discourse. Public culture is in the main agnostic, and the primary emphasis when religion does come up is upon the need for tolerance.

Now, at the end of the twentieth century, the church that is to proclaim the gospel appears to have become unsure of itself and incapable of persuasive witness. There are many reasons that so many Christians and Christian groups have become skeptical about evangelism, but high among them is the inability to formulate a gospel that can break through the individualization and privatization of religion. Moralistic reductions ("we are going to bring about God's kingdom on earth") have little credibility after one century of Christian social activism with minimal results.

---

39. See Lesslie Newbigin, *The Other Side of 1984: Questions for the Churches* (Geneva: World Council of Churches, 1983), and *Foolishness to the Greeks: The Gospel and Western Culture* (Grand Rapids: Eerdmans, 1986), for thoughtful analyses of the impact of the Enlightenment upon churchly thought and practice in the West.

In the conversations of polite and cultivated society, religion is avoided or treated with great caution. The usual parlance is to speak of "values," which may or may not have religious grounds, and to distinguish between them and "facts." Only "facts" are acceptable themes in public discourse. The gospel of God's mission in Jesus Christ, forming a missional community as its witness, and moving out to the ends of the earth to demonstrate the truth of the inbreaking kingdom, has been reduced to a pallid set of values which may not be publicly linked with the name of Christ without offending many. The reductionism is complete.

Those groups that practice aggressive evangelism are, upon closer examination, also proclaiming a very reductionistic gospel. While they claim to be opposing the secularizing and diluting tendencies of modern humanistic skepticism, they too often define the gospel in terms of happiness and evangelize for success, counting upon their mastery of method to produce results. Merwyn Johnson has described the Enlightenment captivity of evangelistic reductionism well:

> Modern Protestants typically set the agenda for evangelism in terms of Paul and the Philippian jailer. "What must I do to be saved?" asks the jailer. To which Paul replies: "Believe in the Lord Jesus Christ, and you will be saved" (Acts 16:30-31). The aim of evangelism here is to get every human being on the face of the earth to pose that question and accept that answer, as the Philippian jailer did, to the salvation of himself and his household (Acts 16:32-34). Following this agenda, the evangelist helps the unbeliever calculate the benefits (advantages or rewards) of being saved and the risks (losses or punishments) of not being saved — a blatant appeal to the individual's self-interest. The evangelist has to motivate the unbeliever to reject the risk and cling to the avenue of salvation, namely, believing in Jesus Christ and faithfully living out the Christian life — all of which requires step by step procedures, techniques, heavy rhetoric, and may even resort to manipulation in order to obtain the unbeliever's "decision for Christ." And since in the end the believer has to do it all — repent, believe, and live it out — naturally he/she is going to take credit (blame) for whatever is done.[40]

40. Johnson, "Calvin's Significance for Evangelism Today," p. 119.

The gospel itself is the issue for a theology of evangelistic ministry. The questions we have to ask, at this point in our history, are well summarized by Coalter, Mulder, and Weeks, in their "theological agenda" for the re-forming of the church: "Who is Jesus Christ? . . . What is the authority for the Christian life? . . . What can we hope for in a world that is increasingly paralyzed by both personal and communal despair? . . . Why, after all, is there a church — an ordered community of Christians?"[41]

41. Milton J Coalter, John M. Mulder, Louis B. Weeks, *The Re-Forming Tradition: Presbyterians and Mainstream Protestantism* (Louisville: Westminster/John Knox, 1992), pp. 281-84. Although this study looks intensively at the Presbyterian developments in the twentieth century, its findings are applicable across the "mainstream."

Chapter Six

The Reduction of Salvation and Mission

The gospel itself is the issue for a theology of evangelistic ministry.

The Gospel Crisis: The Mission-Benefits Dichotomy

Reductionism in our understanding of the gospel and of salvation, linked with old and continuing shifts in eschatology and Christology, has wide-reaching missional implications. The gospel has been reduced to a message focused on the individual's salvation: the fundamental evangelistic question is assumed to be "Are you saved?" The process of evangelization and "discipling" has thus become the program of spiritual and religious exercises that deals with that salvation. The benefits of salvation are separated from the reason for which we receive God's grace in Christ: to empower us as God's people to become Christ's witnesses. This fundamental dichotomy between the benefits of the gospel and the mission of the gospel constitutes the most profound reductionism of the gospel. It is reflected in virtually all evangelistic preaching today, but it is also well established in the classic confessional traditions of both the Catholic and Protestant churches.

Such reductionism in both the theology and the practice of evangelistic ministry must be confronted if we are to develop "an understanding of evangelization rooted in the *missio Dei,* shaped by God's actions in history, faithful to the gospel, and at the heart of ministry" (see p. 25 above).

To foster such an understanding will mean the conversion of the church to the fullness of the gospel of salvation. This mission-benefits dichotomy was a major concern of my earlier work on the theology of evangelism, *Be My Witnesses* (1985). Since writing that book, my conviction has grown that this false dichotomy is one of the great hindrances to a missional renewal of the church. I wrote then: "Our greatest priority, particularly in our theologies of salvation, should be to rejoin the benefits of salvation with the responsibilities and call to the saved to enter into God's mission in the world."[1] Fourteen years later, I am persuaded that the problem is not merely one of "rejoining," but of the continuing conversion of the church as we repent of our gospel reductionism and are summoned by God's Spirit to a more evangelical faithfulness in our witness. The overcoming of this dichotomy is fundamentally the issue of the gospel itself, what it is, what it means, and how we witness to it.

An Excursus: Karl Barth's Interpretation of Christian Witness

This conviction is strongly supported by Karl Barth's exposition of the definition of Christian existence as witness.[2] This discussion provides an incisive analysis of the reductionism in our understanding of the gospel of salvation that inhibits the church today from carrying out its missional vocation faithfully. The conversion of the church can only happen when she recognizes that this reductionism is so pervasive. It constitutes the conformity of the church which must be the focus of her repentance if she is to be "transformed by the renewing of [her] mind" (Rom. 12:2).

In pursuing the question of the purpose of Christian existence, Barth looks for those "lineaments, outlines, and contours of the manner of the Christian" that are the same for all, regardless of their cultural diversity and historical distinctiveness. His argument is an important contribution to today's discussion of Christians' common ground in a

1. D. Guder, *Be My Witnesses: The Church's Mission, Message, and Messengers* (Grand Rapids: Eerdmans, 1985), p. 232; see also pp. 10ff.
2. Karl Barth, "The Christian as Witness," no. 4 in §71 "The Vocation of Man," *Church Dogmatics: The Doctrine of Reconciliation*, trans. G. W. Bromiley, IV, 3/2 (Edinburgh: T. & T. Clark, 1962), pp. 554ff.

global and multicultural church. Barth had already defined Christian existence in this way: "we understand by the Christian a man whom Jesus Christ has called to attachment to Himself, to His discipleship and to living fellowship with Himself, and whom, as we finally say, He has bound and indeed conjoined with Himself."[3] Now, he asks, What are Christians for? Why does God bring about their very existence?

Over the course of Christian history, this question has been answered in two ways, which Barth addresses, assesses, and then dismisses. They should be noted, however, as reductionist understandings that continue to assert themselves within the pluralism of modern Western theology and Christian practice. One of these answers was stronger in earlier ages but has moved to the margins of modern Christianity, often in various forms of fundamentalism as well as some charismatic movements. It describes Christians as "those who, as recipients of the *kerygma* of the eschatological divine act accomplished in the death of Jesus Christ, recognize, affirm, and grasp within the world the possibility of their own non-worldly being, and therefore transcend and leave behind the world even as they still exist within it, and to this degree improperly."[4] Barth acknowledges the importance of these aspects of Christian vocation but asks pointedly if Christian existence is entirely to be defined in terms of the "dialectic of worldliness and unworldliness." Is this not, in fact, a continuing implication of the reduction of eschatology which entered Christianity with the transition to Hellenism? Do we not see in this rejection of the world a profound loss of the missional thrust of biblical faith? Is this not a significant reduction of the witness in and to the world intended as the outcome of the salvation experience of the saints? Was the total purpose of the salvation event of Christ to save Christians? Did John really mean, "For God so loved the *Christians* that he sent his only begotten Son?" "Is this really the principle which controls the structure of Christian existence? Is this really the final goal of vocation?"[5]

3. Barth, *Church Dogmatics*, IV, 3/2, pp. 555f.
4. Barth, *Church Dogmatics*, IV, 3/2, p. 558. The classic text for this approach is Paul's discussion of the unmarried and widows, 1 Cor. 6:25-40. To read this text as a moral argument for a world-renouncing spirituality is a notable example of the reductionism that enters biblical interpretation when the fundamentally missional thrust of the New Testament Scriptures is ignored.
5. Barth, *Church Dogmatics*, IV, 3/2, p. 559.

If the one answer moves to the extreme of other-worldliness and world-renunciation to define why Christians exist, the second answer identifies Christian existence almost entirely with the world. The unique "ethos" of Christianity and its intended impact upon the world are stressed here. Barth describes this emphasis upon Christianity's unique ethos with these words:

> On this view, the call of Jesus Christ is decisively an invitation and demand that the men to whom it comes should adopt a particular inward and outward line of action and conduct of which we have the basic form in the twofold command to love God and our neighbors and a normative description in the imperatives of the Sermon on the Mount or the admonitions of the apostolic Epistles. And the Christian is the man who has accepted and taken to heart this invitation and demand as a binding Word of the Lord, and has begun doing what is necessary in order to obey and to do justice to it.[6]

This emphasis is reflected in the many movements today which stress the primary role of Christianity to be the promotion of social justice or righteousness. It is the dominant emphasis in North American mainline denominations, as they rigorously strategize to bring about the kingdom of God. It contains important insights, especially with regard to the centrality of justice to the inbreaking reign of God. In Jesus' outreach to the poor, the disenfranchised, and the marginalized, he demonstrated that God's justice requires a complete reordering of any and every society. He demonstrated the divinely mandated "preferential option" for the poor, the young, the weak, and the helpless. Jesus trained his followers to form their communities under principles of just order that differed radically from both Jewish and Hellenistic patterns of the first century. He ordained, and the apostles taught, that this new community was not to be characterized by the divisions and hierarchies of human society. He gave them a new commandment that they should love one another (John 13:34). All of the imperatives of the epistles translate that commandment in concrete ways into the life of specific Christian communities. Obedience to Jesus' commandments is a fundamental component of

---

6. Barth, *Church Dogmatics*, IV, 3/2, pp. 558f; translation edited for the sake of Barth's emphasis.

faith. The concern for justice and morality is an essential part of Christian witness.

The obedient practice of justice and morality is, however, an integral part of Christian witness to the redemptive love of God in Jesus Christ. When God's justice, supremely revealed on the cross, is reduced to a humanly managed program of social change, it is inevitably diluted and rapidly becomes an ideology of human creation. When Christian morality is taken out of its context, reduced to an absolute in and of itself, and thus becomes the dominant principle, it loses its distinctiveness, its originality, and its incomparability. It must make its case as one of many ethical systems, of which there are many honorable and impressive examples within the cultures of the world. "A triumphalistic Christian moralism, which elevates itself to the status of a principle, has always resulted in a relativising and leveling down of the difference between Christian and non-Christian existence and the practical sterilization of the former, i.e., the loss of its offensive and defensive power."[7]

One illustration of this loss of distinctiveness lies in those components of the missionary movement which, toward the end of the nineteenth century, began to focus only on educational, medical, and agricultural ministries, and no longer linked them with the proclamation of the gospel.[8] In the Western world, the recasting of the gospel as a program of social justice, without the lordship of Christ and the future tense of the kingdom, would be a further example.[9] This approach is

---

7. Barth, *Church Dogmatics,* IV, 3/2, p. 559; translation edited for the sake of Barth's emphasis. This loss of "offensive and defensive power" is evidenced by the tendency of many Christian organizations to promote programs of social justice divorced from the focus upon the righteousness of God and the lordship of Jesus Christ. This is happening whenever "evangelism" and "justice" are regarded as separate or contending definitions of the church's mission.

8. Kenneth Scott Latourette, *A History of the Expansion of Christianity,* vol. 7 (Grand Rapids: Zondervan, 1970), pp. 48ff.

9. Barth's argumentation relates in a stimulating way to the main lines of John Howard Yoder's and Stanley Hauerwas's understanding of the political meaning of the gospel (see, for example, Yoder, *The Politics of Jesus* [Grand Rapids: Eerdmans, 1994]; or Hauerwas, *The Community of Character: Toward a Constructive Christian Social Ethic* [Notre Dame and London: University of Notre Dame Press, 1981]). This is an intriguing example of theological convergence: Reformed, Wesleyan, and radical Reformation (Mennonite) theologians finding common ground in their critique of Christendom's reductionism of the gospel.

also represented by the various ways in which the kingdom of God is claimed as the program or goal of the church: the language of "building the kingdom," "establishing the kingdom," and "kingdom agenda," betrays this reductionism of the kingdom. As I have noted above (pp. 66-67), the kingdom of God is God's work, God's promise, and we receive it, enter it, respond to it.[10]

The "classic answer" to the question of the purpose of Christian existence, according to Barth, is the tradition which offers the definition of "the Christian as the man who is distinguished from others by the address, reception, possession, use and enjoyment of the salvation of God given and revealed to the world by God in Jesus Christ."[11] This definition, which focuses upon the experience and possession of salvation, can be expanded by describing Christians as "those who are the recipients of grace. They are illumined and awakened by the work of the Word and Spirit of the Lord. They are born again and converted. They have peace with God."[12] They participate in reconciliation, justification, sanctification, the experience of forgiveness of sins, and the power to lead a new life. They look forward to resurrection and to eternal new life, all of this given through the power of the Holy Spirit. They are distinguished from all other people in what "they are and have and may do," and as such they confront the world on the side of God's acting in Jesus Christ. Barth then refers to the theological preoccupation with the *beneficia,* the benefits of faith, which was evidenced by Protestant orthodoxy (e.g., D. Hollaz) and thus firmly established in the thinking and theologizing of the Reformation churches.

The benefits have become predominant in evangelistic ministry in the North American tradition, especially since the revivalist movement of the nineteenth century. These benefits were both individualistic and cultural. The individual Christian received, as Barth summarized above, the benefits of salvation, forgiveness, restoration to a faith relationship with God, assurance of salvation after death, and the empowering

10. See K. L. Schmidt's article on *basileia* in *Theological Dictionary of the New Testament,* ed. Gerhard Kittel and Gerhard Friedrich, trans. Geoffrey W. Bromiley (Grand Rapids: Eerdmans, 1964-1976), 1:581ff; see also Darrell Guder, ed., *Missional Church: A Vision for the Sending of the Church in North America* (Grand Rapids: Eerdmans, 1998), pp. 93ff.

11. Barth, *Church Dogmatics,* IV, 3/2 p. 561.

12. Barth, *Church Dogmatics,* IV, 3/2, p. 561.

strength of God's Spirit to lead life now. The worldwide agenda of Western missions took that gospel of personal salvation throughout the world, linking it with the cultural benefits of Western civilization.

It is clear that Barth is developing an argument against the one-sidedness of the "classical answer." His polemic centers around the very pointed question: "But is then what a person's calling promises, means, and brings about for that person, that is, are the benefits of Christ really the most decisive, the most intriguing, the authentic, the central aspect in the goal of his vocation?"[13]

This question reveals the inadequacy of an emphasis upon the benefits of Christ alone, whether these benefits are understood in terms of the personal, mystical and spiritual, or in terms of the ethical relevance of the gospel. They are, each in their own way, reductionisms of the gospel. As noted above, the reductionist gospel of world improvement dominates much mainline Western Christendom and current "ecumenical theology." Its hold is enhanced by the Enlightenment emphasis upon human reason, competence, and educability, and by the nineteenth-century optimism about progress, which the tragedies of the twentieth century have not completely corrected. This very modern reductionism struggles with the tension between evangelism and social justice, which ultimately will not be resolved, according to Barth, unless and until one finds something beyond them which unites them. That which lies beyond these dichotomies is the gospel, which is greater than these (and many more) reductions. The irony of much of the debate about theological pluralism in North Atlantic post-Christendom Christianity is that it takes place within the confines of a reduced gospel, in which dichotomies between the personal and the corporate, the spiritual and the secular, the church and the world, are still allowed to make sense. The gospel "which is always before us" (Peter Stuhlmacher) can only be heard and responded to as we become aware of these reductions and are prepared to repent of them — that is, as we allow ourselves to be converted anew.

The crux, for Barth, is the question of God's reasons for carrying out the work of salvation. In answering this question, we begin to disclose the subtle power of our reductionism. The egocentricity or anthropocentricity of Western reductionisms from the right to the left

---

13. Barth, *Church Dogmatics*, IV, 3/2; my translation.

end of the spectrum emerges as the real issue. In a sense, the world-renouncing pietist and the world-reforming social activist are both displaying their concern for their own salvation. On the one hand, salvation is secured by means of the spiritual experience one testifies to. On the other hand, salvation is secured by means of the concrete changes one is able to project and implement to make the world a better place to live. Christian existence in both cases is understood from the central point of the Christian who relates the effects or impact of salvation to oneself and one's environment. But, should the goal of all God's actions be defined as my "security or certainty of salvation?" "Now there can be no doubt that the Christian can and should have assurance of his faith and salvation. But can his salvation as known by him be the principle which dominates his Christian existence?"[14]

Certainly we must emphasize the personal and individual expressions of faith. The human side of the experience of faith, however, can become too human, as though the entire purpose of the suffering of Christ were a person's "cozy happiness." This reductionism must make the church into an "institute of salvation" and redefine the gospel as a kind of sacred egocentricity, in which the human person " — in this case, the experience and struggle of the Christian — should be the measure of all things."[15] Barth is quite fair when he points out that this "deeply suspect pious egocentricity" has only rarely existed in a pure form; there has always been a Christian ferment that served as a corrective. For example, the "quietist-mystical" exponents of this classical answer have been moved outward into the world through their concern for pastoral care, diaconic ministry, and also through their literary ministry. Thus Pietism, although often (and perhaps unfairly) seen as world-renouncing, individualistic, and focused upon personal salvation, has often proven to have a profound social impact. Both Protestant missions and continental diaconic mission emerged out of the ranks of European Pietism and its North American counterparts. These movements also generated the revival movements of the nineteenth century which, in turn, affected major social issues of the day (e.g., the Salvation Army, the Social Gospel). A "pure or strict concen-

---

14. Barth, *Church Dogmatics*, IV, 3/2, pp. 565f.

15. Barth, *Church Dogmatics*, IV, 3/2, p. 568; translation edited for the sake of Barth's emphasis.

tration on the personal experience of grace and salvation which is supposed to make a Christian a Christian" has really never emerged in the course of Christian history, except for a few unique instances.[16] Continuing conversion has, in fact, always been at the heart of Christian existence in the world: in this way, God's promised faithfulness is constantly demonstrated.

The ethical reduction of the gospel has also rarely existed in a pure form. This kind of reduction, like the quietist-mystical reduction, finds its expression in highly motivated groups of Christian activists, frequently energized by social, economic, and political issues which challenge the Christian vision of the world under God's rule. Such groups have developed programs for action, mobilized various kinds of political and social pressure and consciousness raising, and made important contributions to improving our social orders. They have found, however, that a program of social activism is not enough. For instance, many Christian activist organizations involved in the social turmoil of the sixties in America, in the civil rights and anti-war movements, found themselves becoming spiritually undernourished. They turned to worship, to the sacraments, to prayer, and to the support of the cell group, in order to find the spiritual power to carry on their public ministry. They have been, at times, forces in liturgical renewal and worship innovation. They have produced devotional literature, liturgies, prayers, and biblical meditations to express their vision of Christian hope in prayers and sermons. Figures like Thomas Merton, Henri Nouwen, Richard Foster, Roger Schütz, James Wallis, and Mother Teresa transcend these reductionist options as living illustrations of the desire for and possibility of a vision and experience of the gospel that overcomes these dichotomies.

Nevertheless, the "classical answer" which focuses upon the benefits of salvation, as well as its aberrations toward the spiritual or the ethical, is not tenable. Barth advances two major theological arguments to show this. The first and prior argument deals with the biblical understanding of the "goal of the event which is described by Scripture as the calling of particular people."[17] He finds the biblical-theological answer in God's calling or vocation of people to serve him. It is clear in the

16. Barth, *Church Dogmatics,* IV, 3/2, p. 569.
17. Barth, *Church Dogmatics,* IV, 3/2, p. 571; my translation.

biblical accounts of the calling of people that their personal spiritual benefits are not contested but at the same time are never "constitutive" in their importance. They do "not play any constitutive role, being for the most part tacitly implied, or it may be merely indicated, as obviously and most decidedly a secondary element according to the meaning and intention of the tradition."[18] The biblical record places no emphasis on the special significance of conversion stories.[19] The experience and significance of grace are amply expounded in the scriptural record, but not in connection with stories of calling. One does not find a concern for "the establishment of their personal well-being in their relationship with God" in the stories of the call of Abraham, Moses, the prophets, the disciples, or Paul. The issue in these encounters is not "the saving of their souls" or "their experience of grace and salvation." To be sure, they experience all the benefits of God's gracious call, "but the fact that this was so, while it definitely belonged in some form to the goal of their vocation, did so only incidentally."[20] The reductionist problem arises when this "incidental" component of faith is made into the major issue.

The spiritual experience of the benefits of salvation is to be regarded, instead, as "encouraging and consoling confirmation" of one's call. It is God's gracious "preparation for the work" to which Christians are called, a "radiance, a *doxa*, a glory" which surprised the Christians precisely because it was neither one's goal nor one's expectation. Proceeding biblically, Barth shows that the experience of the benefits is always subordinated to the call and its purpose. Thus Paul states in Philippians 3:14 that he presses on "toward the goal for the prize of the heavenly call of God in Christ Jesus" rather than looking back upon already received blessings as the source of his salvation security. The "classical" emphasis upon salvation benefits as the reason for God's calling people to be his witnesses is contrary to Scripture and must be rejected. "In its description of what makes a Christian a Christian, this answer gives to the element of his personal experience of grace and salvation, to his reception and enjoyment of the *beneficia Christi,* an ab-

---

18. Barth, *Church Dogmatics,* IV, 3/2, p. 571.

19. Barth illustrate this beautifully in the examples given on pp. 571-72 of *Church Dogmatics,* IV, 3/2.

20. Barth, *Church Dogmatics,* IV, 3/2, p. 573.

stract significance and weight which it does not have in the thinking and utterance of the Old and New Testaments."[21] What Barth calls "shift in emphasis" we are calling reductionism; in either instance it contributes to a problematic distortion of the nature and practice of Christian discipleship and therefore of mission.

The biblical focus is upon the relationship of the benefits of salvation to God's call to serve. "It is common to all the biblical accounts of calling that to be called means being given a task"; Christian existence is "existence in the execution of this task."[22] Thus Christian existence is related to God's mission, into which Christians are called individually and corporately. For this to take place, a complete transformation of the lives of Christians is called for. To use language which complements Barth's approach, the Christian community is to become "a contrast society" (Lohfink), a company of "resident aliens" (Hauerwas and Willimon), "a new covenant community" (Yoder). The biblical warrant for such an understanding is certainly found in 1 Peter with the references there to the "exiles of the Dispersion" (1:1) and to "aliens and exiles" (2:11).

The eschatological tension of "already" and "not yet," which I have already discussed, is paralleled by a tension in the relationship of this community to its cultural context: "As they no longer belong to themselves, they no longer belong to the human society although they do not cease to be part of it."[23] This mission is never something that Christians seek, but rather, they receive it: they are called. In fact, they tend to resist it. But by virtue of God's action, we are called to Christ's side and empowered by God to carry out Christ's commission. "He himself legitimates, authorises, instructs and nourishes them." "It is here that we catch a glimpse of the fact that their vocation does actually include their personal blessing, experience, and endowment as something secondary and accessory, which certainly they will not do without, but which remains bound to the primary and essential element of their status and which thus only in this connection has its own power and constancy."[24]

21. Barth, *Church Dogmatics*, IV, 3/2, p. 573.
22. Barth, *Church Dogmatics*, IV, 3/2, pp. 573f.
23. Barth, *Church Dogmatics*, IV, 3/2, p. 574; translation edited for the sake of Barth's emphasis.
24. Barth, *Church Dogmatics*, IV, 3/2, p. 574; translation edited for the sake of Barth's emphasis.

The reductionism of the gospel that separates the benefits of God's grace from the mission is overcome, for Barth, in the definition of Christian existence as witness. I have already argued, in chapter 3, that this is biblically warranted. To be Jesus Christ's witness is the substance of God's calling of the covenant people. This call, as I have stressed earlier, is not rooted in any human qualifications, nor in any human desires or convictions. It is God's action that addresses and invites us, challenges and empowers us for that mission which is God's work for the salvation of the world. Thus, Christian existence can be defined in these words: "[W]ith their whole being, action, inaction and conduct, and then by word and deed, they have an announcement to make to other people, a definite declaration to communicate. The essence of their vocation is that God makes them His witnesses." They are called to be

> witnesses of the fact that He is, or of who and what He is in and for Himself in His hidden Godhead. He makes them witnesses of His being in His past, present, and future action in the world and in history, of His being in His acts among and upon men. They are witnesses of the God who was who He was, is who He is, and will be who He will be in these acts of His. They are witnesses of the God who in these acts of His, and therefore as God, as God with us, Emmanuel, was, is, and will be with His creation, the world, and all men.[25]

Implications for the Mission of the Church

In the exploration of the missiological implications of reductionism, I have stressed that the reduction of the gospel to individual salvation, with all of its surrounding and resulting implications, is the gravest and most influential expression of the human drive for control. The consequences of this reduction are profound, ranging throughout every dimension and expression of Christian thought and action. A reduced gospel trivializes God as it makes God into a manageable deity. Thus, it violates the profound biblical confession of the holiness of God.[26] It produces, in turn, a reductionist understanding of the church

---

25. Barth, *Church Dogmatics*, IV, 3/2, p. 575.
26. See Donald W. McCullough, *The Trivialization of God: The Dangerous Illusion of a Manageable Deity* (Colorado Springs: NavPress, 1995).

and its mission, and of the relationship of the faith community to its context. This is the situation that calls for the continuing conversion of the church, which will result in the wholehearted commitment to evangelization as the heart of ministry. The evidence of this conversion will be the incarnational witness to the gospel, that is, the being, doing, and saying of the good news of God's love in Jesus Christ.

Over against this pervasive reductionism, there have always been prophetic voices in the church that have summoned her to conversion and thus to greater faithfulness to her missional vocation. Such prophetic voices and movements are a reminder that the fact of reductionism does not mean that there is no gospel left. It means that there is too little gospel; the "breadth and length and height and depth . . . of the love of Christ" (Eph. 3:18f) are deprived of their radical and transforming power; the inbreaking of God's kingdom is hindered or diluted by our redefinitions of it to fit our agenda. But, because God's love is not controlled by our rebellion, it is still powerfully present even in our reductionisms. The gospel is heard even when uttered by the most dubious of evangelists.

Reductionism impedes God's work in us and through us. It is an obstacle to the flow of God's love and grace into the world. But it cannot stop God's grace. Thus, in every reductionist version of the gospel there is the possibility of continuing conversion, of that transformation which results from the renewing of our understanding of the gospel and its claim on us. Similarly, reductionist mission and evangelization can convey, by God's grace, the witness that evokes faith. The critique of Christian reductionism, as blunt and even harsh as it may need to be, must not be construed as a loss of confidence in God, or a diminution of the living hope which is God's promise to us and not dependent upon our faithfulness. When we seek to develop a theology of evangelistic ministry, we are grappling with the shape of our faithful witness, with undiminished confidence in God.

My critique of the church's reductionistic understanding of its calling and mission is not meant as a call to split the church. The American proclivity to solve theological problems (often the issues in such crises are not truly theological) by "starting a new church" must be rejected as patently disobedient to the apostolic instructions for the missional community. As I have emphasized, we receive both with respect and with critical honesty the legacies we inherit. We are not judges of the earlier generations of Christians, but we are responsible for faithful witness in the time and place to which God calls us. Therefore, we proceed in the certainty that God's grace has been and will continue to be sufficient. We learn from earlier generations both the faithfulness of God and the destructive character of our reductionisms.

While we are not called to split the church, we are also not called to preserve reductionisms that weaken the church's faithful witness. Nothing is sacred about the forms and formulations we inherit, as their reductionisms come to light. The continuing conversion of the church includes the possibility that our confrontation with the mission of God might broaden much that is most cherished by us in our particular traditions. Our ability to respond to that challenge modestly and courageously is an important aspect of our witness, as I shall discuss below. We take each step in the full confidence that God's grace is constant: "God is faithful: by him you were called into the fellowship of his Son, Jesus Christ our Lord" (1 Cor. 1:9).

We must, therefore, be profoundly concerned about the implications of a reductionist gospel for the church. As the gospel proclaimed by the church has been reduced to individual salvation, that salvation has itself become the purpose and program of the church. When the church went through the paradigm shift from its initial shape as a movement to its continuing shape as an institution, its focus was more and more upon the administration of salvation. Its worship centered on the message of individual salvation; its sacraments established and regulated the status of salvation; its doctrines sought to define and delimit salvation. The questions it asked and answered were these: Who is saved? Who is not? How can one be sure? How can salvation be lost? How can it be guaranteed? And with time, these questions addressed the church's role in salvation: What does the church do to convey grace? To withdraw it? What do the church's decisions mean with regard to salvation? What are "the keys of the kingdom" if we have reduced the kingdom to individual and personal salvation?

I spoke above of the reification of salvation in the process of doctrinal development. Its primary effect was evident in the sacramental doctrine and practice of the church. But there were and are myriad ways in which reification formed the church. Churchly office moved away from the missional models of the New Testament community, the apostolic leadership that equipped and sent out all followers of Christ to be his witnesses. More and more, the clergy became the special caste of Christians who managed everyone else's individual salvation. They did this with their evolving spiritual power, which came to focus upon what they, in fact, really accomplished when they baptized, pronounced absolution, celebrated the Eucharist, and performed the rite of extreme unction. One of the most significant forms of reifying reductionism was the theology and practice of holy orders. The priest, as the necessary mediator of individual salvation, and the Petrine pope, as the necessary link between God and the church, are powerful agents to control God's free and gracious reign in human history. The doctrinal positions of Roman Catholicism on the male priesthood, priestly celibacy, and the apostolic succession of bishops are continuing evidence of reductionism at work. Other ways in which institutional hierarchies have practiced reification include canonizing saints, issuing indulgences, ascribing salvific powers to certain shrines and pious practices, and consecrating relics.

In the Protestant continuation of that tendency, the restriction of preaching and the administration of the sacraments to the ordained clergy tended to reify their salvific powers, as seen and experienced by the laity. In spite of the "priesthood of all believers," the Reformation churches largely continued to be clerical because they did not refocus the church and its offices upon mission, but pursued the concern for the authentic understanding and practice of individual salvation. Those Reformation traditions that maintained infant baptism and confirmation were still influenced by this same salvation reductionism. Baptism was celebrated as the confession of faith in God that the gift of this child within the community of faith was a sign of God's grace in the life of that child. But confirmation had to follow as the passage of individual appropriation of faith, the young person's own affirmation of God's gift of salvation. Although there have been efforts to view confirmation as "ordination to service," and recent ecumenical theology has stressed that baptism is "general ordination to ministry,"[27] most church members who participate in these rites still see them as primarily focusing upon the personal salvation of the individual being baptized or confirmed.

27. This emphasis emerges in the Faith and Order document *Baptism, Eucharist and Ministry,* as well as in the theological papers produced by the Consultation on Church Union in the United States.

We must conclude that the church as an "institute of salvation" *(Heilsanstalt)* has had a greatly diminished sense of its mission to the world. It has been far more preoccupied with its inner life, thereby failing to grasp the essential linkage between its internal life and its external calling. Rather than understanding worship as God's divine preparation for sending, it has tended to make worship an end in itself. Rather than understanding preaching as the exposition of God's Word to equip the saints for the work of ministry, for the building up of the body of Christ (Eph. 4:11ff), it has become the impartation of clerical wisdom to help the saints prepare for heaven while coping with this "vale of tears." In fact, where the concern for individual salvation grew and the focus upon missional calling decreased in the early medieval church, preaching lost its importance and the sacraments as holy, reified rites became central.

The Reformation restored preaching to a central place, and through its focus upon the Scriptures as authoritative, it unleashed within the church the confrontation with the missional thrust of the gospel. That ferment has contended with the continuing individualization and privatization of faith, now supported by the Enlightenment. As the goal of the gospel has become "the pursuit of happiness," evangelistic preaching has often conceded to the context and presented the gospel as the way to attain happiness, self-fulfillment, self-realization, and even prosperity. Both worship and preaching in much of modern church practice are designed to meet individual needs for the assurance of salvation, even though the language may be that of modern psychology. That assurance may come from personal experience or from active engagement in "building the kingdom" — or both.

Such a reduced church functions relatively well within postmodern North Atlantic society. It fits nicely, fulfills the needed social functions of religious institutions, and serves as the "chaplain" to the world around it.[28] Its practice of evangelism focuses on two institutional concerns: recruitment of new members and planting of new churches. This view of mission is even structurally reductionist: "mission" (or "evangelism")

---

28. John Howard Yoder, "Let the Church Be the Church," in *The Royal Priesthood: Essays Ecclesiological and Ecumenical,* ed. Michael G. Cartwright (Grand Rapids: Eerdmans, 1994), pp. 173-74; see George Hunsberger's discussion of the church as "a people sent or a vendor of religion," in *Missional Church: A Vision for the Sending of the Church in North America,* ed. Darrell Guder (Grand Rapids: Eerdmans, 1998), pp. 83ff.

normally is ranked as one of several commitments or concerns of a church or denomination. There is probably no better example of the reductionist view of the gospel and the church's mission than the organizational chart of many American congregations, where evangelism is a program assigned to one of several committees.

A further evidence of the reductionism of the church and its mission that must issue from a reductionist gospel is the emergence in postmodern Western Christianity of organizations whose sole activity is evangelism. Such entrepreneurial organizations are often called parachurches. This nomenclature originally meant that they were Christian ministry organizations "next to" the established and traditional forms of the church. Although that definition is still valid, there is a prophetically accurate reduction in the prefix, since it implies that the evangelistic mission of the church can be separated out from the rest of the institutional church and function as its own distinctive ministry. That works, of course, when the gospel one proclaims evangelistically is reduced to the individual, the personal, and the private. Although many evangelistic movements stress the need for the Christian to become part of a "local church," their own calling to "save souls" as separate from "call to faithful witness" shows how readily a reduced gospel comes to be taken as all the gospel. The problem is often compounded when such evangelistic organizations ultimately start "local churches" for their converts, in competition with Christian communities already in place, thus dividing the church and its witness even more.

If the gift of salvation is necessarily linked with the vocation to witness, as Karl Barth argues, then it is impossible to separate evangelistic ministry from the life and work of the total church, as divided as it may be. The call to Christ must be a call to his mission. The reason Christians are formed into communities is because of God's work to make a people to serve him as Christ's witnesses. The congregation is either a missional community — as Newbigin defines it, "the hermeneutic of the gospel"[29] — or it is ultimately a caricature of the people of God that it is called to be.

I have located the challenge of gospel reductionism in the constant drive among sinful Christians to bring the gospel of God's sovereign love

---

29. Lesslie Newbigin, *The Gospel in a Pluralist Society* (Grand Rapids: Eerdmans, 1989), pp. 222ff.

under human control. The fundamental form of that reductionism is the mission-benefits dichotomy that has established itself so firmly in the theologies and ecclesiastical practices of virtually all Christian traditions. The impact of this reductionism upon the church, as I have just argued, is to make the church primarily into an institution administering salvation — although late-modern Christianity in North America describes salvation in quite a variety of ways. At the same time, this reductionism profoundly shapes Christian witness as it addresses the world into which we are sent. How the church and its mission engage the cultures reveals, from another side, the scope of Christian reductionism.

The missional community which Jesus intended and which the apostles formed and taught was to testify to the gospel in every dimension of its existence. Its message was never understood as simply a verbal communication about which one might argue, and for which mere mental consent was sought. The gospel of Jesus Christ defines a new reality, under God, in which Jesus Christ has all power in heaven and earth, and his followers are his sent and empowered witnesses. There is a fundamental and radical differentness to this sent-out community, which renders it "in but not of the world." This essential differentness provokes sinful Christians to try to bring it under control and make it manageable. The characteristics of missional differentness are precisely those aspects of the church where reductionism is most likely to emerge.

This differentness evidences itself in the ethical decisions and behaviors of those who follow Jesus. The ethics of discipleship are fundamentally evangelistic, fundamentally demonstration of the gospel, fundamentally witness. In and through this differentness, the gospel of Jesus Christ continues to "become flesh and dwell among us" as it is God's purpose that it do.

This witness takes place in the relationships of Christians to one another as a community called and shaped by God's Spirit. The New Testament speaks of this as the community into which God's Spirit has entered, as the community in which the kingdom of God is present and coming as the King is served.[30] In Christ, who now has all authority in

---

30. See Albert C. Winn, "What Is the Gospel?" in *How Shall We Witness? Faithful Evangelism in a Reformed Tradition,* ed. Milton J Coalter and Virgil Cruz (Louisville: Westminster/John Knox, 1995), pp. 4ff.

heaven and on earth, a new humanity is being formed, and its formation in and before the world is essential to its witness. It is a community in which human categories of social discrimination and privilege are set aside.[31] The gift of the Spirit is general: it comes upon the sons and the daughters, the young men and the old, the servants and the maids (Acts 2:17f); both men and women will pray and prophesy in the new community (1 Cor. 11:4-5); "there is no longer Jew or Greek, there is no longer slave or free, there is no longer male and female; for all of you are one in Christ Jesus" (Gal. 3:28).

Thus, this community must also move against the current of its culture in its relationship to the exercise of domination and power. "Jesus emphatically rejected, as far as his community of disciples was concerned, domination and the structures of domination which are customary in society."[32] The early church understood Jesus' teaching very clearly. They preserved it in the story of the request of the sons of Zebedee and Jesus' teaching about the practice of rulership among Gentiles (Mark 10:35-41, 42-45 and pars.). The issue for Jesus and the early church was not the question of authority in an absolute sense. Jesus both exercised and delegated missional authority, the empowered capacity to be his witnesses. "As my Father has sent me, so I send you" (John 20:21). The practice of Christian authority is always to be that of the servant who radically refuses every form of force and coercion. The model for the practice of authority for the church is Jesus himself, whose authority was "a *paradoxical authority* to the very last, an authority which in its unprotectedness and vulnerability turns any other type of authority upside down."[33] Paul then follows the pattern of Jesus when he reminds the Thessalonians that, as an apostle, he "might have made demands. . . . But we were gentle among you, like a nurse tenderly caring for her own children. So deeply do we care for you that we are determined to share with you not only the gospel of God but also our own selves, because you have become very dear to us" (1 Thess. 2:7-8).

Jesus' rejection of violence is the obvious extension of this radical

---

31. See the discussion of "the elimination of social barriers" in Gerhard Lohfink, *Jesus and Community: The Social Dimension of Christian Faith,* trans. J. P. Galvin (Philadelphia: Fortress, 1984), pp. 87-98.

32. Lohfink, *Jesus and Community,* p. 115; the discussion of "The Renunciation of Domination," is on pp. 115-22.

33. Lohfink, *Jesus and Community,* p. 117.

revision of the structures of authority. The thrust of Jesus' teaching is not merely one of passive submission to external force. It calls for intentional rejection of one's right to self-defense for the sake of witness to the enemy. In summarizing the thrust of Jesus' teaching in Matthew 5:39-42 (par. Luke 6:29f), Lohfink says,

> Jesus' listeners are told to renounce all legal sanctions and all retribution. Do not answer violence with violence. When injustice is done to you, do not remain passive, but take the first step toward your foe. Answer pressure or brutality with overflowing goodness. Perhaps in this way you can win over your adversary.[34]

The same emphasis is found then in Paul's instructions to the Corinthians about lawsuits among believers. Their witness is invalidated by their assertion of rights against each other (1 Cor. 6:1-11). Peter as well follows Jesus in his interpretation of suffering for what is right. By that time, such suffering was becoming the frequent reality of the early church under persecution (1 Pet. 3:8-22). The renunciation of violence is thus not a marginal issue for the early church as it sought to follow Christ the king and serve the coming of his kingdom. This was an ethical definition of the gospel that was essential to its witness. "The radical ethic of renouncing violence is thus addressed neither to isolated individuals nor to the entire world, but precisely to the people of God which has been marked by the preaching of God's reign."[35]

The reductionism of the church's ethical witness became a pro-

---

34. Lohfink, *Jesus and Community*, p. 52; see the entire discussion of "The Renunciation of Violence" on pp. 50-56. See also the fundamental discussion in Yoder, *Politics of Jesus*. The renunciation of violence raises the question of physical and emotional abuse and the Christian response to it. Does the nonviolence taught by Jesus mean that an abused spouse or child should simply submit? Clearly this is not meant. The submission intended here is a voluntary act for the sake of Christian mission. It describes a stance of the entire community within its often violent context. When Christians experience abuse, the community must intervene: provide protection (e.g., safe houses, medical and psychological care) and confront the abusers. As part of society, the Christian community will practice incarnational witness by caring for the weak and the oppressed and working with others to provide refuge. It will also address the systemic causes of such abuse: poverty, broken families, addiction. The church's distinctive witness will be to demonstrate nonviolent ways of confronting violence. These ways of intervention and prevention can be powerful incarnations of the healing good news.

35. Lohfink, *Jesus and Community*, p. 54.

grammatic issue when the church was established as a protected and privileged religion under Constantine. The process that began then has led, over time, to the progressive dilution and even disappearance of fundamental elements of the New Testament witness to the lordship of Christ. This process of reduction has, at the same time, been accompanied by ever more skillful arguments justifying such wholesale disregard for clear scriptural teaching. The cutting edge of the gospel has been blunted precisely where it addresses the realities of government, violence, and war. In order to function as "chaplain" to the public sector and "the soul of the existing society,"[36] the Christian church has made and continues to make very major compromises with its vocation as the community of witness. The protection and power of the church within Christendom made the church into the state's partner, even servant. An attitude of subservience to secular and political culture is still often present in churches that are no longer legally in partnership with the state. The reductionism of salvation to the individual and the recasting of kingdom language to make it irrelevant to worldly culture are necessary companion pieces in this organizational development.

Such reductionism requires that, over time, the Christian ethic be diluted and redefined so that it becomes valid and realistic for everyone.[37] The church will now tolerate and even justify "moderately motivated people" who practice "only a moderate level of devotion." The medieval distinction between "implicit faith" and "explicit faith" begins to make its way into the standard thinking of the church. Those Christians still inclined to take Jesus at his word and respond radically to the radical gospel will be assigned to the margins of the church, where they may even be admired for their rigor and their contributions to the general level of piety in the church. Those critics who go too far in their rebellion against the church's reductionism will be declared both heretics and enemies of the states and removed (e.g., the Waldensians, John Wyclif, Johannes Hus, and, within the Reformation, the Anabaptists).

I have looked briefly at central and typical expressions of the broad reductionistic process that produced Christendom and cultural

36. Yoder, *Royal Priesthood*, pp. 173-74, 178.
37. For the discussion in the remainder of this paragraph, see Yoder, *Royal Priesthood*, pp. 115f. See also Hauerwas, *Community of Character,* especially pp. 37ff.

Christianity. Theologians have devoted much effort to arguing for and justifying these compromises. Even the Reformation churches, as they grappled with many dimensions of reductionism, argued for the principles of *Schonung*, "the indulgence or caution or forbearance with which the reformer takes account of the limited understanding of his faithful."[38] In plain English, the overriding problem repeatedly has been a control-driven combination of concerns for public order, institutional security, and the protection of power. The institutional church has prospered and enjoyed enormous power in Western civilization. Under its sponsorship, the gospel has, to be sure, continued to be witnessed to; people have responded; and faith has been born and shaped. But its compromises have become major problems for Christian witness today.

The incarnation of Jesus Christ is the event that brings about the salvation of the world and establishes the mission of the church. This event also defines how that mission is to be carried out. The reductionism of the gospel in Western Christendom is confronted by the person and work of Jesus as both the content and the criterion of the church's witness. For the church to be and to become Christ's faithful witness will require repentance and conversion.

---

38. Yoder, *Royal Priesthood*, p. 85.

PART III

Implications: The Conversion of the Church

At key points in several of the New Testament letters, such as Romans 12:1 and Ephesians 4:1, the word "therefore" carries considerable weight. It is a word that signals a major shift in the writer's message. What precedes the "therefore" was, in some form, an exposition of the gospel. Then, writing to a specific situation, the apostolic author begins to draw out the implications of the gospel for the Christian witness of that community. In both texts mentioned above, Paul uses the word "therefore" to alert the reader that the great and wonderful truth just explained must have profound consequences: "present your bodies as a living sacrifice," and "lead lives worthy of the calling with which you have been called." What then follows in both epistles is a series of important instructions, shaping these communities for their faithful witness.

In a much more modest sense, I have reached the "therefore" point in my investigation of evangelism as the heart of ministry. Part I laid the foundations for a theology of evangelistic ministry. The larger context, I said, was the broad and exciting understanding of God as *God with a mission,* which the scriptural witness presents to us. The biblical witness reveals to us that God the creator is compassionate and loving toward the lost creation. The concrete evidence of that love is God's action to save and heal the world. God's mission reached its culmination in the sending ("mission" means "sending") of Jesus Christ. Jesus is the sent messenger of God who, in his death and resurrection, becomes the message. He announces the coming of the kingdom, and as the risen Lord, he inaugurates that kingdom as its king. So, his life, death, and resurrection are the good news of God's love and saving purpose for all creation, which defines the calling and the task of the church. I then interpreted that mission as witness: the church is called to bring to all the world its witness to what God has done, is doing, and will do in and through Jesus Christ, the reigning Lord.

Part II confronted the major challenges to a theology and practice of evangelistic ministry. The basic challenge is rooted in the vocation of the witness to translate the gospel into every human culture humans. That is what God's Spirit empowers the church to do: to be the witness which carries, translates, communicates, and demonstrates the good news of God's love in Christ "to the ends of the earth." But, as a community of forgiven sinners, we constantly try to bring this gospel under our control. We do that by reducing it to manageable proportions. In a great variety of ways, that reductionism has become characteristic of our Christian witness, especially in the Western world, among the heirs of the oldest traditions. For evangelistic ministry, that reductionism is displayed in its most potent way in the division of the gospel into "benefits" and "mission." What the believer receives from responding to Christ has become the focus: forgiveness, new life, and assurance of salvation. These truly blessed benefits may not, however, be separated from the calling of the Christian community to be Christ's witness. Thus, the heart of the church's evangelistic ministry is its own continuing conversion to the fullness of Christ and his mission.

In this third section, "therefore," I will discuss some of the concrete implications of the continuing conversion of the church. The essence of the church's credible witness is its own ongoing evangelization. As the love of God in Jesus Christ is incarnated in the faith community, that love is demonstrated to the world. Witness happens in all that the church is, does, and says, but always in and through its forgiveness and its dependence upon God's grace. In these two concluding chapters and an epilogue, I will consider what such an incarnational witness might mean for the practice of the local congregation, and for the church as an institution.

Chapter Seven

Converting the Church:
The Local Congregation

---

*A vital instrument for the fulfillment of the missionary vocation of
the Church is the local congregation.*[1]

As we move to the end of the twentieth century, there has been a growing consensus in worldwide Christianity that the local congregation is
the basic unit of Christian witness. The quotation above from *Mission
Evangelism: An Ecumenical Affirmation*, written in 1982-83, would probably be rephrased by now to define the local congregation as "*the* vital instrument for the fulfillment of the missionary vocation of the Church."
It bears many names: parish, congregation, community, fellowship —
or the name I favor: mission community. It is defined in many ways,
but the concept of "local" is present in virtually every definition.

"Local" implies "place," a "particular, identifiable place." The basic unit of Christian community is formed and lives out its witness in
particular places, where its members can gather regularly for worship
and work. Proximity, frequency of direct contact with one another, mu-
tually supportive relationships, sharing of resources, struggling and

---

1. World Council of Churches, *Mission and Evangelism: An Ecumenical Affirmation*
(Geneva, 1982), ¶25.

145

growing together in the faith — these characteristics of a Christian community define its shape. The people of God must have a visible, tangible, experiencable shape. This is not, however, simply a sociological or organizational necessity. It is essential to the *missio Dei*. The witness to God's loving and saving work in history is through the people God calls and sets apart for this mission.[2] Every mission community is a historical witness to the work of God being carried out; it is concrete evidence of God's purposeful action. This is what the Holy Spirit does: it forms mission communities so that the gospel may be incarnated in particular places, to be the witness to Jesus Christ. Any understanding of the Christian church which does not emphasize the concrete and historical reality and the centrality of local and particular communities is docetic: it is not taking with great seriousness God's mission and the incarnation of that mission in Jesus Christ and his church.

But the concrete shape of the local community will differ from place to place, from culture to culture. When the gospel is translated into a particular culture, then that culture's patterns of human relationships are used in the formation of local churches. In tribal and clan societies, the local congregation can be large and numerous, more or less approximating the network of relationships defined by such social structures. In societies where family is the dominant social form, the local congregation will often function as an extended family. Since the days of Charlemagne in Europe, "local" has meant the geographical parish in which people were joined in churches with their neighbors, all of whom were (at least nominally) Christians. The congregation brought together everyone within walking or reasonable riding distance. The parish embraced everyone within earshot of the church tower's bells. In a Christendom structure, where virtually everyone bore the identity "Christian," the geographical parish system made sense.

In some societies, especially in the industrialized West, the dominant social form of organization has become the "voluntary society." Local congregations in such settings are made up of people who choose to come together in a particular Christian community. Their motives no longer have to be geographical, although that is often still relevant. Proximity in major urban areas is no longer measured in terms of

2. The magisterial study of the formation of God's people is Paul D. Hanson, *The People Called: The Growth of Community in the Bible* (New York: Harper & Row, 1987).

neighborhoods but rather in terms of accessibility. Mass transportation and the automobile create new kinds of local congregations. In the typical American city, Christians will drive or ride past numerous church buildings to get to "the church of their choice." That choice may be based upon denominational tradition, ethnicity, program, theological outlook, worship style, children's education, perceived social advantage, aesthetics, parking availability, proximity to the bus line or subway stop — or a combination of these and other factors.

This range of factors indicates the missional challenge of community formation. On the one hand, the faith community can and should be formed in ways that relate to the culture in which the witness is to be carried out. There is no normative way to organize local congregations. The church's mission that forms faith communities should also guide their organization. The formation of local communities for continuing witness is an essential part of the gospel translation process. There are, however, aspects of any culture which are hostile to the gospel, or conversely, which are threatened by the gospel. Much of the reductionistic process is related to such cultural hostility. These cultural components can lead to organizational forms that are not faithful to the gospel mission. The culture can take the organized church captive. In tribal societies, tribal norms can be equated with gospel values. In the parish system of Christendom, nominalism emerges easily when everyone "belongs" and more or less behaves "the way a Christian should." In the entrepreneurial voluntarism of North America, the values and assumptions of the competitive market can take over the church and make it into a business. This ever-present reality of cultural conformity makes continuing conversion a spiritual necessity.

As we come to the turning of the century, the growing emphasis upon the local congregation is accompanied, in churches of the Western tradition, by the diminishing significance of regional and national church structures. They are both getting smaller and are being redefined. This is a very complex process that has been exhaustively studied and variously explained. As they decrease in size and authority, denominational structures in the North Atlantic context increasingly affirm the local congregation as the prime unit of mission. They are describing themselves as agencies that support and encourage local congregational ministry and mission. In those countries where church and state are separated (as in North America), the local congregation must support denominational structures financially. When the congregations cut back on funding, these structures are forced to regroup or (perhaps) disappear. That process has been going on in the last decade of this century, and the prognosis for denominational structures is unclear, but many signs are more threatening than encouraging. It seems to be certain that, while the local congregation will continue, the connecting structures are going to look very different.[3]

Regardless of the actual shape and name adopted, the local congregation is the basic unit of Christian witness if we understand witness incarnationally. The gospel is always to be embodied by the people of God in a particular place. The sent-out community is sent out into the specific context in which it is located. There, it must grapple with the challenge to be faithful to its mandate while translating relevantly, which will mean that it struggles with the pressures to conform found in every cultural setting. Nevertheless, the communal and particular character of God's mission in Christ is essential to the biblical understanding of God's saving work in history. And, therefore, it has been a constant refrain in the development of a theology of evangelistic ministry.

The survey of the biblical foundations of evangelistic ministry in chapters 2 and 3 stressed the corporate and plural character of the New Testament's teaching about the church. When I defined mission as witness in chapter 3, I began by emphasizing the formation of the mission community. When I summarized my understanding of witness at the end of chapter 3, I stressed that witness is ecclesiological (point 6). When I speak of the "conversion of the church," I am stressing the communal character of faith and trying to correct the reduction of conversion to the experience of the individual, as important as that is.

"Incarnational witness" defines the way the community is to function as Christ's body. The "one another" passages, almost one hundred New Testament imperatives emphasizing the mutuality of Christian community, only make sense within a community whose members are committed to Christ and to one another. Such relationships require frequency of contact and communication, common worship and Christian activity, and mutual responsibility and support. Incarna-

---

3. For a discussion of the missional issues related to structures see Darrell L. Guder, ed., *Missional Church: A Theological Vision for the Sending of the Church in North America* (Grand Rapids: Eerdmans, 1998), chapters 8 and 9.

tional witness happens in the specific and concrete actions and relationships of intentional communities. This has been true of the Christian movement since Pentecost.

Therefore, the concrete and tangible reality of the local congregation must be emphasized. To illustrate the challenge of continuing conversion, I will turn to my own experience, both as a teacher and a pastor. My students often return to the classroom from their field education experience in local congregations with serious missional concerns. Next to encouraging reports about spiritual vitality and missional energy in some churches, we hear statements like these:

> "The congregation I am in does not want to grow; it does not want new members; it does not want to change. They want the pastor to ensure that things will continue to be done the way they have always been done."

> "My congregation is dying, and they expect me to accompany the process and make sure that it is a dignified death."

> "My congregation is divided into opposing camps. Meetings of the council are a battlefield. Everyone is trying to get the pastor to take sides."

> "The people are really nice in my congregation; they've made me feel very welcome. But they really want their church to be a religious social club. There is no interest in adult education or in Bible study. What they really want me to do is set up a youth program to keep their kids out of trouble."

To complicate the confusion, most of these congregations have "evangelism committees." What they mean by "evangelism" is, in most cases, "new member recruitment." There is virtually no sense of the calling of the entire community to be an evangelizing community in every dimension of its life. When we discuss these experiences, it becomes clear to my students and to me that the "renewal" or "redevelopment" of such congregations in our context is really a question of their conversion, their own evangelization.

What does the conversion of the church, of any particular local congregation, look like? How does a local congregation become a mission community? If the local congregation is the basic unit of mission, how is it supposed to happen there? Everything I have said up to now focuses on these questions.

The Continuing Conversion of the Church

The Reformed tradition emphasizes that "the church once reformed is always in the process of being reformed according to the Word of God." That phrase, *ecclesia reformata secundum verbi Dei semper reformanda,* is used a great deal in North Atlantic Reformed circles these days, probably because of the crisis in which most of these churches find themselves. It is indeed a work of God's Spirit when we recognize that under the guidance of the Word of God the church must constantly experience re-shaping, re-forming. It might well be, however, that re-forming is not enough. In view of our reductionism and our cultural captivity, it might be evidence of greater spiritual honesty if we were to describe ourselves as churches continually needing conversion. The emphasis upon reform can, in fact, ignore the central missional vocation of the church, or narrow our focus to questions of our shape and organization, that is, issues of "form." There is a tendency, especially in North American churches, to solve problems by reorganization. What I have tried to make clear is that the church's crisis is one of fundamental vocation, of calling to God's mission, of being, doing, and saying witness in faithfulness to Jesus Christ, the Lord. Our missional challenge is a crisis of faith and spirit, and it will be met only through conversion, the continuing conversion of the church.

> *The continual conversion of the church happens as the congregation hears, responds to, and obeys the gospel of Jesus Christ in ever new and more comprehensive ways.*

Or, to put it more succinctly:

> *If evangelization is the heart of mission, then evangelization must be the heart of ministry.*

In chapter 2 I reviewed the evangel that is the content of evangelization. This is where we always start, with the person who is the message and the messenger, the Savior and the Lord, Jesus Christ. This is the theme of our life together in the mission community. This is what separates the mission community from every other human assembly: the presence and power of Jesus Christ.

I then examined the many ways in which we, as a human and sinful church, reduce the gospel of Jesus Christ, bringing it under our control. This reduction fatefully infects evangelistic ministry when the gospel is proclaimed as only personal salvation but leads no further. The gospel is always the message of God's salvation resulting in the call to God's service as Christ's witness. The perspective of the gospel is universal: "God so loved the world" *(cosmos)*. Any local church that wants to be renewed must, therefore, confront its own gospel reductionism — I return to this theme below.

This is a work of God's Spirit that we cannot manage or program. "Revival" is not a program we can put on a calendar and post on a banner hung out in front of a church. But we can start with what God has given us: the biblical witness. We can ask Scripture the questions that will open us up to a reviving encounter with the gospel. We can ask Scripture what a gospel-centered church looks like and how it functions.

In one of my classes, we were discussing the implications of incarnational witness for the local congregation. One of my students commented on the mission-benefits dichotomy with a statement which caught me up short: "I see a lot of people in the church who don't have any experience of the blessings of the gospel anymore but are still trying to do the mission!" Her observation is sadly true of many congregations and perhaps even denominations. It illumines the essential fact of the gospel-centered community: It is itself experiencing continuing conversion. Its own evangelization is constantly going on. The evangelizing congregation is continuously being evangelized. This is happening individually and communally: the lines here cannot be easily separated. As individuals in the congregation hear and respond to the gospel in ways that convert them, then the community's continuing conversion happens. As the community is shaped by God's Spirit so that it risks being intentionally alternative to the dominant pressures of its cultural setting, then it is being converted.

I experienced this in my first pastoral assignment as an outreach pastor to upper-school youth in a region of the Lutheran church of northern Germany. One summer I took a group of about thirty young people between the ages of sixteen and twenty to spend time at the Protestant monastic community of Taizé in south central France. My ministry with these young people had been going on about one and one-half years. We had done a lot together: weekend conferences on challenging themes, debates about the issues of the faith, time building relationships. But it was a program ministry very much based on how effectively I could market and attract them to the themes and events I could organize.

In Taizé we worshiped every day with the brothers. We worked with them, and we had a fascinating series of conversations with some about their calling to monastic life and their desire to serve Christ by submitting to his rule in their lives. We also worked as a group, studying the Bible and opening ourselves up to its confrontation of our very controlled faith commitment. The example of these committed Christian men and their community had a profound impact upon my students. After almost two weeks in Taizé we set off on our return bus journey to northern Germany. As the hours rolled by, I noticed that there was a lively discussion going on in the back of the bus. Finally, one of the students came up and asked me to join them. When I went back, it was obvious that they were very excited about something. They said to me, "Herr Doktor Guder [we were still using titles and last names at this point], we feel that something has to change in the way we are doing the student ministry at home. We need to spend more time studying the Bible, finding out what it means to be a Christian, and acting like a Christian community. Can we do that? Would you mind?"

An amazing thing happened in those few hours. We became a converted and thus a converting community. We dropped the titles and the formality; we committed ourselves to becoming a community that was open to God's call to us in Christ. We returned home with a new kind of joy and a whole new set of challenges. We moved from being a program to being a mission community, with all of its risks. We were more aware than ever of our weakness and incompleteness. But we knew that what was happening was God's gift to us. Individuals changed, and the community changed, yet it was never possible to talk about this process as cause and effect. It happened in the experience of the community in obvious and subtle ways. Separations between personal conversion and the continuing conversion of the church are neither possible nor relevant.

> *Evangelization as the heart of ministry means that the gospel-centered community continually encounters and celebrates Christ. This is the purpose and witness of public worship.*

When the community gathers for public worship, it claims, affirms, and celebrates the promised real presence of Jesus Christ as Savior and Lord in its midst. The various components of public worship announce the good news of God's healing love in Jesus. Therefore, "one of the primary and irreplaceable ingredients in evangelism is the quality of worship in the Christian community."[4] The ancient practice of the gospel text for every Sunday defines the public worship of the community: it is gospel-centered and thus evangelizing. We gather in the name of Christ because we are called to be his people, his witnesses, and because his Spirit gives us the power to express our responses of joy, praise, and commitment to him. In large assemblies and in small groups, at many different times and a variety of places, we hear the Word proclaimed, and we receive the visible Word in the sacraments. We praise God; we confess our sins and are assured of our pardon; we respond to gospel proclamation with affirmation of faith and acts of giving and commissioning. We provide each other the opportunity to share our experiences of the reality of God's love in our lives and to encourage each other. Members bring their struggles, doubts, disappointments, and fears into the community where they become the common concern for shared prayer and action. In this assembled community, members encounter the risen Lord in word, sacrament, and fellowship, and they are sent back out for their continuing ministry of witness as light, leaven, and salt.

Every time we gather for public worship and hear the gospel, we are invited to respond anew to God's call in Christ. Our conversion continues because God is faithful and is completing the good work which He has begun in us (Phil. 1:6). God invites us, receives us, heals and blesses us, and sends us.

---

4. William J. Abraham, *The Logic of Evangelism* (Grand Rapids: Eerdmans, 1989), p. 168.

What I am saying here is, of course, obvious and simple. The community's encounter with and celebration of Christ is the common ground that unites every strand of Christian tradition together. Our history is a wonderful resource for discovering how true and powerful this gospel experience is. When a storefront church gathers in an American inner city and praises Jesus Christ with the emotion and fervor of voices, clapping, shouting, drums, and guitars, it is witnessing to this central fact of our calling. When a liturgical procession forms in an Anglican cathedral to carry the Bible out into the middle of the nave, surrounded by candles and incense, with the entire congregation standing and facing toward the priest and the open book, and the gospel is read as the holiest moment in the service, then Christ's presence is being witnessed and celebrated.

But this obvious and simple truth of the gospel is perhaps its most daunting challenge. We frequently hear that the major problem with the church is that its public worship is boring. This complaint is closely linked, I think, to the profound issue raised by my student when she spoke about the people who don't experience the blessing but still try to do the mission. Public Christian worship is the most sensitive indicator of the spiritual health or lack of it in the body of Christ. Much has been and will be written about the challenge of public worship. There are many aspects of this question which merit careful attention. I am persuaded, however, that for us in the mission field of the post-Christendom West, the essential issue for all public worship is the Christological question. In a nutshell, what is the formative and pervasive theme of our assembled worship?

After six volumes of research on one of the mainline church traditions in North America and its decline in the latter third of the twentieth century, Coalter, Mulder, and Weeks formulated the "theological agenda for the church." The first and most urgent question they raised was this:

Who is Jesus Christ? . . . What affirmations about the uniqueness of Christ can we make in the midst of the pluralism of American culture and world religions? What does it mean to confess that Jesus Christ is savior of the world? What do we mean when we say that in Jesus Christ God became human and that in Jesus Christ God forgives human sin and reconciles the world? How does this good news change the way we live and the structures of society?[5]

Our questioning must start here: "How does this good news change the way we worship, the way we confess our faith as a local congregation?" The continuing conversion of the church happens and is demonstrated here, when we encounter and celebrate Jesus Christ as our risen and present Lord, in our midst. Our worship is therefore the first demonstration before the world of our sentness, as we respond to God's grace in the good news of Jesus Christ.

Ironically, our worship can be thoroughly Christocentric and still be overshadowed today by what we may now call "the worship wars." We find more and more preoccupation with the styles and methods of worship, with camps forming around "contemporary," "traditional," and "blended" worship. As our culture becomes progressively non- if not anti-Christian, there is a growing concern to find new ways to translate the story and practice corporate worship. Such a concern is obviously missionally important: the sent community is empowered to communicate the gospel so that it can be heard and understood. Others are just as exercised about preserving the great liturgical and musical traditions of Christendom, which also has missional validity. It is part of our witness to demonstrate the presence and work of God through all the centuries since Pentecost. Both the "contemporary" and the "traditional" worship camps can be wholeheartedly Christ-centered and yet their struggles with each other can invalidate their witness to the watching world.

There are others who are primarily concerned that their experience of worship "meet their needs." However their "needs" are defined, this approach to worship invariably reveals the problematic consequences of gospel reductionism. It is missionally relevant in the way it shows how much we are captive to our culture and its priorities. The "gospel which meets my needs" must be replaced with the good news that reveals needs I did not know I had while providing healing I never dreamed was possible.

5. Milton J Coalter, John M. Mulder, and Louis B. Weeks, *The Re-Forming Tradition: Presbyterians and Mainstream Protestantism* (Louisville: Westminster/John Knox, 1992), pp. 281-82. See also, by the same authors, *Vital Signs: The Promise of Mainstream Protestantism* (Grand Rapids: Eerdmans, 1996), pp. 130-32.

The struggles with the character and practice of worship are an especially telling evidence of the turmoil that our passage out of Christendom is causing. Since everything around us is changing, there must necessarily be change in the church if it is to be an evangelizing community. The way we change is itself a form of witness, which is often forgotten in the divisive and hurtful battles that go on inside local congregations. Merely changing the externals of worship will not meet the crisis. The missional faithfulness of the church is not ultimately a question of organs versus guitars, baroque versus rock. The real problem today is a general lack of understanding of what worship is really all about. We need to probe the gospel itself in order to discover what corporate worship truly is, and what it is not.[6] The process here, as everywhere else, is basically biblical and theological, before it becomes methodological. What does it mean to assemble in the confidence of God's presence, to address God corporately, and to hear and respond to God's address to us? In how many ways can that happen? How translatable are the modes of Christian worship into our diverse cultures? The answers to these questions are not simple ones, and the discussion of them is for many very threatening. But it needs to be joined, for the sake of our calling.

There is one dimension of the worship wars which calls for particular scrutiny. The primary emphasis of much innovation is upon effective communication to the secularized participant. If modern Americans do not respond to organs, hymns, and gowned preachers in pulpits, then let us have bands, praise songs, and a casually clad storyteller on a stool. Communication in such programs is certainly happening, but one must ask if it is always worship. The focus in worship is upon God as the one with whom we communicate. When we shift the focus of worship to the possible participants from our mission field, then there is a great risk that we have replaced worship with something else. Many would jump to the conclusion that we have reduced worship to entertainment. I do not want to make such sweeping generalizations.

One question needs to be raised, however. Why do we assume that every time we gather in any kind of assembly to "do Christian

6. For one modest attempt, see Darrell L. Guder, "The Missional Center of Reformed Worship," *Reformed Liturgy and Music* 32, no. 2 (1998): 100-104.

things" that we are conducting a worship service? Is it not possible for us to envision a whole range of communication events within the church's mission, which move from personal conversations about the faith, through a great variety of informational and evangelistic presentations, to the God-centered worship of the believing community? I suspect that many of our so-called seeker-friendly or contemporary worship services are really evangelistic gatherings which, quite rightly, are translating the gospel into the language and culture of people who do not know what worship is nor how to do it. They have to find out who God is through their encounter with Jesus Christ. They are not capable of worship yet. So they must hear the gospel in understandable ways; they must experience Christian witnesses who are seeking to be "Jews to the Jews and Greeks to the Greeks." Paul spent hours in the courtyards of Mediterranean homes, expounding the gospel to household members and any stranger who might wander in from the street. These were not worship services. They were evangelistic gatherings, which must take place if the witness is to be said and heard. But the believing community gathered at a riverside or in a private space to share bread and wine, hear the gospel, and respond with praise and prayer.

The mission field in which we find ourselves requires that the church diversify its ways of communicating. That is obvious. We need to become more creative in finding ways to translate the message. Jesus' use of the parables will always stand as a challenge to the missional church to find clear and confrontive ways to make the story plain. Our changing cultural context also requires that we change our worship forms so that Christians shaped by late modernity can express their faith authentically and honestly. What we need to grapple with is this: Not all evangelization is worship, but all worship is evangelization. Not every way we communicate the story is focused upon the reality of God in our midst. But when we are gathered to worship God, everything we say and do is a witness to the good news.

As we said above, public worship is the first and central form of witness to the world. It is at the same time a demonstration of the reality of God that cannot be, in every way, understandable and accessible. The watching world must see a community of people who love the God they are addressing, who love each other, and who desire to carry their

God's love into the world. That watching world will not necessarily understand the significance of broken bread, poured out wine, or baptismal washing. They will not know what is happening when people pray, communicating with our unseen God whose presence we do not doubt. But even as they do not understand, they will witness the difference that the presence of God makes in the midst of this community. They will see good news happening, whether they can join in worship of the one true God or not. They will, in some way, hear the same message that all Christians need to hear, although they will hear it in obviously different ways.

That message must constantly be heard and witnessed by Christian worshipers and unbelieving observers alike. What they all need to hear, to respond to, and to share, has been beautifully summarized by Shirley Guthrie with these words:

> Before you ever thought of seeking out God to ask for God's love, God sought you out and acted in self-giving love for you. Before you even considered choosing Christ and making a decision for him, Christ chose you and made a decision for you. Before you even heard about opening yourself to the freeing and renewing work of the Holy Spirit, the Spirit has already been at work in your life and in the world around you. Before it occurred to you to ask for your own and the world's salvation, while you were still trapped and dead in your sin and unbelief, it already happened in the life, death, and resurrection of Christ, and is happening through the presence of the living Christ and his Spirit in your life and in the world. Therefore accept and live by this good news. Not because you must, but because you may. Not because you are or want to be a godly, spiritual person, but because God loves, Christ died for, and the Spirit comes to ungodly, worldly sinners. Not because God is soft and indulgent in dealing with sin and sinners like you but because in Jesus Christ God has already taken on God's self the consequences of your sin and the sin of the whole world. Not because God will damn and punish you if you don't, or pay off with all kinds of good things if you do, but out of sheer thankfulness for the loving and powerful grace of God in Jesus Christ. Accept and live by this grace not because the kingdom of God cannot come unless you seek it and work for it, but because the kingdom of God is coming and is already on the way. Accept and live by it because God always has been, is and always will be a loving and pow-

erful gracious God — even in those times when you are not sure you believe and despite the massive unbelief and disobedience in the world around you.[7]

That message must not stop with the "you" to which it is addressed, but lead on to the mission for which we are reconciled with God and brought into the community of Christ.

> *Evangelization as the heart of ministry happens as Christ commissions the community to be his witnesses, to do his witness, and to say his witness. Continuing conversion is to Christ's salvation and thus to his mission.*

As the blessings of the gospel are shared, affirmed, and renewed, the congregation receives its commission, its calling to be God's people in its particular place. Continuing conversion is always a turning to mission, to the sending for which the Christian church is gathered and blessed. The benefits of the gospel, as I have emphasized, equip and empower the mission community for its witness. The witness that begins in the corporate event of public worship now continues in the life of each individual Christian. They leave the public worship with a renewed sense of being called and set apart. They are challenged and encouraged to place their trust in Jesus Christ the Lord to make them faithful witnesses every day of the week.

Whether the community is gathered or scattered, the mandate to be Christ's witnesses defines every dimension of the community's life. This is what is meant by incarnational witness: demonstrating concretely the reality of God's love in the ways the community functions. The relationships among the members of the community are intended to incarnate the powerful and transforming love of the gospel. The compassion with which the community cares for its own as well as for its neighbors (those next to it) incarnates the gospel. The dependence upon God's forgiveness is incarnated in the way that the community forgives, practices tolerance, bears one another's burdens.

---

7. Shirley C. Guthrie, "A Reformed Theology of Evangelism," in *Evangelism in the Reformed Tradition*, ed. Arnold B. Lovell (Decatur: CTS Press, 1990), pp. 80-81.

The Holy Spirit shapes God's people for mission through the continuous encounter with the Scripture. Continuing conversion happens as the community "indwells" Scripture.[8]

Rigorous biblical learning must be the missional congregation's priority. The congregation intentionally commits most of its time together to biblical study — which takes place in many different ways. It encourages and equips its members to continue biblical study individually. Through its continuing encounter with the biblical word, the congregation experiences the conversion which is the result of the "transformation of the mind" (Rom. 12:2). This means that the members are learning to think Christianly; they are learning how to see the world through the eyes of Jesus; they are becoming biblically literate in order to be effective translators of the gospel into their world.

[W]e get a picture of the Christian life as one in which we live in the biblical story as part of the community whose story it is, find in the story the clues to knowing God as his character becomes manifest in the story, and from within that indwelling try to understand and cope with the events of our time and the world about us and so carry the story forward. At the heart of the story, as the key to the whole, is the incarnation of the Word, the life, ministry, death, and resurrection of Jesus. In the fourth Gospel Jesus defines for his disciples what is to be their relation to him. They are to "dwell in" him. He is not to be the object of their observation, but the body of which they are a part. As they "indwell" him in his body, they will both be led into fuller and fuller apprehension of the truth and also become the means through which God's will is done in the life of the world.[9]

8. Lesslie Newbigin uses Michael Polanyi's epistemological concept "indwelling" to describe how the Christian community's witness can truly "challenge the reigning worldview," in *The Gospel in a Pluralist Society* (Grand Rapids: Eerdmans, 1989), pp. 97ff. "[I]t can do so through the witness of a community which, in unbroken continuity with the biblical actors and witnesses, indwells the story the Bible tells [p. 97]. . . . [T]he important thing in the use of the Bible is not to understand the text but to understand the world *through* the text [p. 98]. . . . What is required is that one lives in the text and from that position tries to understand what is happening in the world now [p. 98]."

9. Newbigin, *Gospel in a Pluralist Society,* p. 99.

As the people are formed biblically, they learn to speak the language of faith. Each Christian finds ways to say what he or she believes and has the opportunity to do so. This happens through the "spiritual conversation" of the community, which may and should be constantly practiced. The members of the congregation need constantly to be helped to "say their faith" when they are together, so that they can learn how to say it when they are apart — that is, when they are the sent-out people of God in mission.

> *Christ gives the ministry of the Word to the community to equip it for its mission through the encounter with the biblical witness (Eph. 4:7, 11f).*

The ministry of the Word in any mission community is carried out by individuals who are given to the community by Christ. They continue the work of the "apostles, prophets, evangelists, and pastor-teachers" which is "to equip the saints for the work of ministry" (Eph. 4:11-12).[10] Their common and most important characteristic is that they are ministers of the Word. In a very special way, they are essential because of their function as the Spirit's instruments for the Word-centered equipping of the saints. Their office is not the important thing about them, but rather their calling and gifting to serve the community as students and expositors of the Word.[11] Thus, these persons can be "ordained" or "lay," for the forms of ministerial office are not the issue here, but rather the particular and essential function of those whom Christ gives to the church "to equip the saints for the work of ministry" (Eph. 4:12). What this means is that all formally structured offices of the church as mission community are defined in terms of that mission. They are to be understood as functional to the church's mission. The organizational dimensions of these "ordered offices of ministry" are

10. For the most thorough investigation of the "constitution of the church" in Ephesians 4:1-16, see Markus Barth, *Ephesians: Translation and Commentary on Chapters 4–6*, The Anchor Bible, 34A (Garden City, NY: Doubleday, 1974), pp. 425-97.

11. Calvin is instructive here: "[W]e must here remember that whatever authority and dignity the Spirit in Scripture accords to either priests or prophets, or apostles, or successors of apostles, it is wholly given not to the men personally, but to the ministry to which they have been appointed; or (to speak more briefly) to the Word, whose ministry is entrusted to them"; John Calvin, *Institutes of the Christian Religion*, IV, viii, 2.

subject to change and redefinition as the circumstances and demands of the particular mission of the church in a particular context require. But there must always be the ministry of the Word if there is to be missional church.

What will always be true of all ministers of the Word is summarized in Ephesians 4:11. They will, firstly and most importantly, always be *apostolic*. They will continue the basic apostolic ministry of gospel proclamation, which was demonstrated and defined normatively by the apostolic witness of the New Testament church. Ministers of the Word must be faithful both to the apostolic message and the apostolic mission, which is the incarnational witness to that gospel message. They will equip the saints both by proclaiming the apostolic message and by forming the community as a sent people. Everything else that the ministry of the Word implies is subsumed importantly under this fundamental definition: apostolic.

The apostolicity of this ministry means that it must be *prophetic*. The gospel Word is always to be translated into the particular context in which the mission community is present and is sent. Ministers of the Word are called and empowered by the Holy Spirit to unfold the implications of the gospel as it invites people to be forgiven and healed, and to become transformed evidence of God's saving love. The gospel is never articulated in a vacuum, but in particular contexts that are both affirmed and challenged by the claims of Christ. The prophetic witness makes those challenges to every culture clear and explicit. It addresses God's Word to the structures and systems that shape people and societies, and its address will always extend the invitation to follow Christ and often link that invitation with the word of judgment over human sinfulness. So, ministers of the Word equip the saints for the work of ministry as they carry out the prophetic translation of the gospel. That translation, which is often risky and dangerous, guides the mission community to behaviors and actions that demonstrate the good news of God's reign in Christ.[12]

At the heart of these basic functions of the ministry of the Word stands the work of the "evangelist." For many years, I pondered this

12. Richard Hays, *The Moral Vision of the New Testament: Community, Cross, New Creation: A Contemporary Introduction to New Testament Ethics* (San Francisco: HarperSanFrancisco, 1996).

term at the center of this five-dimensional definition of the ministry of the Word that equips the saints for the church's mission. If one understands the term "evangelist" too narrowly, that is, if it is restricted only to communication of the gospel to unbelievers, then it is difficult to see how this ministry "equips the saints." If we understand the necessity of the church's continuing conversion, however, then the function of evangelist is essential to the church's missional equipping. The apostolic and prophetic ministry of the Word must constantly evangelize the community so that it can be about its work, its evangelizing witness. The community should experience the constant challenge of the gospel to our reductions and conformities. The gospel itself, through the proclamation and exposition of the Word, will uncover our need for conversion as the Spirit is faithful and makes that miracle happen.

Our congregations today urgently need to be ministered to by evangelist-pastors. That does not mean that they should hear a sermon every Sunday about accepting Christ. They should hear, instead, the constant and empowered message of good news which calls all Christian to continuing conversion, to growth and healing in the life of faith, and to greater and more radical obedience as sent-out witnesses. Seminaries should be preparing evangelists to be sent into the churches, so that they might become evangelizing communities. This will also mean that the ministers of the Word themselves require constant evangelizing, constant encounter with the gospel as healing good news. It would revolutionize the structures of the church if the primary purpose of our polity were mutual evangelization.

Finally, the functions of the ministry of the Word which equip the church for its mission are both pastoral and instructive, or as Paul says, "pastors and teachers." The preponderance of exegetes sees these two terms as one function, joined with a hyphen: pastoral-teachers, or teaching-pastors. The equipping ministry of the Word guides the community as a shepherd guides the flock, gently, firmly, with attentiveness to its true (rather than its "felt") needs. It does so instructively, teaching the faith at every step and providing the community the understandings of the gospel and the world which are needed for faithful witness. The interaction of these two images is profoundly formative for our practice of ministry: all pastoral care is to teach the faith, and all teaching of the faith is to be carried out pastorally. Rooted in the Word, pastoral care will not be content with the merely therapeutic but will strive for the "cure of souls." Similarly, the pastoral-teacher will guide the community beyond superficial understandings of the gospel to grapple with its radical and life-transforming claims.

If this five-dimensional ministry of the Word is necessary for the equipping of the church for its mission, then it is immediately clear that no one person can ever do it all. The concept of the "solo minister" is foreign to the missionary congregation. The apostolic ministry in the New Testament was carried out by teams, such as Paul, Sylvanus, and Timothy (see 1 Thessalonians). Paul appointed groups of elders to lead the communities he founded. The Spirit is not stingy in its gifting of the church for its mission. Every community's task is to discern those who are Christ's gifts to the church as part of the apostolic-prophetic-evangelistic-pastoral-teaching Word ministry that is to equip it for its calling. Here, the conversion of the church will necessarily mean the conversion of many of our concepts and practices of office, ordination, and leadership. The legacies of Christendom reductionism weigh heavily upon our church constitutions today and hinder us from moving out in mission into the changed context in which God has placed us.

Our centeredness and dependence upon the ministry of the Word means that neither the collegial leadership nor the congregation owns the gospel. It means that, together, they are engaging the gospel as openly and honestly as they can. As this happens, they "come to the unity of the faith and of the knowledge of the Son of God, to maturity, to the measure of the full stature of Christ" (Eph. 4:13).

> *Christ converts the community by confronting its conformities. Evangelism as the heart of ministry grapples with gospel reductionism.*

Jesus Christ enables the congregation to confront its conformities. This confrontation is linked with the constant endeavor to understand our calling more fully and respond to it more faithfully. The community that is continually being converted knows that it is involved in compromises within its world which can only be dealt with through repentance and healing. It intentionally submits itself to the scrutiny of Scripture and hears Christ's call to greater faithfulness. It knows that it is dependent upon God's forgiveness and grace. It is constantly discovering how the "Gospel is always before us" and responding to that challenge.

I have summarized in brief theses some of the most important characteristics of the gospel-centered community, as it is continually being converted by that gospel. The vocation and practices of the church as mission community have been thoroughly explored in the expanding worldwide discussion of the church's missionary calling.[13] There are many specific challenges in the situation of the churches of the West which call for more detailed treatment. I shall examine two of them: the question of disagreement among Christians and the question of church membership. In these areas, the conversion of the church is urgently called for if she is to be able to incarnate the gospel faithfully.

The Witness of Christian Disagreement

The community which is continually being converted "makes every effort to maintain the unity of the Spirit in the bond of peace" (Eph. 4:3). Precisely when there are disagreements within the community, it incarnates the gospel by grappling with these problems and remaining united in Christ. Disagreeing Christianly is one of the most powerful forms of incarnational witness the church can practice.[14]

It should not surprise us that there are differences and disagreements within the faith community. This has been true since Pentecost. Only if the church were fully converted, that is, had arrived at a complete and final understanding and practice of the gospel, would this not be true. The New Testament depicts the church realistically as a church being continually converted. The ongoing evangelization of the

13. Among the many theologians whose writings focus upon the character of the mission community, I refer to Dietrich Bonhoeffer, *Life Together,* trans. John W. Doberstein (New York: Harper and Row, 1954); Johannes Blauw, *The Missionary Nature of the Church: A Survey of the Biblical Theology of Mission* (New York: McGraw-Hill, 1962); Stanley Hauerwas, *Community of Character: Toward a Constructive Christian Social Ethic* (Notre Dame and London: University of Notre Dame Press, 1981); Gerhard Lohfink, *Jesus and Community: The Social Dimension of Christian Faith,* trans. J. P. Galvin (Philadelphia: Fortress, 1984); John Howard Yoder, *The Royal Priesthood: Essays Ecclesiological and Ecumenical,* ed. Michael G. Cartwright (Grand Rapids: Eerdmans, 1994).

14. Germane to this discussion is Inagrace Dietterich's exposition, "Reconciliation: Cultivating Communities of Mutual Accountability," in Guder, *Missional Church,* pp. 166ff, and the literature cited there.

community happens precisely in the give-and-take of disagreement among Christians. There is where the powerful love of Jesus Christ as the Prince of Peace is incarnated.

Acts develops its missional theology as it documents early Christian disagreements that led to profound passages of continuing conversion. Suspicion of the expanding mission of Christ in Samaria (Acts 8:4-25) is replaced by joy at the unexpected work of the Spirit there. Deeply engrained prejudices are transformed by the conversion of the Ethiopian eunuch (Acts 8:26-40). Peter's encounter with Cornelius (Acts 10) leads him through a spiritual battle with God to a conversion to the gospel that crosses all boundaries and leaves no one out. The controversy about Gentile Christians is resolved by the Council of Jerusalem (Acts 15) in a way which serves as a model for the incarnational witness in situations of disagreement. There, the Christian community confesses that God's Spirit works through compromises that are the result of honest struggle among disagreeing Christians.

In Paul's letters, we see reported instances of such struggles. The apostle's response is invariably a combination of clear teaching and even-handed correction, coupled with compassion and the acknowledgment that those with whom he disagreed were no less Christian than he. Every one of those controversies was, in fact, an occasion for the continuing conversion of the church. Maintaining unity in the midst of disagreement and controversy was, for the apostle, a priority of the church that is faithful to its Lord.

If a congregation is experiencing its own continuing conversion, it will be unsettling to many who are part of it. There will be many responses to the missional gospel message. The missional thrust of the biblical account will not always please everyone. We are not necessarily open to hearing what it meant in Jesus' day for him to spend time with lepers and Samaritans and women of the street. When we begin to grasp that Jesus chose his disciples from the margins of society, we may be offended. We may not want to hear about the profound threat to faith which wealth always means. Loving our enemies is not everyone's idea of "victorious Christian living." We would rather not see ourselves reflected in the religious leaders of Jesus' day, against whom Jesus' most trenchant criticism was (and is) directed.

While some will not like hearing familiar passages interpreted in unfamiliar ways, others will be challenged and grateful. Every minister can report about such diverse reactions. They are unavoidable in the church that is moving toward conversion: such change is threatening to some and exciting to others. The pace and rhythm of congregational converting is not uniform.

Our contemporary situation contributes in many ways to divisiveness and controversy in the church. The history of modern skepticism has created theological factions in the church, as I noted in chapter 1. Those who respond to the canons and claims of modernity by adapting the faith to it come down in very different places from those who resist every compromise with modernity. On every side, we see threats to the church's incarnational witness, especially in the so-called single-issue battles such as abortion, human sexuality, capital punishment, and pluralism. Such concerns must receive the serious attention of Christians. They are all potent expressions of gospel faithfulness as well as risky possibilities for gospel betrayal. Yet, the real challenge for the church is not so much these difficult problems as it is the way we deal with them. Clarity about the church's missionary nature and honesty about its need for continuing conversion will enable us to deal with these problems in more authentically evangelizing ways.

The worldwide expansion of the church has produced a great variety of ways in which Christians worship, organize themselves, and do mission. Often, these cultural differences are a bone of contention. Now, in North America, we live daily with multicultural realities. Our colonial history has meant that, from the outset, North American society would be multicultural. Our conquest of the Native Americans, our history of slavery, and our formation by waves of immigrants have ensured that we must always contend with the fact of many cultures living within the same country and contributing to the same culture. This is the fundamental cultural challenge for our churches as well. It is also sadly true that our primary way of dealing with this challenge has been through various forms of segregation and of domination of minorities by the white majority. The integrity of the incarnational witness of predominantly white American denominational churches is on the line when they address the multicultural reality of North America. It starts, for many of them, with the way they deal with the Korean, Chinese, Southeast Asian, Hispanic, and Native American congregations that are a part of the churchly reality in North America. These communities are rapidly growing and often threaten the established forms of the church, creating tension and disagreement. Here again is a specific place for faithful incarnational witness to the gospel in an area of possible tension. The majority traditions may experience their own conversion as they discover in these challenges by marginal or burgeoning minorities that they are in fact instruments of the gospel calling the majority to repentance and new life.

The whole process of disestablishment raises questions about the Western church's appropriate role within society. Church people often disagree on these issues. Every American congregation that has an American flag standing somewhere in the sanctuary is inviting a discussion about the relationship of the church to public culture, and that discussion is seldom without heat. Some Christians decide to enter military service, even to become military chaplains. Other Christians see in pacifism the only responsible form of obedience to Christ in our violent world. These views must be worked through within the community as a witness to the reconciling power of the gospel.

It is never easy. Once, while I was a theology student, I taught an adult Sunday School lesson on the theme, "What the church is not for." After the class, I was confronted by an outraged layman. He could barely speak, he was so beside himself. I had stressed in my lesson that the church was called and set apart by God for its witness to Jesus Christ. That witness meant that it was not the primary task of the church to serve other purposes and organizational goals than those of Christ and his kingdom. Being young and brash, I used some examples that were risky. I said that it was not the mission of the church to serve a particular party's political agenda. It was not the mission of the church to assert the superiority of a particular culture or social order. It was not the mission of the church to preserve a particular liturgical or musical tradition, or a particular kind of architecture. Certainly Christianity could not be equated with American nationalism. Nor was it the mission of the church to devote itself to anticommunism. That week in that city, there had been a major Christian effort to mobilize churches against the threat of communism. My outraged critic, as it turned out, was a major organizer of that effort. For him, there was only one thing the church was for: to fight communism. He could not grasp how "loving one's enemies" or "being zealous to maintain the bond of unity in the Spirit of peace" had anything to do with the gospel. The gospel was a defined cultural territory that we had to defend, especially against its communist enemies. Our conversation that day was not an example of how Christians can disagree in a way that still points to the lordship and love of Christ!

It was important to me then (and now) to stress that the biblical summons to follow and to obey Christ means that our marching orders have to do with the gracious kingdom of God. To witness to Christ incarnationally must always mean that we are moving between the fronts drawn by warring human parties, both inside and outside the church. Where others draw lines and assign people to camps, the mission community demonstrates that, in Christ, we can tear down walls and become friends, even brothers and sisters, of those who are completely different from us or even disagree profoundly with us. That is what happened in the circle of Jesus' disciples when a Jewish Zealot, opposed to Roman occupation, and a tax collector serving the Roman authorities became followers of the same Lord and brothers of each other. Our Lord is our king, and that divine royalty supersedes all other loyalties. If that powerful gospel message is going to make any sense at all in a divided and rancorous environment like ours, then it is all the more urgent that the mission community demonstrate the peace-making power of Christ inside our ranks.

Those responsible for the ministry of the Word in a church which is being converted will lay out the biblical story as God's good news and let the biblical witness challenge us constantly in our reductionisms. As I said, our continuing conversion does not proceed at the same pace and in the same way. The continuing conversion of the church is, therefore, evidenced in the ways that we learn to be patient and honest with each other. Paul put it succinctly: "lead a life worthy of the calling to which you have been called, with all humility and gentleness, with patience, bearing with one another in love" (Eph. 4:1-2). "Bearing with one another" really means, "Put up with each other!"

The Witness of Church Membership[15]

In the Western tradition of Christianity, Christian identity is usually defined as church "membership." This way of describing what it means

15. See also my discussion in *Missional Church*, pp. 243ff.

to be Christian is probably rooted in Paul's extensive use of the term "member," especially in 1 Corinthians. "Now you are the body of Christ and individually members of it" (1 Cor. 12:27). Here, the image of the body with its members is the context. The emphasis is upon the way in which Christians are linked to each other in Christ and depend upon each other. It is a very important interpretation of our calling. As we study Paul's usage missionally, we can say a lot about how incarnational witness functions organically, that is, as the concerted action of related members. Membership, in this organic sense, is an essential aspect of the "how" of Christian mission.

Gospel reductionism has, however, led us far from that dynamic and incarnational understanding of membership. As the church focused more on the benefits of salvation enjoyed by the individual Christian, membership came to mean "saved." In the same way, as the church redefined itself as the institution that administers salvation, its membership was understood as the rights and privileges of those who were receiving the benefits of that salvation. Baptism came to be understood as the event that put the person into the status of "saved," which was then maintained within the disciplines of the church. Following the passage called confirmation, admission to the Lord's Supper was then primarily admission to the main source for the continuing grace of salvation. As a communicant, one was a full member of the church. Nonmembership meant "unsaved": *extra ecclesiam nullus salus* — "outside the church there is no salvation" (Cyprian). Excommunication was a very threatening thing, because it put one's salvation in jeopardy.

That reduced understanding of membership has persisted over the entire history of Western Christianity, through the Reformation into the modern period. With it, there has been a constant awareness of the problem of "nominal" Christianity, that is, people who "name" themselves Christian, who maintain a minimal level of faith commitment and practice, but for whom the vocation to serve Christ does not define their lives. For vast numbers of those within the culture of Christendom, church membership has been, as a rule, nominal. As I discussed in chapter 1, the actual emergence of the term and practice of "evangelism" was largely a reaction to growing nominalism in late Christendom. There have always been reactions, of course. The monastic movements were a reaction to the shallowness of general church membership. So were the pre-Reformation movements such as the Waldensians and the Hussites.

The Reformation attempted to deal with the issue of nominal Christianity in a variety of ways. The translation of the Bible into the vernacular languages, the formulation of catechisms, the establishment of parish schools to train the laity — all these were important steps to move people from the "implicit faith" of medieval Catholicism to the "explicit faith" of biblically literate Christians. Luther could imagine what it would be like to have a church made up of "people who with all seriousness wanted to be Christians," but he concluded that he was not going to find them. The disciplines of the Swiss Reformed churches were a serious attempt to develop more consciously Christian communities, but they often foundered in legalism and a rigidity that was not an incarnational witness to the gospel. The spirit of nominal Christianity was unavoidable in the establishment structure of the church, which the major streams of the Reformation preserved. From the sixteenth century onward, the "believers' churches" of the Radical Reformation have been a very instructive and prophetic alternative to the structural patterns of the major Reformation traditions with their nominal membership.[16] The way in which the Radical Reformation movements were persecuted by both Catholic and Protestant established churches testifies to the church's failure to incarnate the gospel faithfully.

After the Reformation, the challenge of nominal membership in the established traditions was reflected in the emergence of movements like Pietism. In such movements, various attempts were made to bring Christians to a more conscious and disciplined commitment to Christ and his mission. Membership in the larger church was so often a diluted reality that special movements and organizations instituted something like a second level of membership. That way of dealing with reductionistic membership continues today. There are innumerable networks and movements which draw together Christians who want to "go beyond" the normal level of commitment of the nominal church member.

Membership has become a spiritually even more questionable de-

16. See Donald F. Durnbaugh, *The Believers' Church: The History and Character of Radical Protestantism* (New York: Macmillan, 1968).

scription of Christian identity in North America. When membership is defined in terms of the church as voluntary society, it becomes almost entirely a matter of an individual's decision. It is an organizational matter. People choose their church membership in ways that parallel other memberships they opt for. There is, for many, little of the sense of mission and Christian interdependence that were at the heart of Paul's teaching about membership. At the beginning of the American experiment, there was some rigor attached to church membership, at least in the New England colonies. But over time, these practices have become less demanding. American revivalism in the nineteenth century, with its emphasis upon personal salvation and the benefits of religion, contributed to the dilution of membership as a discipline. As a result, most mainline churches maintain what is, interestingly, called a "low threshold" to church membership. It is more difficult to become a member of many service clubs than to join most Protestant congregations.

Every minister of the Word has struggled with the resulting superficiality of general understandings of church membership. Many are the attempts to realign the practices of church membership. Congregations set up rigorous church membership classes and require that prospective members comply. Many congregations take the task of confirmation very seriously and work with their young people to ensure that when they become adult members they know what they are doing. But the dilution of membership is clearly deeply rooted now in our culture. Nothing illustrates that more than the ease with which people stop being members of churches.

When I was on the pastoral staff of a large congregation on the West Coast of North America, a woman came to me to ask me to baptize her infant child. I asked her, as a matter of course, if she were a member of our congregation. She said that she was not, but was on the rolls of a sister congregation in another part of the city. I said that she should go to her own church to have her child baptized, since it was really an act of the whole community and not just her action. But she was not attending that church regularly anymore and did not like it. Instead, she was going regularly to a third Presbyterian congregation in yet another part of the city. When I asked her why she did not transfer her membership to the church she was now attending and have her infant baptized there, since that would be the Christian family in which her child would grow up, she replied with some annoyance, "Well, they have this requirement that you attend eight membership classes, and I don't want to do it." It was my duty then to explain to her that I could not baptize her child in our congregation, with which she had no real ties. I suggested that she resolve the problems of her own church membership and then celebrate her child's baptism in that part of the family where these vows were going to be fulfilled in practice. It was hard for her, with her very typical understandings of nominal membership, to understand what was at stake here.

This reductionism of the concept and practice of membership is a compelling example of the church's need for conversion. It reveals how far from the missional understanding of her vocation the church has moved in practice. We reveal what we think Christian witness is all about with the standards and practices we establish for becoming a Christian. If we accept a "lowest common denominator" definition of Christian commitment, then we should not be surprised that our congregations evidence so little commitment to gospel mission.

This problem is clearly seen by many theologians. Karl Barth's comprehensive discussion of baptism, and especially of infant baptism, fleshed out many of the fundamental problems of nominal Christian membership as practiced in the churches of the Western tradition.[17] William Abraham has suggested that evangelism must be understood as "initiation into the kingdom"[18] and should require a process over time that is "corporate, cognitive, moral, experiential, operational, and disciplinary."[19] This means that there must be a process of initiation which moves from pre-baptismal instruction, through baptism, to thorough grounding in the creeds and spiritual disciplines of the church. Rather than a low threshold, there will be a carefully conducted catechetical process which leads to an understanding and practice of membership that is shaped by the mission of the kingdom of God.

Patrick Keifert, from the Lutheran tradition, is arguing in the same direction: "The church needs to move beyond making members to making Christians, disciples of Jesus the Messiah."[20] He shares this

17. Karl Barth, "Baptism with Water," *Church Dogmatics,* trans G. W. Bromiley, IV/4, fragment (Edinburgh: T. & T. Clark, 1969), especially pp. 165ff.

18. Abraham, *Logic of Evangelism,* p. 95 and passim.

19. Abraham, *Logic of Evangelism,* p. 103.

20. Patrick R. Keifert, *Welcoming the Stranger: A Public Theology of Worship and Evangelism* (Minneapolis: Fortress, 1992), p. 118.

conviction with Robert Webber, who has also argued that there must be a disciplined process of incorporation into the Christian community through liturgical worship.[21] Both propose that the church revive traditions going back to the third-century practice of the catechumenate. Keifert envisions a two-year process in which the prospective member of the church is led through seven passages: "(1) a period of inquiry; (2) the rite of entrance, which marks the beginning of (3) the time of instruction; (4) the rite of election, which precedes (5) an intense spiritual preparation for baptism; and finally (6) the rite of baptism and (7) the process of continuing nurture in the church."[22]

I strongly concur with these writers and their trenchant critique of the reductionism of church membership that is so pervasively rooted in our Western Christian institutions. To go one step further, one might ask if the conversion of the church must mean that we do away with the understanding and practice of membership as we have developed it over centuries. It is so laden with the gospel reductionism that is our problem that it cannot function for the incarnational witness to which we are called. Robert Webber and Rodney Clapp have stated the challenge concisely:

> The church is not a club where people with common hobbies meet. It is not a voluntary association, such as the American Medical Association, in which members guard and tend to their shared interests. Nor is it simply a helping organization, an Alcoholics Anonymous that people seek out after they determine they have an unmanageable problem. People choose to join AA or a civic club but, in that sense, no one really "joins" the church. The members of the church are called, gathered together by the God who showed himself in Jesus Christ.[23]

The public worship of the mission community should be open and welcoming to all. There should be no threshold at all with regard

---

21. Robert Webber, *Celebrating Our Faith: Evangelism through Worship* (San Francisco: Harper and Row, 1986).

22. Keifert, *Welcoming the Stranger,* pp. 100-101; the process is described in detail on pp. 101-7.

23. Robert Webber and Rodney Clapp, *People of the Truth: A Christian Challenge to Contemporary Culture* (Harrisburg: Morehouse Publishing, 1993), p. 53.

to the witness of faith that takes place in public worship. Our worship should be like the wonderful experience of worship in burgeoning African churches. The Christian community in a village puts up a framework with a roof in the middle of village, and the Christians gather under the roof to praise God and hear the gospel. Around the building, the villagers who are not yet Christians stand, sharing in the entire experience — there are no walls to obstruct their seeing and hearing of all that Christians do when they worship. The evangelistic witness of such public worship bears fruits as they move from the ranks of observers to join in the worship.

Although there is much about the movement of "mega-churches" and "seeker-friendly" churches in North America to raise concerns, they are demonstrating one thing in a compelling way: it is needful and possible to gather for public worship in ways which can include the non-believer.[24] This is an essential aspect of incarnational witness. One should not have to be a member to be a participant in the public worship of the church.

Nor should membership be linked primarily with financial support. This is an extremely important aspect of incarnational witness whose implications go far beyond the limits of this book (although they will be addressed to a degree in the next chapter). It is, however, a fateful reductionism to link membership with regular giving as its major concrete expression. As important as sacrificial giving to the work of Christ's church is, it must be interpreted in such a way that it never appears to function as "membership dues" or as "the price of admission." One might envision a structure of financial support that invites people to accept a responsibility for the congregation's life, regardless of where they might be in their spiritual pilgrimage. The observer who is on the fringes of faith but moving gradually into the circle, to use the African image, should be invited, never pressured, to support the community as much as the most committed member. It is clear that this is an area fraught with problems. Fundraising is both a major preoccupation of congregations and a major source of resistance to the church in our

---

24. The difficulty, as I stated above, is that often today the entire communicative system of contemporary worship is shaped by the unbelieving world and what it wants and needs; the task is to communicate in culturally understandable ways while confronting the culture with the undiluted gospel.

secular society. Nowhere is the continuing conversion of the church more urgently needed than in its bondage to the bottom line.

For the local congregation to become truly a mission community, the seventh step in "liturgical evangelism" proposed by Keifert, Webber, and Clapp needs to be developed much more extensively. Keifert describes this step as the "time of continued instruction" following initiation, in the six weeks of Easter. The early church spoke of it as *mystagogia*, a passage which focuses upon "the deepening of the awareness that baptized ones have of the Eucharist, the church, and the world. . . . In contrast to the usual pattern of conversion and evangelism, this period tries deliberately to integrate the newly baptized into the down-to-earth mystery of the church in the world."[25] This should be expanded into a comprehensive definition of the congregation's ministry with regard to the calling to "be Christ's witnesses." The concept of membership as a status, an accomplished level of spiritual attainment, must be replaced with a lifelong process of calling and response that could be called "vocation to mission." This should take place at a number of levels within a congregation.

At the level of the individual Christian, the process of initiation described above leads to incorporation in the mission community as one who shares responsibility for its mission. In a process similar to the catechesis leading to incorporation, Christians should be challenged singly, as families, and as groups with a common sense of their specific vocation to seek out the specific shape of their ministry. The community should provide forms of instruction and spiritual formation that lead Christians to identify a specific vocation, perhaps for a specific period of time. Often, in Western societies, this will be linked with the place and form of their daily work. The mandate "to lead lives worthy of the calling to which we have been called" must be translated into specific arenas of ministry for the local congregation.

Let me illustrate what I mean with some experiences I have had with people who were committed to serving Christ's mission and who found that their experience as church members did not help them very much in pursuing that goal. My father is a particularly important example for me. He was a certified public accountant who wanted very much to carry out his vocation as a Christian witness in his profession. He

25. Keifert, *Welcoming the Stranger,* p. 106.

struggled with the ethical conflicts of the world of finance and taxes. He carried his faith in his own very quiet and noncoercive way into all his en-counters with clients, often challenged by their desire to cut corners and manipulate the system. He remarked more than once that it was very dif-ficult to find some way within our church to learn biblically and doctrin-ally how to incarnate Christ's rule in the practice of public accounting. The tendency was rather to compartmentalize life and leave those broad areas relatively untouched by the rule of God. This he could not do. He did talk about his concerns with other lay persons in the business world and found some encouragement and guidance. But most of what he did he worked out alone, interpreting his own lifelong study of the Bible and the faith in his daily professional life. He spoke about it little; he was modest in the claims he would make about his faithfulness as a mission-ary in the business world. But when he died (at the age of forty-nine), the business community in the city where he had his company came to the family in surprising numbers to tell us that he had been a man of distinc-tive integrity. They knew that he was doing his business with different goals and attitudes from most. He was trusted, respected, relied upon. He became for many the definition of an honest businessman. But he had to do that without any sense of commissioning from his church that this was his calling, nor was he ever able to find support or guidance in di-rectly relevant ways.

A lawyer told me once that he could never tell his pastor what he was really dealing with every day in his office. The kinds of decisions he was having to make fell completely outside the perspective of the themes one could discuss at church. He felt himself to be alone as a Christian witness in the turbulent world of litigation, and yet he also knew that he was called to incarnate the gospel there. I could repeat in-stances of such conversations with people from every aspect of the world of work.

My understanding of this challenge was profoundly changed by a short conversation one day with Margaret. She and her husband were pillars of our church, gifted, committed, gracious representatives of Christ. She was a children's librarian at the main library of our city. She took her work very seriously. I was constantly going to her to ask her to serve on this committee or take on that responsibility in the church. She would always refuse, in a kind but very firm way. Finally, in my frustration, I asked her why she would not take on more work in the congregation, when we needed such talent desperately. She said to me, "Darrell, my calling is to be a children's librarian. It takes a great deal of work and study to be good at what I do. I want to represent Christ there, and that has to be my priority." That experience was a step of continuing conversion for me. I began to realize then, and continue to explore this insight now, that every Christian community should see itself as a community of missionaries. Its responsibility to them is to guide them to identify God's calling, to recognize the gifts and opportunities they have, to provide them the biblical and theological training to incarnate the gospel in their particular fields, and then to commission them to that ministry. Our structures of membership need to be transformed into disciplines of sending.

Some congregations have adopted the practice of speaking of the whole congregation as "the ministers" or the "servants" of Christ. One could make that understanding much more tangible by continuing the process of liturgical evangelism in a congregational discipline of calling and commissioning to mission. This should take place with individuals, families, and groupings in the congregation. Individuals might explore their vocation in their places of work or avocation. Or they might sense God's calling in the particular relationships in which they live: as parents, as adult children of aging parents, or as friends. Families might be encouraged to examine their place and opportunities in their neighborhoods or extended families as vocations to mission. For whoever seeks the congregation's support and guidance for mission, there should be a process of nurturing which leads to the commissioning of individuals or families.

In a similar way, groups in congregations which sense a common interest in a particular mission should be prepared for that work and mandated to it by the congregation. This is done in many congregations for functions within the parish program, such as Sunday School teachers and church officers. But it should be open to all who sense God's Spirit calling and gifting them for a particular expression of incarnational mission. People like Margaret, my father, and the lawyers in the congregation should all be invited into a process of spiritual nurture leading to their formal commissioning to their ministry. The group which sees a great opportunity for incarnating Christ in prison ministry should have the opportunity to deepen their vocation in focused Bible study and be commissioned for that work. The retired people who want to tutor inner-city children can receive support and guidance for that difficult task, both in the form of commissioning and continuing support.

Such structures of vocation to ministry should become the basic understanding of membership in the mission community. In public worship, there should be regular celebrations of calling and commissioning. The intercessory prayer of the community should specifically support the congregation's "local missionaries." Within the gatherings of the congregation, their experiences, challenges, disappointments, and blessings should be reported and learned from.

If a mission community saw itself primarily as the Spirit's steward of the calling and gifts of its members, its internal activities would, in one sense, diminish. It would spend much less time on providing activities that take its members out of the world. It would devote more of its times of gathering for the equipping, support, and accountability of its member-missionaries. The ancient sense of the conclusion of public worship as the sending out of God's people (*ita, missa est* – go, you are sent) would be translated into the concrete forms of congregational life. Our concept of "active church member" would, of course, have to change. We would expect to see less of our more mature and accountable members, and focus more of our gathered time on the young, the new Christians, those in training for their missionary vocation.

Every aspect of congregational life, shaped by the legacy of previous generations, is subject to conversion by God's Spirit for mission. We have looked at the difficult problems of disagreement and of membership as representative of the local congregation's need for conversion. As we come to terms with the Christendom legacy, there are obviously many forms of reductionism that could and need to be addressed. The issues of disagreement and membership ultimately relate to one of the broadest and profoundest of contextual adaptations made by the Western church: the compromises with power brought about by the Constantinian establishment. The church, which was once pacifist, found itself within a few centuries endorsing theologies of just war. This reduction of the gospel stands as a symbol of the challenging conversions which lie yet ahead of the post-Christendom church.[26] An even

---

26. See especially John Milbank, *Theology and Social Theory: Beyond Secular Reason* (Oxford, UK, and Cambridge, MA: Blackwell, 1990).

more daunting task awaits us as we gradually begin to question the implications of the centuries-long debate about usury and the ecclesial decisions made from the sixteenth century onward not only to allow but to regulate the taking of interest.

Evangelism is truly the heart of ministry when the gospel's mission shapes both the purpose and the methods of all that we do in our local congregations, beginning with our corporate repentance. "God through his revelation, especially through the Incarnation, set the agenda for the Church."[27] The promised Holy Spirit can empower every mission community to use its redeemed creativity to discover what the specific shape of that agenda in its locale will be. What connects all local congregations to one another and forms the church catholic is the dominical mandate: You shall be my witnesses. That witnessing community evangelizes, communicates good news, as it is itself evangelized. Its evangelization and continuing conversion will always begin with its contrite struggle with its conformities. As we respond to the gospel, we become its messengers to the world into which God is sending us. Our continuing conversion is essential to our sending.

---

27. Louis J. Luzbetak, *The Church and the Cultures: New Perspectives in Missiological Anthropology* (Maryknoll, NY: Orbis Books, 1988), p. 43.

Chapter Eight

The Conversion of the Institutional Church

[T]he way the church must always respond to the challenge of our polity is to be herself. This does not involve a rejection of the world, or a withdrawal from the world; rather it is a reminder that the church must serve the world on her own terms. We must be faithful in our own way, even if the world understands such faithfulness as disloyalty.[1]

The Basic Tension

Very early on in his magisterial study of mission, *Transforming Mission: Paradigm Shifts in Theology of Mission,* David Bosch makes some rather sweeping statements about the failures of the early church. He addresses two related "failures." The first is the more basic one: the very early dilution and reduction of the gospel of the kingdom of God to a manageable religion whose adherents' concern was their survival as a distinct religious group.[2] This reductionism of the gospel of God's reign is, as I have suggested above, the major challenge to incarnational

---

1. Stanley Hauerwas, *A Community of Character: Toward a Constructive Christian Social Ethic* (Notre Dame and London: University of Notre Dame Press, 1981), p. 85.
2. David Bosch, *Transforming Mission: Paradigm Shifts in Theology of Mission* (Maryknoll, NY: Orbis Books, 1991), pp. 50-52.

mission, and it is the place where the church is constantly called to its own continuing conversion. Bosch's second "failure" addresses the theme of this gospel reductionism as it relates to the institutional church: the transition of the early Christian movement into an institution.

Calling on distinctions made by H. Richard Niebuhr, Bosch defines the difference between institution and movement with these ideas: "[T]he one is conservative, the other progressive; the one is more or less passive, yielding to influences from outside, the other is active, influencing rather than being influenced; the one looks to the past, the other to the future."[3] He adds, "[T]he one is anxious, the other is prepared to take risks; the one guards boundaries, the other crosses them." Across Christian history the challenge has been to form the church's institution to serve its mission, and the problem has been the ways in which the institution has taken over and shaped the mission. That institutional takeover has invariably been reductionistic of the gospel and the church's missional vocation.

This much-discussed tension can be described in many ways. We hear of the distinction between "order" and "ardor" in Christian ministry. Others prefer to distinguish between "organism" and "organization," implying that the organism is vital, pulsing, energetic, full of the Spirit (and it is assumed that this Spirit is Holy), and the latter is stolid, arid, lifeless, lacking in all spirituality. One should then, at all costs, continue as an organism and avoid becoming an organization.

The missional problem posed by institutional structures may be illumined by considering Ralph Winter's approach. He describes this tension in a less judgmental and more helpful way as the interaction between the "modality" and the "sodality" of the church.[4] By modality, Winter means the comprehensive, cross-generational, cradle-to-grave Christian community that embraces all followers of Christ, however one distinguishes between the visible and the invisible church. The so-

---

3. Bosch, *Transforming Mission,* pp. 50f.

4. Ralph D. Winter, "The Two Structures of God's Redemptive Mission," *Missiology* 2, no. 1 (January 1974): 121-39; Ralph D. Winter and R. Pierce Beaver, *The Warp and the Woof: Organizing for Mission* (South Pasadena: William Carey Library, 1970); Ralph D. Winter, "The New Missions and the Mission of the Church," *International Review of Mission* 60, no. 237 (January 1971): 89-100.

dality, on the other hand, is the intentional, decisional grouping of like-minded Christians who focus their energies upon a particular task within the larger mission of the church, which links us all to each other. For Winter, the sodality is represented by the Pauline mission, by the religious orders, by modern missionary societies, and to some degree, by the so-called parachurch movements and organizations of the twentieth century.

There are many other examples of this tension and attempts to understand it. The powerful influence of "enthusiasm" as defined by Ronald Knox[5] is a case in point: the so-called enthusiastic movements, ranging from first-century to twentieth-century charismatics, and including many important renewal movements, have both enriched and divided the church.[6] These movements are always defined in contrast to the more stable, traditional, continuing church structures, out of which they emerge and with which they interact. They usually claim to have received some particular guidance or gift from the Holy Spirit that empowers and authorizes them to move outside the existing church structures. Often they can be interpreted as a reaction to deficiencies in the church's traditional structures. Their rejection of the church's authority has frequently meant that they have become divisive and ended up as marginalized sects. In other instances they have found ways to integrate their particular calling into the diversity of the church's ministries. The Catholic orders and the Protestant missionary societies are an example of such integration. With regard to the development of evangelistic ministry in the twentieth century, the case can be made that many of the evangelistic movements that have sprung up next to the established church structures (parachurch organizations) are contemporary forms of enthusiasm.

Karl Barth made the constructive suggestion that we distinguish between the more traditional and ongoing structures of the church and what he called the "special working fellowships of the church" — stipulating that they were all validly part of "the commu-

---

5. Ronald A. Knox, *Enthusiasm* (New York/London: Oxford University Press, 1950).

6. Students of the Protestant Reformation encounter this phenomenon in the *Schwärmer* with whom Luther fought so strenuously. The term *Schwärmer* means "fanatics," but it is usually translated "enthusiasts" in the technical sense developed by Knox.

nion of the Holy Ghost."[7] His criteria for such working fellowships can help us to analyze the real points of tension today among the diverse forms of ministry institutions which have become a major characteristic of the church's organizational geography. His approach to the institutional diversity of such "special working fellowships" is thoroughly missional. He understands that the one unifying mission of the church can express itself in a variety of organizational ways. Such organizations will carry out "the activity demanded of all Christians," but they will do so in a distinctive way: they will render "a particular service . . . in common in a particular form of thought, speech, and action, Christian witness being given in a particular way." Their validity is determined, for Barth, by three tests. First, their particular ministry must be based "on divine gifts and endowments received in concert, and not on the arbitrariness and self-will of common whims and impressions." Second, their ministry should take place "within the 'communion of the Holy Ghost,'" and not disrupt it.[8] Finally, they should be genuine working fellowships whose purpose is not to meet the needs of their members, but "to achieve in closer fellowship the ministry and witness of the community in the world." This approach to a difficult institutional tension illustrates a profoundly missiological way to deal with the concrete questions of ministry's form and function.

When we look over the entire organizational history of the church, we can see a genuine and necessary multiplicity of forms of missional ministry, which is rooted in the very nature and calling of the church. It appears that the work of God's Spirit in carrying out the mission of God is not to be restricted to one institutional form. Whenever

---

7. Karl Barth, *Church Dogmatics*, trans. G. W. Bromiley, IV, 3/2 (Edinburgh: T. & T. Clark, 1962), p. 856. The discussion summarized below is found on this page.

8. This test does not work in North America, of course. There is no ecclesiastical agency that could "certify" a ministry organization as being "within the communion of the Holy Ghost." Every religious organization is, by definition, a private and voluntary society with equal legal status. For Presbyterians, for instance, any organization or ministry that is not under the umbrella of the General Assembly is a problem. Barth's test works in Europe for both the Roman Catholic Church and the established Protestant churches. For the church in North America, this deficiency points to an ecumenical need which is not currently being addressed: the development of structures of relationship, cooperation, and fellowship among the diversity of ecclesial organizations, denominations, and parachurch agencies.

the church tries to do that, there is reaction, both in the form of renewal and in the form of division. In terms of institutional structure, the Spirit does list where it will. This is a major place for the practice of incarnational witness: the way that various mission structures (including denominations) of the church relate to each other and work together is a demonstration of the character of our common faith and calling. Or, to put it negatively, where there is competition, rancor, and mutual renunciation, the gospel witness is diminished profoundly. The institutional formation of the church is unavoidable. There is no continuation of the Christian movement within history without institutional forms and patterns. Whether or not the missional church is an institution is, therefore, not really a question to be debated. The question, rather, is whether its institution supports and serves its missionary vocation. Does the institutional dimension of the church, as one necessary aspect of its existence in the world, incarnate the gospel of God's reign in Christ?

Diversity of Forms of Ministry in the New Testament

This tension is already found in the New Testament. New Testament scholars have helpfully pointed out that there was a pattern of diverse forms of ministry in the New Testament churches. One of the most instructive expressions of this diversity can be seen in the life and work of the Antiochene community, and the itinerant apostolic ministry of Paul and Barnabas, as both are described in Acts. The Antiochene community was the incarnational witness to Christ in that place, in that major city. Paul and Barnabas were among its most important leaders. In that resident community in Antioch, incarnational mission happened first of all in its corporate life as it lived out its witness within its pagan environment. Linked with that, the Antiochene church also sent out and supported the apostolic missionaries Paul and Barnabas, following closely the pattern established by Jesus as he sent out his missionaries. Thus, we have both modality and sodality in the Antiochene church. In addition to these two fundamental patterns of mission in the New Testament, we can also discern the mission activity of Johannine wandering preachers, especially in Palestine and Syria, mission patterns that ultimately fed into the ascetic forms of ministry that emerged in this area a few centuries later.[9]

There were always problems and challenges among these forms of mission community, as Bosch goes on to say. These tensions became the agenda of the "Apostolic Council" described in Acts 15 and Galatians 2. But the New Testament indicates that a creative tension was maintained between these types of ministry. Furthermore, the common conviction of all forms of New Testament community was that they were missional. They knew that the reason for their existence was their sentness, the calling to be the witness to Jesus Christ.

As I have discussed in chapters 2 and 3, this common sense of mission united the early Christian communities in all their diversity. It informed their struggles with their environments. It was the underlying issue in the problems addressed by the New Testament writings. "Mission is the mother of theology," as Martin Kähler said, and mission was the overriding identity and purpose of the first-century Christian communities. This consensus is underlined by the fact that the Gospel of John, probably one of the latest New Testament writings, is still so thoroughly missiological in its thrust. "As my Father has sent me, so send I you" is the basic theme of this Gospel, equipping Christian communities at the end of the first century for their mission.

The struggle of the institutional church, in all its diversity, has always been with the comprehensive claim of this gospel to define every aspect of the mission community's life, including its institutional structures and practices. This does not appear to have been a matter of debate for the New Testament church. It is abundantly clear from a study of all levels of the New Testament that these communities understood themselves to be sent out as representatives of Christ, as his Body, and thus to represent him in his self-giving love to the world. The way in which the New Testament communities were to live was what Stuhlmacher has called "the missionary lifestyle of the congregation,"[10] asserting that

---

9. Peter Stuhlmacher, "Weg, Stil, Konsequenzen urchristlicher Mission," *Theologische Beiträge* 12. Jahrgang, 1981, pp. 130ff; Georg Kretschmar, "Das christliche Leben und die Mission in der frühen Kirche," in Heinzgünter Frohnes u. Uwe W. Knorr, Herausgeber, *Kirchengeschichte als Missionsgeschichte, Bd. I, Die alte Kirche* (München: Chr. Kaiser Verlag, 1974), pp. 94-100.

10. P. Stuhlmacher, "Weg, Stil, Konsequenzen urchristlicher Mission," *Theologische Beiträge* 12. Jahrgang, 1981, p. 118.

there is throughout the New Testament a continuing emphasis upon "the way, style, and consequences of primitive Christian mission."

Thus, it is essential to New Testament mission that the Christian community, as it necessarily institutionalizes, do so in an incarnational fashion, that is, in a way which continues to demonstrate, invite, and initiate people into the knowledge and service of Christ. This is where our history and our current reality confront us. How can an institution be incarnationally missional? Is this perhaps to require the impossible? Can we as Christian communities so be shaped by God's Spirit that our institutional structures themselves enflesh the compassionate and healing purposes of God?

The Inevitability of Institution

The problem with the transition from movement to institution, according to Bosch, is the loss of a creative tension, still found in Antioch, between the "settled ministry of bishops (or elders) and deacons, and the mobile ministry of apostles, prophets, and evangelists."[11] He goes on to say that this transition is unavoidable and inevitable. Movements do not remain movements: they either become institutions or they disappear. This is a sociological axiom. When a group of people gathers the second time to continue doing what they did when they gathered the first time, they have become an institution. Thus, the issue is not one of avoiding institutionalization. Movements that claim that they are not institutions are practicing self-delusion. In fact, the attempt to conceal the institutional reality, the attempt to maintain the facade of a movement while actually functioning as an institution, is a very dangerous one. The apparent spontaneity, charismatic adventurousness, and flexibility of such groups often camouflage highly manipulative and authoritarian leadership styles that are not subject to the controls and challenges which open institutional structures can provide.

The real problem, then, is not that movements become institutions. The problem is what happens to the central and driving mission

---

11. Bosch, *Transforming Mission,* p. 51. One is reminded of the way that Calvin conflates all the offices or functions in Eph. 4:11 into "the pastoral office" (*Institutes,* IV, iii, 4).

of the movement when this necessary transition takes place. Bosch speaks of this problem as a "loss of much of [the movement's] verve."

> Its white-hot convictions, poured into the hearts of the first adherents, cooled down and became crystallized codes, solidified institutions, and petrified dogmas. The prophet became a priest of the establishment, charisma became office, and love became routine. The horizon was no longer the world but the boundaries of the local parish. The impetuous missionary torrent of earlier years was tamed into a still-flowing rivulet and eventually into a stationary pond.[12]

This is a process that we observe over and over again in the history of the church. We see the same kind of loss of energy as we move from the generation of the Protestant Reformers into the period of Protestant orthodoxy. Before that, we can see similar fluctuations in the history of medieval monasticism, itself a reaction against the institutional deadness of the established church. New religious orders emerged to renew the church, but with time, they themselves had to struggle with the powers of institutional conservatism, the pressure to maintain what had now become its own institution.

It appears that the problem is more basic than a "loss of verve." It is not simply a psychological or emotional issue. There is, at the core of this constant pattern, a basic theological issue, which I have already addressed with the theme "reductionism" in chapters 5 and 6. I have described how, throughout our history, this recurring reductionism of our institutional mission means that we have forgotten how to read the New Testament as it was intended to be read, as the equipping of God's people for mission. When that interpretive key is missing in our biblical study, then every aspect of our ministry is reductionistic, that is, captive to a reduced and diluted version of the gospel.

Reductionism and the Institutional Church

I have described in considerable detail how the core of the church's missiological problem has always been the temptation to reduce the gospel to a manageable size. This is the first and most important "fail-

12. Bosch, *Transforming Mission*, p. 53.

ure" to which Bosch speaks. I examined that problem primarily with regard to the gospel reductionism that profoundly shapes the church's evangelistic ministry. Here, we need to examine the parallel impact upon the church's institutional shape. Whereas the early Christian community was established by Christ and empowered by the Holy Spirit to be a missionary people sent into the entire world as salt, light, and leaven, it began to be concerned with itself, with its identity, structure, and survival. "Their survival as a separate religious group, rather than their commitment to the reign of God, began to preoccupy them."[13]

This survival as a religion was linked with the church's growing perception that the gospel was primarily directed to meeting individual human needs. This meant from very early on, as discussed above, the reduction of the gospel to an individually and privately defined vision of salvation. This salvation was, quite rightly, understood as a fundamental change in the relationship between the person and God, and the assurance of life after death in heaven. Reductionism does not mean that what remains is wrong: it means that what remains is too little. The church, as it institutionalized, did not set aside the gospel; it reduced it and made it manageable. For the gospel of Jesus Christ, the King and the Lord to whom all authority has been given on heaven and on earth, is a message about God's healing and saving purposes which affect all the world, not merely each individual's eternal fate. It is, to use Newbigin's constant refrain, "public truth," and its implications are comprehensive, embracing all dimensions of life within God's creation.

The reduction of the gospel to the individual and personal dimensions of salvation had profound reductionistic implications for the institutional shape of the church. To summarize what was discussed at length in chapter 5: This reduced gospel shaped a church with a reduced mission. It was now to be focused upon the issue of personal salvation. This salvation was to be managed by the church with the administration of the sacraments and the distribution of grace, and it was all dependent upon the development of special offices of the church empowered to administer God's grace in churchly actions. Bosch calls this "the ecclesiasticization of salvation."[14] To restate an important qualification, the

---

13. Bosch, *Transforming Mission*, p. 50.
14. Bosch, *Transforming Mission*, pp. 217ff.

problem was not that the gospel was no longer heard. The problem was and is that the gospel is larger, more cosmic, more transforming, more revolutionary in its scope than such an individualized and privatized reduction of it reflects. The world of the principalities and powers is little challenged by a private and personal, vertical-relationship gospel. And that suits the powers and the principalities fine.

What this means for the problem of the institution is fundamentally missiological: the gospel mission in its incarnational breadth and depth is reduced and loses its formative power to shape the church. Rather, the church as institution shapes the gospel, that is, reduces the gospel to a message and a practice that fit within the necessary requirements of the church in order for this institution to maintain itself, to survive, to "conserve" itself. There is always pressure to tame the gospel. There is always resistance to the claims of Christ for total lordship. There is always a desire to move humans from the posture of sinners dependent upon grace to the stance of co-workers with God for the improvement of the world. In one way or another, we always find ourselves trying to fit the gospel into our categories, making it what the Germans call *salonfähig* (socially acceptable), assigning it the function of religion within our society.

As we have seen, this reductionism of the gospel has meant, almost invariably, a separation of the gospel message of salvation from the gospel message of the kingdom of God.[15] One of the continuing evidences of that fateful separation is the kind of evangelism, still widespread in North America, which claims that it can justify separating between the saviorhood of Jesus Christ and the lordship of Jesus Christ. There the reductionism is complete. Jesus as the source of a person's salvation is reduced to the level of one's salvation need; the claims of Jesus as Lord of life and history are reserved for another time and place. In effect, they are never heard, because such claims burst the boundaries of the safely reduced gospel which ensure that Christianity will never be as radical in our social setting as in fact it must be.

This separation is often linked to the fact that, since the revival movements of the last century, much evangelistic ministry is conducted by specialized organizations that exist next to the church for

---

15. Mortimer Arias, in *Announcing the Reign of God: Evangelization and the Subversive Memory of Jesus* (Philadelphia: Fortress, 1984), explains this "fateful separation" lucidly.

the purpose of evangelism. The so-called parachurch organizations, as a rule, make no claims to be the church or to function as congregations. "Evangelism" is their program or their product. The gospel proclaimed by such movements must necessarily be reductionistic, because it is separated from the incarnational witness of the mission community. Such an evangelistic message can have little sense of the incarnational witness that must be carried out by the people of God in every dimension of their life in the world. When evangelization is divided from the incarnational witness of God's people in community, the danger is very great that the gospel will be reduced to the minimum of personal salvation and private faith.[16]

Incarnational Mission and Institutions

I am defining incarnational mission as Christ's formation and sending of God's mission community, as Christ's witness and witnesses, to be the demonstration of, the invitation to, and the initiation into the kingdom of God. A truly incarnational definition of such mission, that is, a definition that is rooted in the person and work of Jesus Christ, must have profound implications for the way we make the transition from movement to institution. Its implications must relate to what happens to the connectional structures that the church forms, that is, to the various ways in which local congregations are linked with each other. The incarnational understanding of mission must continue to define the ways in which we function as institutions of mission, be it locally, regionally, nationally, or internationally. Whether we are in traditional ecclesiastical structures, such as an established church in Europe

---

16. It is not the purpose of this book to address the complex problem of church/parachurch tensions and relationships in North America, although they certainly are related to the continuing conversion of the church. The challenge to the many evangelistic parachurch organizations is to develop their communities as "special working fellowships" of the church, using the criteria proposed by Barth. The challenge to the traditional church structures is to take the initiative to form networks or structures of relationship and interaction with the parachurch agencies, so that through conversation, joint projects, and organizational cooperation, much of the present tension and competition could be reduced. Such steps would move toward the integrity of incarnational witness in the way all the affected institutions function.

or a North American voluntaristic denomination, or in a special working fellowship of the church or a parachurch agency, we are all confronted by the fundamental mandate of the incarnation of Christ as the content of our message and the definition of the way we carry out our mission institutionally.

The ecumenical discussion of the last twenty years has shown a growing interest in incarnational understandings of mission. We see this, for instance, in the growing emphasis upon our calling to go about our mission "in Jesus Christ's way."[17] When talking about incarnational ministry, mission, and witness, we recognize that we are being shaped by the continuing encounter with Jesus Christ as the one who is both the message bringer and the message himself. We respond to the wonderful and joyful news of God's love in Christ with the conviction that the witness to that love must itself be loving. We recognize that Jesus wants to be made known to others the way he made himself known during his earthly ministry: in love, in companionship, in relationships, in that unique compassion which is really suffering with and for us. We continue to explore the dimensions of incarnationally understood gospel and mission, and we continue to be challenged, if not converted, by what we discover. Regardless of the institutional shape of our ministry, we affirm that unconditional love is the way that God desires and empowers the gospel to be enfleshed.

As we embrace an incarnational understanding and practice of ministry, we also become aware of a profound inconsistency in our institutions. We watch our ecclesial structures struggle with numerical decline and financial jeopardy. We see power brokering and factions jockeying for privilege and money. Society's widespread suspicion of all institutions has become a fundamental attitude among church members. We must ask, Are our missional institutions, our churches and organizations, incarnational? Are we applying the fundamental biblical standard of gospel faithfulness to our institutional behavior? This is, I think, a true crux for us all in our desire to be faithful in our witness to Jesus Christ, our incarnate Lord.

17. Darrell Guder, "Incarnation and the Church's Evangelistic Message," *International Review of Mission* 83, no. 330 (July 1994): 417-28.

Institutional Captivities

Institutional structures, including those adopted by the church over time, are not invented out of thin air. They are adapted, in complex processes, from the institutional givens in the context into which the church enters. We know, for instance, that the early Christian churches were influenced by the synagogue as well as by public assemblies in the Hellenistic world, from which the apostolic community adopted the word *ecclesia* for this new mission community. We know that the secular patterns of authority from top down were gradually absorbed by the churches from somewhere in the second century on, with the result that we had monarchical bishops and ultimately a bishop over all the bishops, the pope in Rome. We can identify good reasons for many of these institutional developments. It is not seemly for us to judge the decision-making of our Christian predecessors, although we must deal responsibly and critically with the heritage of those decisions as they shape us and often restrict our faithful witness.

The institutionalization of the Christian mission community is one of the central aspects of what missiologists call "inculturation," or, in the words of Luzbetak, the "incarnation" of the gospel into a culture.[18] When the Christian message is translated into a culture, as I discussed in chapter 4, a mission community is formed in response to the gospel to continue that witness within that culture. Its institutional shape will be influenced by (1) the culture of the evangelist, who often came from another culture;[19] (2) the institutional givens of the receiving culture; and (3) the gospel itself as it enters, sanctifies, and converts cultures. When we look back over the history of Christian mission, we

18. Louis J. Luzbetak, *The Church and the Cultures: New Perspectives in Missiological Anthropology* (Maryknoll, NY: Orbis Books, 1988), pp. 69ff.

19. Another missional pattern is emerging today, as a result of the massive movement of peoples as refugees and economic migrants from Third to First World countries. Vietnamese settlers in North America, for example, are becoming Christians and returning to Vietnam as missionaries and church planters. The process of cultural translation has already begun before the mission process and continues with much less of the cultural clash which was frequently present in colonialist mission. There are similar patterns with many other ethnic groupings, suggesting that the North Atlantic missionary is being replaced by the missional witness of the North Atlantic churches within their own societies. There are, of course, precedents for this kind of evangelistic mission throughout the history of the church.

see fascinating processes where these three forms of cultural incarnation are at work. Many times, the evangelist has defined the cultural shape of the newly formed Christian community. Thus, we find in Africa Gothic churches and pastors clad in black gowns designed in medieval Europe. But, at the same time, God's Spirit has worked to re-shape faith communities in order to incarnate the gospel witness faithfully in different cultures. We are experiencing profound examples of this process in the base communities of Latin America, as well as in rapidly expanding Christian communities in Africa and southeast Asia. It has become very clear that Eurocentric or North Atlantic culture no longer defines the shape of Christianity around the world, as powerful as it still is in many ways.

It is in the third function that the dynamic power of the gospel is often curtailed in favor of cultural reductionism. Often, the culture makes the gospel captive. Any sense that the gospel must continue to challenge and convert the culture, must continue to summon the Christians to enflesh Jesus Christ, to "prolong the logic of Christ's ministry" (Bosch), is lost or greatly diluted. The most virulent forms of such cultural conditioning of the church and gospel reductionism are seen in the area of the church as institution. It appears to be a "principalities and powers" question: the gospel is quickly reduced when confronted with questions of institutional power, wealth, and influence. When Christian priests and pastors of warring nations bless the weapons and encourage the soldiers of their respective fronts with the message that their nationalist military goals may be equated with the Christian mission, then this reductionism is seen in its most dreadful form.

We can observe in the past and present many examples of institutional captivity to culture that effectively reduce the gospel and dilute Christian mission. In our Western history, the institutional church has allowed itself over and over again to be reshaped as a royal or imperial agency, serving the interests of the state. Although the German established church, the *Volkskirche,* is not a state church, one must still raise questions about the reductionism at work when the church is so profoundly conditioned by its privileged status within the German legal system. The church-state partnership continues to haunt us in our North American church traditions as well. One needs only to think of those American flags in sanctuaries across the country, which constantly baffle international visitors. Linked with the flags is the recurring theme of "America as the promised land" and "Americans as God's chosen people," ideas which are deeply rooted in our culture.

We have also shaped our mission after military models, whether it be the Crusades as perhaps the most disastrous model, or the rigorous militarism of Loyola's Jesuits, or the legalism of many discipleship movements today. Combined with the model of state agency, the military model has constantly led the Christian church to move far from the gospel in its appropriation and use of power. One might well say that the most telling form of institutional reductionism in our history resides at this point. Western Christianity has consistently removed from its understanding of the gospel Jesus' own renunciation of human power. It has interpreted away his command to love one's enemies, and replaced "taking up one's cross" with religious apologies for one's rights to self-defense, just war, capital punishment, carrying concealed arms, and political power-brokering. In spite of Jesus' admonition at the end of Matthew's Gospel that the mission community was to "teach the nations all that I have commanded you," our reductionism with regard to Jesus' concrete teaching in Matthew has been massive. David Bosch's trenchant comment bears repeating, that the Sermon on the Mount "expresses, like no other New Testament passage, the essence of the ethics of Jesus. Through the ages, however, Christians have . . . found ways around the clear meaning of the Sermon on the Mount."[20] For today's discussion in America, especially with regard to our institutional integrity, these questions are raised with probing clarity by Letty Russell, John Howard Yoder, Stanley Hauerwas, Walter Brueggemann, and Wilbert Shenk. Particularly, the corrections of gospel reductionism that have been offered by the Radical Reformation movements, the so-called peace churches, require not only our respect but our careful attention. They reveal how deeply engrained in classic Western theologies and ecclesiastical structures this reductionism is.

Let us focus, however, upon a particular aspect of institutional captivity with which many are struggling in North America. Recent studies on the religious development of American society in the twentieth century have revealed a fascinating aspect of our present situation,

20. Bosch, *Transforming Mission*, p. 69.

which is profoundly and alarmingly reductionistic. Toward the end of the nineteenth century, American business began to emerge as the dominant cultural force in our society. The large American corporation evolved as the most effective way to marshal our resources and meet the challenges of an expanding economy. As we refined our version of the free-market system, the values which rooted themselves deeply in our national psyche and which came to control our thinking and decision-making were focused upon profit, independence, efficiency, market-ability, and manageability. What was in fact happening was the translation of fundamental concepts of the Enlightenment into our social, economic, and cultural constructs: the primacy of reason, science, and technology; the rational solvability of all problems, especially through exploitation of the cause and effect nexus; the belief in unceasing progress; and over it all, the pursuit of personal happiness in liberty, which justified it all.[21]

It is now clear, as we look back over the last 100 to 125 years, that the value systems and operating structures of the large American corporation have become the dominant model for the institutional church, whether it was the denomination or the independent mission society. Over the last century, the Christian religion has become a big American business. We have centralized for efficiency and good management, developed major headquarters, accepted numerical and financial growth as the most important indications of success, introduced statistical measurement to determine that success, and made religion into a product. Denominational headquarters have generated programs and curricula. Marketing has become an essential function of religious management. Public relations and the canons of effective advertising define our activities. Local congregations are run as businesses, where giving, membership numbers, growth, and attendance

---

21. The Presbyterian version of this process is well analyzed in Milton J Coalter, John M. Mulder, and Louis B. Weeks, eds., *The Organizational Revolution: Presbyterians and American Denominationalism* (Louisville: Westminster/John Knox, 1992), especially Louis B. Weeks, "The Incorporation of the Presbyterians," pp. 37-54; Richard W. Reifsnyder, "Managing the Mission: Church Restructuring in the Twentieth Century," pp. 55-96; and more generally, Craig Dykstra and James Hudnut-Beumler, "The National Organizational Structures of Protestant Denominations: An Invitation to a Conversation," pp. 307-31. See also Ben Primer, *Protestant and American Business Methods* (n.p.: UMI Research Press, 1979).

are all evaluated as evidence of a healthy religious bottom line.[22] In many polities, they tend to function as "branch offices" of "central headquarters."

This institutional reductionism of the church's mission has meant that evangelism has been reshaped into a program of the church "business." We have noted before that it is always reductionistic to speak of the church's evangelistic ministry as "church member recruitment" and "new church planting." These aspects of evangelistic witness surface as priorities in a church whose ethos is defined by the values of the large corporation. This is where evangelism becomes something that can be counted, evaluated, and "re-tooled."

The nondenominational agencies that have proliferated in North America in this century have been even more profoundly dominated by the model of the large American corporation. The entrepreneurial spirit of American business is reflected in the ways that Christian visionaries have built their organizations. The multiplication of parachurch organizations in America must be understood within the larger context of the American glorification of the entrepreneur. Especially within the world of evangelistic organizations, the idea of "building a better mousetrap to bring the world to your door" is translated into developing a more effective method to convert more people, build more and larger churches, and demonstrate more Christian success on the market's terms. Profit and loss, growth, bottom line, and efficiency are sacrosanct standards in most of these organizations. In both denominational and nondenominational institutional structures, perhaps the most telling evidence of cultural captivity and gospel reductionism will be found in the complex undertaking called "fundraising."

In a fascinating twist in the English language, we now speak in secular America of "corporate mission," and we mean by that term the goals, achievements, and products a corporation intends to generate. AT&T, General Motors, and IBM all have their missions now. Conversely, churches now speak of their facilities as "plants"; they have "staffs" and describe pastoral responsibilities with terms like "chief of

22. See Philip D. Kenneson, "Selling [Out] The Church in the Marketplace of Desire," *Modern Theology* 9 (October 1993): 319-48; and R. Laurence Moore, *Selling God: American Religion in the Marketplace of Culture* (New York: Oxford University Press, 1994). One publication which represents the problem (and which Kenneson analyzes) is George Barna, *Marketing the Church* (Colorado Springs: NavPress, 1988).

staff" and "executive pastors." Churches and Christian organizations have accepted the secular reductionist redefinition of mission: we work with goals and objectives and measurable results as if it were more than obvious that this is what Christ meant we were to do when he defined our calling and sending as witness. Fully in line with our cultural context, we now define Christian mission institutionally in terms of results, normally measurable results. Thus, the decline in membership of virtually all traditional denominational structures is a compounded trauma, for it not only raises questions about our faithfulness to our mission mandate but also threatens the bottom line.

The Incarnational Integrity of Christian Institutions

This chapter began by raising the question of the relationship between incarnational witness and institutional structure. The primary effect of the institutional cultural captivity I have been describing is to reduce severely the incarnational integrity of our Christian institutions. The compromise of the institutional church is really a conquest: the gospel has been reduced to its barest minimum when the institutional forms of mission community are so thoroughly controlled by secular concerns for power, image, profitability, and success. Howard Snyder was not overstating the case when he wrote, "It is hard to escape the conclusion that today one of the great roadblocks to the gospel of Jesus Christ is the institutional church."[23]

How, then, shall we approach and assess the challenge of the incarnational witness of our ecclesiastical institutions? I have stressed, first of all, that a diversity of institutional and organizational forms of mission community is both biblically and historically validated. The issue for the incarnational witness of the institutional church, especially in its larger connectional structures, is not necessarily structural uniformity, but rather unity in diversity. That means that the gospel continues to be the definitive criterion for incarnational witness at every level of the institutional church. The basic concern for congruence be-

---

23. Howard A. Snyder, *The Problem of Wine Skins: Church Structure in a Technological Age* (Downers Grove, IL: InterVarsity, 1975), p. 21.

tween the evangelical message and how we go about witnessing to it must guide our institutional process.

This review of the history of gospel reductionism exposed by the institutional compromises of the church gives reason to proceed with caution. It does appear that the churches' accumulation of wealth and power, linked with the evolution of large institutional structures invested in their own maintenance, constitutes a profound challenge for the integrity of incarnational witness. Whether we are looking at the Roman Catholic Curia, denominational bureaucracies, or parachurch administrations, the tension between maintenance and mission is obvious. It appears that the inherent conservatism of institutions is far stronger and more assertive the more complex the institutional structures become. Jesus' statement about the difficulty for rich people to enter the kingdom of God applies here: we might paraphrase the saying to read, "It is easier for a camel to go through the eye of a needle than for an ecclesiastical institution to replace maintenance with mission as its commitment."

It is, in fact, far easier for a local congregation to close down than for a sophisticated ecclesiastical structure to place itself in question. We are accustomed to seeing buildings that were formerly local churches now used as restaurants, bookstores, or even private residences. None of the seven churches to which the seer of the Revelation of John directed his letters exists today. At every level of the church, we need to accept the basic fact that the maintenance of particular organizational expressions of the mission community is not the priority of our vocation to be Christ's witness. The church itself is not the goal of the gospel, but rather is called to be its witness and servant. This means that the continuation of all institutional forms of the church must take place under the scrutiny of the gospel and our missional vocation. No organized form of the church may claim to be normative for all organized expressions of the Body of Christ.

The cultural captivity of the institutional structures is a formidable obstacle to missional renewal. "Do not be conformed any longer to this world" constitutes a very profound challenge for the institutional renewal of ecclesiastical structures. It is likely that such renewal will happen only as a result of broad missional renewal of local congregations. Rarely do we see the Holy Spirit reforming the church from the top down. When connectional institutions attempt to reform, they reorganize or restructure. There is a profound difference between the re-shuffling of bureaucracies, which has become the consistent pattern of denominational reform in the last several decades in North America, and the missional renewal that transforms the church toward greater faithfulness in witness.

Where there is a serious concern for the integrity of incarnational witness in the hierarchies and administrations of ecclesial institutions, then the spiritual process will have to start with the challenges of power and money. This is where the legacy of Christendom is such a daunting challenge. Stanley Hauerwas represents many theologians asking hard questions about the challenge of institutional reformation of the church:

> Constantinianism is a hard habit to break. It is particularly hard when it seems that we do so much good by remaining "in power." It is hard to break because all our categories have been set by the church's establishment as a necessary part of Western civilization.[24]

This caution is not a reason to retreat from the challenge. While missional ferment is changing the face of local congregations across our societies, there are opportunities to begin the parallel process at the various levels of the institutional church. This needs to become a disciplined undertaking, informed especially by the content and methods of contemporary missiology. What is needed urgently is a missiology of the institutional church. For, in spite of the skepticism (or better, the sober realism) registered here, it will continue to be true that the concrete witness of the church must express itself in connectional structures linking congregations, confessional traditions, and mission endeavors across all cultural boundaries.

The skepticism we have described is leading many to conclude that the solution is to turn one's back on the connecting structures and pursue mission independently at the local level. Denominational structures are in jeopardy; councils and federations are struggling to survive;

---

24. Stanley Hauerwas, *After Christendom? How the Church Is to Behave If Freedom, Justice, and a Christian Nation Are Bad Ideas* (Nashville: Abingdon, 1991), pp. 18-19. For the most probing study of the challenges facing the institutional church in Western society, see John Milbank, *Theology and Social Theory: Beyond Secular Reason* (Oxford, UK, and Cambridge, MA: Blackwell, 1990).

the national offices of many regionalized mission organizations are facing similar challenges. We are speaking now of an expanding "congregationalism" in American organized religion. The suspicion of all power clustered somewhere far away from the grass roots is shaping both the political and the ecclesiastical process in North America. It may be that the question, "Can our institutions be incarnational?" is becoming moot.

This solution is not acceptable. The basic problems of institutionalism are not limited to the connectional structures of denominations and religious organizations. The local congregation is profoundly susceptible to cultural captivity and gospel reductionism. Money and power are as much a problem for the local congregation as they are for the denominational hierarchy. The danger is great that, at the local level, these dangers will go unrecognized. One of the necessary functions of the larger connectional structures of the church is to relate local mission communities to the larger church. Through such relationships, important experiences of accountability emerge which are often opportunities for the continuing conversion of the church.

My home church got involved shortly after the end of World War II in the program of ecumenical work groups coordinated by the World Council and other ecumenical agencies. Every summer large groups of young adults went to Europe and Asia to work in areas of great human need, especially with refugees, as well as in the rebuilding of destroyed churches. The work that was done was important, no doubt. But the impact upon our congregation in America was truly converting. These men and women returned with a profound sense of the gospel's depth and breadth that challenged the shallowness of our American reductionistic gospel of happiness. They experienced human suffering, people relying upon God in hopeless situations, miracles of healing and transformation — the incarnating of Christ in ways they had never seen or heard of. What they brought back from the larger church in other cultures was essential to the continuing conversion of our congregation. That form of continuing evangelization is, if anything, an even more urgent priority today.

Strategies for the missional renewal of the institutional church are undoubtedly as questionable as strategies to lead a person to Christ in twelve easy steps. The conversion of the church at every level is the work of God's Spirit and the earnest theme of Christians' prayer. Nevertheless, I shall risk concluding with some concise theses and questions which attempt to summarize what I have explored as the continuing conversion of the church. If evangelization is truly the heart of ministry at every organizational level of the church, then in some form or other, the institutional church in all its configurations will need to grapple with these questions. If evangelization is becoming truly the heart of ministry, and the church is being continuously converted to greater faithfulness to its missional vocation, then it will look like this:

Its fundamental commitment is to incarnational witness. The incarnational integrity of a Christian institution is rooted in its commitment to incarnational witness to Jesus Christ. Although the emphases and formulations will vary, every institutional expression of the church must be able to define itself in terms of our common vocation: "You shall be my witnesses."

It demonstrates congruence between the gospel it proclaims and the way it goes about its work. What the gospel means is shown by the institution in how it carries out its mission. Its desire is to "lead lives worthy of the calling to which you have been called" (Eph. 4:1).

It intentionally confronts its conformities. As the institutional church, it assumes that it has inherited and preserves a reductionist gospel. It seeks, through rigorous engagement with the Bible, the Christian traditions, and the ecumenical diversity of the church, to discover and repent of these reductions of the gospel, so that it can become more faithful as incarnational witness.

It will be open to its continuing conversion. Its repentance of its conformities and its gospel reductionism will lead to renewal as the result of the "transforming of the mind" (Rom. 12:2). Such conversion is a work of God; we cannot program it for any level of the church. But we can begin to explore earnestly how an institutionalized church practices corporate confession. Pope John Paul II has proposed in his official letter on the jubilee to be celebrated in the year 2000, *Tertio Millennio Adveniente,* that the church "cannot cross the threshold of the new millennium without encouraging her children to purify themselves, through repentance, of past errors and instances of infidelity, inconsistency, and slowness to act."[25] Perhaps the most profound form of ecu-

---

25. "Don't Apologize Yet, Say Some Catholic Leaders," *Ecumenical News International,* June 14, 1996.

menical action in the years which lie immediately ahead will be corporate confession of the church's reductionism of the gospel and cultural captivity.

To discover its conformities, give substance to its corporate confession, and thus be open to the Spirit's work of continuing conversion, the churches of the West must risk grappling with these questions:

- What are the assumptions and attitudes that shape our definition of the gospel and our mission?
- Who, for us, is Jesus Christ?
- What does the rule of Christ mean for us?
- What are the assumptions about power which guide our institutions?
- Where do those assumptions about power come from?
- How do our assumptions about power incarnate the gospel of Jesus Christ?
- How do our institutions' decision-making processes witness incarnationally to the gospel of Christ?
- What are the assumptions about success that guide our institutions?
- How does our understanding of our success incarnate the gospel?
- How does the relationship between *what* our institutions do and *how* they do it embody the gospel of Jesus Christ?
- How do the institutions' policies and practices with all those who work in them or are members of them incarnate the gospel?
- What are the assumptions about money, property, and investments that guide our institutions?
- How do these assumptions incarnate the gospel?
- How do we understand and interpret the significance of our inherited wealth over against our mission vocation today?
- How do our institutions relate to their past, and what role does their past history play in their present decision-making?
- What are the obstacles and problems that prevent Christian institutions from converting to a more incarnational way of functioning?
- How do our institutions identify their need to repent, to seek forgiveness, to receive the transforming gift of newness, and thus to change?

The entire church in the Western world faces the problem of the incarnational integrity of the institution today. Perhaps the greatest obstacle to faithful witness on the part of Western Christianity is our failure to address the institutional compromises that we have made over the centuries. These compromises are at the level of fundamental gospel issues: power, pride, ambition, fear, and hypocrisy. If we cannot incarnate the gospel in the way we function as institutions, then we betray the gospel. The problem is old, as the letters to the seven churches in the Book of Revelation indicate. The need is urgent for us, in our various arenas of ministry, to ask about the incarnational integrity of our institutions. Only when the institutional church becomes the church penitent, the church candid about its compromises and reductions, can its renewal be expected. This renewal will come about as we submit our cultural captivities to the transforming scrutiny of Scripture. To do that, we need to let Christian brothers and sisters from other cultures, other parts of the worldwide church, engage with us in our discipline of reflection and contrition.

Christ the Lord calls and equips us to become those who not only hear but do the Word of God, and who thus incarnate the good news of God's healing love for all the world. "Do not be conformed to this world [any longer], but be transformed by the renewing of your minds, so that you may discern what is the will of God — what is good and acceptable and perfect" (Rom. 12:2).

A Final Word

Several years ago, the Evangelism Office of the Presbyterian Church (U.S.A.) proposed a definition of evangelism with the following text, which I amended while working on it with my students:

> Evangelism is GOD'S PEOPLE joyfully sharing the good news of the sovereign love of God and GOD'S SPIRIT calling all people to repentance, to personal faith in Jesus Christ as Savior and Lord, to active membership in the church, and to obedient service AND WITNESS in the world.[1]

If this definition is taken seriously, then clearly evangelization can no longer be regarded merely as a set of methods and programs for recruiting church members. Nor can it be just a program of a denominational office or a parachurch evangelistic organization. It cannot be reduced to "twelve steps to soul-winning" or "four spiritual laws." It cannot be narrowly defined as the process that leads to a particular kind of individual faith decision.

Donald McCullough has commented on the "well-meant evangelical exhortation to 'invite Jesus' into your heart'":

> I assume this imagery comes from Revelation 3:20 ("I am standing at the door, knocking; if you hear my voice and open the door, I will

---

1. Evangelism and Church Development Unit, Presbyterian Church (U.S.A.), Louisville, 1990; the capitalized terms are my amendments.

come in to you and eat with you, and you with me"). But why, on the basis of one verse, has an entire theology and language of "personal acceptance" of Jesus swamped the far more pervasive apostolic call to confess "Jesus is Lord"? The reason, I submit, is that it fits more comfortably with our American sensibilities. So long as *I* invite Jesus in *my* heart, I'm still in control of things and my personal freedom is in no way threatened.[2]

His comments and my amendments to the definition all point to the comprehensive nature of the church's evangelistic vocation. Evangelization has to do with the fundamental calling of the church to respond to Jesus as Savior and submit to him as Lord. It is the vocation for which the Holy Spirit is given. The only way for the church to carry out its calling to be Christ's witness is to seek, in all humility and in total dependence upon God's gracious enabling power, to incarnate the gospel of Jesus Christ. We are to be, to do, and to say witness to the saviorhood and lordship of Jesus Christ as God's good news for the world.

To do this, the church must be continually converted from her reductions of the gospel to its fullness. Rather than reading that famous passage in the Revelation as an evangelistic text directed to the non-Christian, we should remember that Jesus is knocking at the door of the church, asking to come in. The challenge in the letter to the church at Laodicea is profoundly relevant for the church of the post-Constantinian West. We are described here in our need to be converted: we are neither hot nor cold, but lukewarm; we think we are rich and need nothing; we do not realize that we are in fact "wretched, pitiable, poor, blind, and naked" (Rev. 3:17). We need to be clothed anew in the baptismal gown of those who are continually being converted to the service of their reigning Lord. We need to respond to the Lord who loves his church and therefore reproves and disciplines it.

The Holy Spirit began the conversion of the church at Pentecost and has continued that conversion throughout the pilgrimage of God's people from the first century up to now. The conversion of the church will be the continuing work of God's Spirit until God completes the good work begun in Jesus Christ.

2. Donald McCullough, *The Trivialization of God: The Dangerous Illusion of a Manageable Deity* (Colorado Springs: NavPress, 1995), p. 23.

The time has come to move beyond the well-intended observation by Stephen Neill, "If everything is mission, nothing is mission."[3] That remark assumed that mission was one dimension of the church's larger vocation. In the context of Christendom, the church's purpose could be defined by referring to the preaching of the Word and the administration of the sacraments within the faith community. Next to these central tasks of the church, one could also list mission, evangelism, and service. When we define the church within God's mission, then all of these dimensions of the church's work are drawn together into the comprehensive calling to be, to do, and to say witness to Jesus Christ as Savior and Lord.

Whatever is not mission is not part of the church's vocation. Evangelization, carried out as incarnational witness, is the heart of the church's mission and ministry. All that the Body of Christ is and does must be linked to that heart just as every part of the human body must be linked to the human heart.

This is not an impossible task. It is precisely what Jesus himself intended when he called and formed a community for the continuation of his mission. Mark's Gospel makes this particularly clear in the story of Jesus' calling of the twelve (Mark 3:13ff). Jesus chose these twelve men as disciples with the express purpose that they should become apostles, "sent ones." "He appointed twelve, whom he also named apostles." As his disciples, they were "to be with him," to learn from him all that they would need to be his messengers and witnesses. But they were not to stay with him, not to reduce their vocation as his "called out people" (*ecclesia*) to their internal life and all that they would do as a gathered community. Rather, they were "to be sent out to proclaim the message, and to have authority to cast out demons." Their gathered life was always to lead into their scattered life, as the witnessing church, evangelizing as they were evangelized. The reductionisms that make our continuing conversion essential are always, in some way, a dividing of what should not be divided. One shall not divide discipleship from apostolate, gathering from sending, community with Christ from witnessing for Christ.

The challenge and the possibility of the good news that is Jesus Christ is its life-embracing and life-transforming character:

3. Stephen Neill, *Creative Tension* (London: Edinburgh House, 1959), p. 81.

"All authority in heaven and on earth has been given to me. Go therefore and make disciples of all nations, baptizing them in the name of the Father and of the Son and of the Holy Spirit, and teaching them to obey everything that I have commanded you. And remember, I am with you always, to the end of the age" (Matt. 28:18-20).

The gospel of these "alls" — *all* authority, *all* nations, *all* that I have commanded you, *always* I am with you — is the transforming power that will continue to convert the church until Christ comes.

Resources Cited

Aagaard, Johannes. "Trends in Missiological Thinking During the Sixties," *International Review of Mission* 62 (1973): 8-25.

Aagaard, Marie. "Missio Dei in katholischer Sicht," *Evangelische Theologie* 34 (1974): 420-33.

Abraham, William J. *The Logic of Evangelism.* Grand Rapids: Eerdmans, 1989.

———. "A Theology of Evangelism: The Heart of the Matter," *Interpretation* 48, no. 2 (April 1994): 117-30.

Anderson, Gerald A. *Bibliography of the Theology of Missions in the Twentieth Century,* 2nd ed. New York: Mission Research Library, 1960.

———. "The Theology of Mission among Protestants in the Twentieth Century," in *The Theology of the Christian Mission,* edited by Gerald A. Anderson. New York: McGraw-Hill, 1961.

Anderson, Gerald A., ed. *The Theology of the Christian Mission.* New York: McGraw-Hill, 1961.

Anderson, Gerald A., and Thomas F. Stransky, eds. *Mission Trends No. 2: Evangelization.* New York: Paulist; Grand Rapids: Eerdmans, 1975.

Arias, Mortimer. *Announcing the Reign of God: Evangelization and the Subversive Memory of Jesus.* Philadelphia: Fortress, 1984.

Arias, Mortimer, and Alan Johnson. *The Great Commission: Biblical Models for Evangelism.* Nashville: Abingdon, 1992.

Armstrong, Richard S. *Service Evangelism.* Philadelphia: Westminster, 1979.

Arnold, Walter. *Evangelisation im ökumenischen Gespräch: Beiträge eines Symposiums (Genf 1973).* Erlangen: Verlag der Ev.-Luth. Mission, 1974.

Barna, George. *Marketing the Church,* Colorado Springs: NavPress, 1988.

Barrett, David B. *Evangelize: A Historical Survey of the Concept.* Birmingham, AL: New Hope, 1987.

Barth, Karl. *Church Dogmatics.* IV, 3/2. Translated by G. W. Bromiley. Edinburgh: T. & T. Clark, 1962.

————. *Church Dogmatics.* IV/4, fragment. Translated by G. W. Bromiley. Edinburgh: T. & T. Clark, 1969.

————. "Die Theologie und die Mission in der Gegenwart." In *Theologische Fragen und Antworten.* Vol. 3. Zollikon Zürich: Evangelischer Verlag, 1932.

————. *Protestant Theology in the Nineteenth Century: Its Background and History.* Valley Forge: Judson, 1973.

Blauw, Johannes. "The Biblical View of Man in His Religion." In *The Theology of the Christian Mission,* edited by Gerald A. Anderson, pp. 31-41. New York: McGraw-Hill, 1961.

————. *The Missionary Nature of the Church: A Survey of the Biblical Theology of Mission.* New York: McGraw-Hill, 1962.

Bonhoeffer, Dietrich. *Life Together.* Translated by J. W. Doberstein. New York: Harper & Row, 1954.

Bosch, David. "Evangelism: Theological Currents and Cross-currents Today," *International Bulletin of Missionary Research* 11, no. 3 (July 1987): 99-103.

————. "Mission and Evangelism: Clarifying the Concepts," *Zeitschrift für Missionswissenschaft und Religionswissenschaft,* 68. Jahrgang, 1/1984, Heft 1, pp. 161-66.

————. "Reflections on Biblical Models of Mission." In *Towards the Twenty-first Century in Christian Mission,* edited by James M. Phillips and Robert T. Coote, pp. 175-92. Grand Rapids: Eerdmans, 1993.

————. "The Scope of the 'BISAM' Project," *Mission Studies* 6-1, no. 11 (1989): 61-69.

————. "Towards a Hermeneutic for 'Biblical Studies and Mission,'" *Mission Studies* 3, no. 2 (1986): 65-79.

————. *Transforming Mission: Paradigm Shifts in Theology of Mission.* Maryknoll, NY: Orbis Books, 1991.

————. *Witness to the World.* London: Marshall, Morgan & Scott, 1980.

Bright, John. *The Kingdom of God: The Biblical Concept and Its Meaning for the Church.* Nashville: Abingdon, 1953.

Bromiley, Geoffrey W. *Historical Theology: An Introduction.* Grand Rapids: Eerdmans, 1978.

Brownson, James. "Speaking the Truth in Love: Elements of a Missional Hermeneutic," *International Review of Mission* 83, no. 330 (July 1994): 479-504; also included in *The Church Between Gospel and Culture,* edited by George Hunsberger and Craig Van Gelder, pp. 228-59. Grand Rapids: Eerdmans, 1996.

Brueggemann, Walter. *Biblical Perspectives on Evangelism: Living in a Three-Storied Universe.* Nashville: Abingdon, 1993.

Castro, Emilio, and Gerhart Linn. "Evangelisation." In *Evangelisches Kirchenlexikon.* Göttingen: Vandenhoeck & Ruprecht, 1986.

Coalter, Milton J, and Virgil Cruz, eds. *How Shall We Witness? Faithful Evangelism in a Reformed Tradition.* Louisville: Westminster/John Knox, 1995.

Coalter, Milton J, John M. Mulder, and Louis B. Weeks, eds. *The Organizational Revolution: Presbyterians and American Denominationalism.* Louisville: Westminster/John Knox, 1992.

Coalter, Milton J, John M. Mulder, and Louis B. Weeks. *The Re-Forming Tradition: Presbyterians and Mainstream Protestantism.* Louisville: Westminster/John Knox, 1992.

———. *Vital Signs: The Promise of Mainstream Protestantism.* Grand Rapids: Eerdmans, 1996.

Costas, Orlando. *Liberating News: A Theology of Contextual Evangelization.* Grand Rapids: Eerdmans, 1989.

Cullmann, Oscar. *Christ and Time: The Primitive Christian Conception of Time and History.* Translated by F. V. Filson. Philadelphia, Westminster, 1964.

"Don't Apologize Yet, Say Some Catholic Leaders." *Ecumenical News International.* June 14, 1996.

Durnbaugh, Donald F. *The Believers' Church: The History and Character of Radical Protestantism.* New York: MacMillan, 1968.

Durrwell, F. "Christian Witness: A Theological Study," *International Review of Mission* 69, no. 274 (April 1980): 121-34.

Dvornik, Francis. *Byzantine Missions among the Slavs: SS. Constantine-Cyril and Methodius.* New Brunswick: Rutgers University Press, 1970.

Fitzmier, John R., and Randall Balmer. "A Poultice for the Bite of the Cobra: The Hocking Report and Presbyterian Missions in the Middle Decades of the Twentieth Century." In *The Diversity of Discipleship: Presbyterians and Twentieth Century Christian Witness,* edited by Milton J Coalter, John M. Mulder, and Louis B. Weeks. Louisville: Westminster/John Knox, 1991.

González, Catherine Gunsalus. "'Converted and Always Converting': Evangelism in the Early Reformed Tradition." In *How Shall We Witness? Evangelism in a Reformed Tradition,* edited by Milton J Coalter and Virgil Cruz, pp. 73-91. Louisville: Westminster/John Knox, 1995.

González, Justo. "Ecumenical Tensions of the Church in the West: A North American Perspective." Unpublished manuscript of lecture delivered in Paris, January 1996.

Green, Michael. *Evangelism in the Early Church.* Grand Rapids: Eerdmans, 1970.

Guder, Darrell L. *Be My Witnesses: The Church's Mission, Message, and Messengers.* Grand Rapids: Eerdmans, 1985.

———. "Incarnation and the Church's Evangelistic Mission," *International Review of Mission* 83, no. 330 (July 1994): 417-28.

———. "The Integrity of Apostolic Ministry: I Thessalonians 2:1-13," *reo: A Journal of Theology and Ministry* no. 1 (November 1996): 12-19.

———. "Locating a Reformed Theology of Evangelism in a Pluralist World." In *How Shall We Witness? Faithful Evangelism in a Reformed Tradition,* edited by Milton J Coalter and Virgil Cruz, pp. 165-86. Louisville: Westminster/John Knox, 1995.

Guder, Darrell L., ed. *Missional Church: A Vision for the Sending of the Church in North America.* Grand Rapids: Eerdmans, 1998.

Günther, Wolfgang. *Von Edinburgh nach Mexiko City: die ekklesiologischen Bemühungen der Weltmissionskonferenzen (1910-1963).* Stuttgart: Evangelischer Missionsverlag, 1970.

Guthrie, Shirley C. "A Reformed Theology of Evangelism." In *Evangelism in the Reformed Tradition,* edited by Arnold B. Lovell, pp. 70-84. Decatur: CTS Press, 1990.

Hahn, Ferdinand. *Mission in the New Testament.* Translated by F. Clarke. London: SCM, 1965.

Hauerwas, Stanley. *A Community of Character: Toward a Constructive Christian Social Ethic.* Notre Dame and London: University of Notre Dame, 1981.

———. *After Christendom? How the Church Is to Behave If Freedom, Justice, and a Christian Nation Are Bad Ideas.* Nashville: Abingdon, 1991.

Hayes, Richard B. "Ecclesiology and Ethics in I Corinthians," *Ex Auditu,* 1994, pp. 31-43.

———. *The Moral Vision of the New Testament: Community, Cross, New Creation: A Contemporary Introduction to New Testament Ethics.* San Francisco: HarperSanFrancisco, 1996.

Henderson, Robert T. *Joy to the World: An Introduction to Kingdom Evangelism.* Atlanta: John Knox, 1980.

Hengel, Martin. "The Origins of the Christian Mission." In *Between Jesus and Paul: Studies in the Earliest History of Christianity.* Philadelphia: Fortress, 1983.

Hollenweger, W. J. *Evangelisation gestern und heute.* Stuttgart: J. F. Steinkopf Verlag, 1973.

Hordern, William. *A Laymen's Guide to Protestant Theology.* New York: MacMillan, 1967.

Hunsberger, George. *Bearing the Witness of the Spirit: Lesslie Newbigin's Theology of Cultural Pluralism.* Grand Rapids: Eerdmans, 1998.

————. "Is There Biblical Warrant for Evangelism?" *Interpretation* 48, no. 2 (April 1984): 131-44.

Hunsberger, George, and Craig Van Gelder. *The Church Between Gospel and Culture*. Grand Rapids: Eerdmans, 1996.

Johnson, Ben Campbell. *Pastoral Spirituality: A Focus For Ministry*. Philadelphia: Westminster, 1988.

————. *Rethinking Evangelism: A Theological Approach*. Philadelphia: Westminster, 1987.

————. *Speaking of God: Evangelism as Initial Spiritual Guidance*. Louisville: Westminster/John Knox, 1991.

Johnson, Merwyn. "Calvin's Significance for Evangelism Today." In *Calvin Studies V: Papers Presented to the Davidson Colloquium on Calvin Studies,* edited by John Leith, pp. 119-33. Richmond: n.p., 1990.

Kähler, Martin. *Schriften zur Christologie und Mission*. Munich: Chr. Kaiser Verlag, [1908] 1971.

Kantonen, T. A. *The Theology of Evangelism*. Philadelphia: Muhlenberg, 1954.

Keifert, Patrick R. *Welcoming the Stranger: A Public Theology of Worship and Evangelism*. Minneapolis: Fortress, 1992.

Kelley, J. N. D. *Early Christian Thought*. New York: Harper & Row, 1968.

Kenneson, Philip D. "Selling [Out] the Church in the Marketplace of Desire," *Modern Theology* 9 (October 1993): 319-48.

Kettler, Christian, and Todd H. Speidel, eds. *Incarnational Ministry: The Presence of Christ in Church, Family, and Society*. Colorado Springs: Helmers & Howard, 1990.

Knox, Ronald A. *Enthusiasm*. New York and London: Oxford University, 1950.

Kretschmar, Georg. "Das christliche Leben und die Mission in der frühen Kirche." In *Kirchengeschichte als Missionsgeschichte, Bd. I, Die alte Kirche,* Heinzgünter Frohnes u. Uwe W. Knorr, Herausgeber, pp. 94-100. München: Kaiser Verlag, 1974.

Latourette, Kenneth Scott. *A History of the Expansion of Christianity*. 7 vols. Grand Rapids: Zondervan, 1970.

LeGrand, Lucien. *Unity and Plurality: Missions in the Bible*. Translated by R. R. Barr. Maryknoll, NY: Orbis Books, 1990.

Loetscher, Lefferts. *The Broadening Church: A Study of Theological Issues in the Presbyterian Church since 1869*. Philadelphia: University of Pennsylvania Press, 1954.

Lohfink, Gerhard. *Jesus and Community: The Social Dimension of Christian Faith*. Translated by J. P. Galvin. Philadelphia: Fortress, 1984.

Lovelace, Richard F. *Dynamics of Spiritual Life: An Evangelical Theology of Renewal*. Downers Grove, IL: InterVarsity, 1979.

Luzbetak, Louis J., SVD. *The Church and Cultures: New Perspectives in Missiological Anthropology.* Maryknoll, NY: Orbis Books, 1988.

Macky, Peter. *The Bible in Dialogue with Modern Man.* Waco: Word, 1970.

McCullough, Donald. *The Trivialization of God: The Dangerous Illusion of a Manageable Deity.* Colorado Springs: NavPress, 1995.

Milbank, John. *Theology and Social Theory: Beyond Secular Reason.* Oxford, UK, and Cambridge, MA: Blackwell, 1990.

Moltmann, Jürgen. *The Church in the Power of the Spirit: A Contribution to Messianic Ecclesiology.* London: SCM, 1977.

Moore, R. Laurence. *Selling God: American Religion in the Marketplace of Culture.* New York: Oxford University Press, 1994.

Mott, John. *The Evangelization of the World in This Generation.* New York: Student Volunteer Movement for Foreign Missions, 1900; reprint, New York: Arno, 1972.

Motte, Mary, FFM. "Roman Catholic Missions." In *Toward the Twenty-first Century in Mission,* edited by James M. Phillips and Robert T. Coote. Grand Rapids: Eerdmans, 1993.

Neill, Stephen. *Creative Tension.* London: Edinburgh House, 1959.

Newbigin, Lesslie. "Cross-currents in Ecumenical and Evangelical Understandings of Mission," *International Bulletin of Missionary Research* 6, no. 4 (October 1982): 146-51.

———. "Ecumenical Amnesia," *International Bulletin of Missionary Research* 18, no. 1 (January 1994): 2-5.

———. *Foolishness to the Greeks: The Gospel and Western Culture.* Grand Rapids: Eerdmans, 1986.

———. *The Gospel in a Pluralist Society.* Grand Rapids: Eerdmans, 1989.

———. *The Household of God: Lectures on the Nature of the Church.* London: SCM, 1953.

———. *The Open Secret: Sketches for a Missionary Theology.* Grand Rapids: Eerdmans, 1978; rev. ed. 1995.

———. *The Other Side of 1984: Questions for the Churches.* Geneva: World Council of Churches, 1983.

———. "Reply to Konrad Raiser," *International Bulletin of Missionary Research* 18, no. 2 (April 1994): 51-52.

———. "A Sermon Preached at the Thanksgiving Service for the Fiftieth Anniversary of the Tambaram Conference of the International Missionary Council," *International Review of Mission* 77, no. 307 (July 1988): 326-27.

———. "Witness in a Biblical Perspective," *Mission Studies* 3, no. 2 (1986): 80-84.

Pauck, Wilhelm. "Theology in the Life of Contemporary American Protestantism." In *Religion and Culture: Essays in Honor of Paul Tillich,* edited by Walter Leibrecht. New York: Harper & Brothers, 1959.

Pelikan, Jaroslav. *The Emergence of the Catholic Tradition (100-600).* Vol. 1 of *The Christian Tradition: A History of the Development of Doctrine.* Chicago and London: University of Chicago Press, 1971.

Phillips, James M., and Robert T. Coote, eds. *Toward the Twenty-first Century in Christian Mission.* Grand Rapids: Eerdmans, 1993.

Presbyterian Church (U.S.A.). *Book of Confessions: The Constitution of the Presbyterian Church (U.S.A.).* Part 1. Louisville: Office of the General Assembly, 1994.

Primer, Ben. *Protestant and American Business Methods.* N.p.: UMI Research, 1979.

Raiser, Konrad. *Ecumenism in Transition: A Paradigm Shift in the Ecumenical Movement?* Geneva: WCC Publications, 1991.

————. "Is Ecumenical Apologetics Sufficient? A Response to Lesslie Newbigin's 'Ecumenical Amnesia,'" *International Bulletin of Missionary Research* 18, no. 2 (April 1994): 50-51.

Ramey, Robert H., Jr., and Ben Campbell Johnson. *Living the Christian Life: A Guide to Reformed Spirituality.* Louisville: Westminster/John Knox, 1992.

Rasmusson, Arne. *The Church as* Polis: *From Political Theology to Theological Politics as Exemplified by Jürgen Moltmann and Stanley Hauerwas.* Notre Dame: University of Notre Dame Press, 1995.

Rice, Howard K. *Reformed Spirituality: An Introduction for Believers.* Louisville: Westminster/John Knox, 1991.

Richardson, Alan. *The Bible in an Age of Modern Science.* Philadelphia: Westminster, 1961.

Robinson, P. J. "Mission as Ethos/Ethos as Mission," *Missionalia* 18, no. 1 (April 1990).

Rogers, Jack B., and Donald K. McKim. *The Authority and Interpretation of the Bible: An Historical Approach.* San Francisco: Harper & Row, 1979.

Rudnick, Milton K. *Speaking the Gospel through the Ages: A History of Evangelism.* St. Louis: Concordia, 1984.

Samuel, Vinay, and Albrecht Hauser, eds. *Proclaiming Christ in Christ's Way: Studies in Integral Evangelism.* Oxford: Regnum, 1989.

Sanneh, Lamin. "Christian Missions and the Western Guilt Complex," *The Christian Century* 104, no. 11 (8 April 1987): 330-34.

Sanneh, Lamin. *Translating the Message: The Missionary Impact on Culture.* Maryknoll, NY: Orbis Books, 1991.

Schmidt, K. L. "Basileia." In *Theological Dictionary of the New Testament.* Edited by Gerhard Kittel and Gerhard Friedrichs; translated by Geoffrey W. Bromiley, 1:581ff. Grand Rapids: Eerdmans, 1964-76.

Schweizer, Eduard. *Das Evangelium nach Markus* (NTD 1). Göttingen: Vandenhoeck & Ruprecht, 1967. Translated by E. H. Madvig under the title *The Good News According to Mark.* Atlanta: John Knox, 1970.

Seeberg, Reinhold. *History of the Doctrines in the Early Church: Text-Book of the History of Doctrines.* Translated by C. E. Hay. Grand Rapids: Baker, 1977.

Selwyn, E. G. "Eschatology in I Peter." In *The Background of the New Testament and Its Eschatology,* edited by W. D. Davies and D. Daube. Cambridge: Cambridge University Press, 1956.

Senior, Donald, and Carroll Stuhlmueller. *The Biblical Foundations for Mission.* Maryknoll, NY: Orbis Books, 1983.

Sider, Robert D. *The Gospel and Its Proclamation.* Vol. 10 of *Message of the Fathers of the Church.* Wilmington: Michael Glazier, 1983.

Snyder, Howard A. *The Problem of Wine Skins: Church Structure in a Technological Age.* Downers Grove, IL: InterVarsity, 1975.

Soards, Marion L. *The Speeches in Acts: Their Content, Context, and Concerns.* Louisville: Westminster/John Knox, 1994.

Spindler, Marc. "Visa for Witness: A New Focus on the Theology of Mission and Ecumenism," *Mission Studies* 3-1 (1986): 51-60.

Stuhlmacher, Peter. "Die Mitte der Schrift — biblisch-theologisch betrachtet." In *Wissenschaft und Kirche: Festschrift für Eduard Lohse,* edited by Kurt Aland and Siegfried Meurer, pp. 29-56. Bielefeld: Luther Verlag, 1989,

———. *Jesus of Nazareth — Christ of Faith.* Translated by Siegfried S. Schatzmann. Peabody, MA: Hendrickson, 1993.

———. "Weg, Stil und Konsequenzen urchristlicher Mission," *Theologische Beiträge* 12. Jahrgang, 1981, pp. 107-135.

Terry, John M. *Evangelism: A Concise History.* Nashville: Broadman, 1994.

Thielicke, Helmut. *Modern Faith and Thought.* Translated by G. W. Bromiley. Grand Rapids: Eerdmans, 1990.

Trites, Alison A. *The New Testament Concept of Witness.* Cambridge: Cambridge University Press, 1977.

van Pelt, J. R. "Witness." In *Dictionary of Christ and the Gospels,* 2 vols., edited by J. Hastings, 2:830. Edinburgh: n.p., 1980.

van Ruler, Arnold A. "A Theology of Mission." In *Calvinistic Trinitarianism and Theocentric Politics: Essays Toward a Public Theology,* translated by J. Belt. Lewiston: Edwin Mellon, 1989.

Walls, Andrew. "Missiology." In *Dictionary of the Ecumenical Movement,* edited by Nicholas Lossky et al. Geneva: WCC Publications; Grand Rapids: Eerdmans, 1991.

Walton, Martin. *Witness in Biblical Scholarship: A Survey of Recent Studies, 1956-1980.* IIMO Research Pamphlet No. 15. Leiden/Utrecht: Interuniversitair Instituut voor Missiologie en Oecumenica, 1986.

Webber, Robert, and Rodney Clapp. *People of the Truth: A Christian Challenge to Contemporary Culture.* Harrisburg: Morehouse, 1993.

Webber, Robert. *Celebrating Our Faith: Evangelism through Worship.* San Francisco: Harper & Row, 1986.

Weber, Otto. *Foundations of Dogmatics.* 2 vols., translated by D. L. Guder. Grand Rapids: Eerdmans, 1981-83.

Westermann, Claus. *Our Controversial Bible.* Translated by D. H. Beekmann. Minneapolis: Augsburg, 1969.

Winn, Albert C. *A Sense of Mission: Guidance from the Gospel of John.* Philadelphia: Westminster, 1981.

———. "What Is the Gospel?'" In *How Shall We Witness? Faithful Evangelism in a Reformed Tradition,* edited by Milton J Coalter and Virgil Cruz, pp. 3-26. Louisville: Westminster/John Knox, 1995.

Winter, Ralph D., "The New Missions and the Mission of the Church," *International Review of Mission,* 60, no. 237 (January 1971): 89-100.

———. "The Two Structures of God's Redemptive Mission," *Missiology* 11, no. 1 (January 1974): 121-39.

Winter, Ralph D., and R. Pierce Weaver. *The Warp and the Woof: Organizing for Mission.* South Pasadena: William Carey Library, 1970.

World Council of Churches. *Mission and Evangelism: An Ecumenical Affirmation.* Geneva, 1982.

Yoder, John Howard. "'But We Do See Jesus': The Particularity of Incarnation and the Universality of Truth." In *The Priestly Kingdom: Social Ethics as Gospel,* pp. 46-62. Notre Dame: University of Notre Dame Press, 1984.

———. "Let the Church Be the Church." In *The Royal Priesthood: Essays Ecclesiological and Ecumenical,* edited by Michael G. Cartwright, pp. 168-80. Grand Rapids: Eerdmans, 1994.

———. *The Politics of Jesus.* Grand Rapids: Eerdmans, 1994.

———. "To Serve Our God and to Rule the World." In *The Royal Priesthood: Essays Ecclesiology and Ecumenical,* edited by Michael G. Cartwright, pp. 127-40. Grand Rapids: Eerdmans, 1994.

———. "Why Ecclesiology Is Social Ethics: Gospel Ethics Versus the Wider Wisdom." In *The Royal Priesthood: Essays Ecclesiology and Ecumenical,* edited by Michael G. Cartwright, pp. 102-26. Grand Rapids: Eerdmans, 1994.

Subject Index

Anti-Semitism, 88, 89; as reductionism, 105

Barth, Karl, 17-18, 77, 173; critique of classic definition of Christian, 17-19, 121-31; as missional theologian, 19; "special working fellowships of the church," 183-84
Bible translation, 98-99
Biblical interpretation, 86, 188
Bosch, David, 11n.5, 20, 25, 181-82, 186-88, 195

Canon of the New Testament, 51, 54
Catholicity, 54
Christendom, 85, 91, 102, 110-12, 114-15, 140, 146, 164, 207; deterioration of, 6-8, 10-11, 16-17, 24, 92-93, 156
Christian identity. See Vocation
Church. See Institutional church; Mission community; Missio Dei; Witness
Church membership, 169-79
Clericalism, 133-35
Congregation (local). See Mission community
Constantinianism, Constantinianization, 9, 11, 85-87, 105-13, 114, 140, 179-80, 200

Continuing conversion, 25-27, 71-72, 81-82, 85, 128, 149-50; and church membership, 174-79; in ecumenical exchange, 90; as Gospel obedience, 150, 159; of institutional church, 202-4; in response to reductionism, 103-4, 121, 131-41, 144, 149; as scriptural encounter, 160-61; as translation, 87-92, 97-98
Control. See Reductionism; Sin
Corpus Christianum, 7, 93
Cultural bilinguality, 94-95
Cultural transformation. See Translation of the Gospel

Denominations: decline, 184-88
Disestablishment, 7, 168

Enlightenment, 4-5, 7-8, 15-16, 65; and Gospel reductionism, 116-17, 126, 135; and North American business ethics, 196-98
Enthusiasm, 183
Eschatology: decline of, 107n.16, 108-9, 116, 122. See also Witness as eschatology
Evangelism, evangelization: and continuing conversion of the church, 150-53, 164-65; defined, 205-6; as

218

Scripture Reference Index

74억 이유리 - 조애